There Is a Garden in the Mind

DATE DUE

There Is a Garden
in the Mind

A Memoir of Alan Chadwick
and the Organic Movement in California

Paul A. Lee

North Atlantic Books
Berkeley, California

Published by
North Atlantic Books
P.O. Box 12327
Berkeley, California 94712

Book design and typography by Jack W. Stauffacher of The Greenwood Press and Kina Sullivan. San Francisco. Set in Nicholas Kis types.
Cover design and photography scans by Dennis Letbetter
Cover photo by Elizabeth Kennard
Printed in the United States of America

There Is a Garden in the Mind: A Memoir of Alan Chadwick and the Organic Movement in California is sponsored by the Society for the Study of Native Arts and Sciences, a non-profit educational corporation whose goals are to develop an educational and cross-cultural perspective linking various scientific, social, and artistic fields; to nurture a holistic view of arts, sciences, humanities, and healing; and to publish and distribute literature on the relationship of mind, body, and nature.

North Atlantic Books' publications are available through most bookstores. For further information, visit our website at www.northatlanticbooks.com or call 800-733-3000.

Library of Congress Cataloging-in-Publication Data
Lee, Paul A.
  There is a garden in the mind : a memoir of Alan Chadwick and the organic movement in California / Paul A. Lee.
     p. cm.
  Includes bibliographical references.
    ISBN 978-1-58394-559-9
1. Chadwick, Alan, 1909-1980. 2. Gardeners—England—Biography. 3. Gardeners—California—Biography. 4. Organic gardening—California. 5. Organic farming. I. Title.
 SB453.5.L44 2012
 635.9'87092--dc23
 [B]
                    2012022634

1 2 3 4 5 6 7 8 Sheridan 17 16 15 14 13

for Charlene
gardening partner for life

Contents

Illustrations

Unless indicated, photographs are of Alan Chadwick.

Preface

Alan Chadwick's garden is a "garden in the mind" as much as it is of the soil, and like all genuinely inspired creations it has the power to stir us to new dreams, to a new vision of what man and nature can do, together. —Page Smith

The vision that Alan Chadwick transmitted so freely and generously, tantamount to an economy of gift, has inspired and sustained me over the last four decades while I have worked on this book. Alan Chadwick planted a garden in my mind that has taken root and blossomed like the heritage roses he so loved. One of his favorites—Madam Carrière—which we planted in his memory, is in bloom in my garden right now.

This book is a memoir of my experience as the founder of the Chadwick Garden at the University of California, Santa Cruz, and the part I played in the subsequent gardens developed by Alan Chadwick at the Green Gulch Farm Zen Center; Saratoga; Covelo; and New Harmony, West Virginia.

I concentrate on the story of the origins of the Chadwick Garden at the University of California, and then what it was like to work with Alan over the course of his gardening career. It is my story about what I have learned from this remarkable adventure. I have learned a lot since its inception over forty years ago, in 1967.

It is not a biography of Alan per se, even though I found out about Alan's past from contact with relatives while writing this book. I leave the biography and a more concentrated appraisal of Alan's ideas and methods—his French intensive and biodynamic system—for someone else.

One of the reasons it has taken so long to organize my thoughts in print is the intellectual and scholarly construction the garden inspired me to work out after it opened up for me: what I came to appreciate as the deepest split in our culture—the physicalist/vitalist conflict, a scholarly retrieval in the philosophy of science. Physicalism stands for the ideology of positivist/reductionist scientism, and vitalism for the beleaguered and assumedly insupportable defense of the integrity of organic nature. This line of thought became so elaborated in my pursuit of it, nothing less than a critique of Western culture, taking me back to Galileo and what has been called the mathematization of nature, that I had a hard time attaching it to the story of a three- or four-acre garden plot. I was worried that it intruded on the story of the founding of the Chadwick Garden and the other gardens that followed, so I reduced the philosophical pursuit to a minimum; the gardens that Chadwick developed and the garden in my mind that developed as a response, hopefully, will complement one another in this telling without too much scholarly overload.

The roots of the organic movement in Chadwick's work began in Santa Cruz, at the University of California, in 1967, and ended with his death, in 1980, at the Zen Buddhist farm at Green Gulch, Muir Beach, California, where he had begun a production garden some years before and where he returned to die. The garden in my mind is a long excursus on what I have learned from my association with Chadwick and his gardens, and the split in the culture: industrial technocracy against organic nature, accounting for the current environmental crisis. This conflict was revealed to me when the idea of an "organic" garden was viewed negatively by some of the scientists on the campus when we started in the late 1960s. Aside from thinking an organic garden was a hippie plot to further embarrass them, they thought that "organic" was the exclusive property of organic chemistry. "Organic," in this case, is equated with "artificial synthesis"; organic nature was reduced to the realm of the inorganic after it became possible to artificially synthesize anything organic from inorganic sources, once the chemistry is known. After all, as they say, chemicals are chemicals. That, for me, was the great eye-opener.

The reductionist trend in modern science, begun by Galileo on the part of mathematical physics[1] in the sixteenth century, was further advanced in the early nineteenth century, when the chemical blow to organic nature was added to the blow of mathematical physics, accounting for the radical shift from nature to matter. This shift turned out to be the key to my pursuit; the refutation and elimination of vitalism was the outcome of this development within modern science. Vitalism represented organic nature and physicalism matter. Vitalism had lost—physicalism had won. A victorious physicalism still tries to enforce the rule that matter is all that matters and only the mathematized sciences count for knowledge. Take it or leave it.

This shift is fundamental to the foundation of industrial technocracy as a world "above" the given world of nature, a world that is fundamentally artificial and synthetic, now in the late stage of self-destruction, to which the environmental movement, which I see as neo-vitalism, based on a reaffirmation of the integrity of organic nature, protests against.

As Paul Tillich put it:

I would say the most universal expression of the demonic today is a split between the control of nature by man and the fate of man to fall under the control of the product of his control. He produces, and then he falls under the power of what he has produced, the whole system of industrial existence. It has liberated him, it has given him control over nature and now it puts him into a servitude in which he loses more and more his being, his person. This form of dehumanization was what we fought against in Germany; we must continue this fight now on a much larger basis.[2]

As Hans Jonas put it in a section he calls "The Universal City as a Second Nature":

For the boundary between "city" and "nature" has been obliterated: the city of men, once an enclave in the nonhuman world, spreads over the whole of terrestrial nature and usurps its place. The difference between the artificial and the natural has vanished, the natural is swallowed up in the sphere of the artificial, and at the same time the total artifact (the works of man that have become "the world" and as such envelop their makers) generates a "nature" of its own, that is, a necessity with which human freedom has to cope in an entirely new sense.[3]

The emergence and triumph of industrial society and the collusion of modern science in the undermining of the integrity of organic nature are central to the Chadwick story. The formulation of Tillich about the late stage of the self-destruction of industrial society was to haunt me like a mantra—I found myself repeating it again and again in an effort to understand it. We were engaged in a struggle against the whole system of industrial existence, and the plight of organic nature and the effort to salvage it had put the fight on a larger basis, just as Tillich had indicated—even though it was played out on a small plot of land on a university campus. This was the place where the forces of physicalism and vitalism were enjoined, and where the struggle between these contending forces showed itself. Unbeknownst to us at the time, we were a neo-vitalist revolt in the midst of the physicalist stronghold.

Along with the influence of Tillich, it was the work of Hans Jonas that has meant the most to me in this pursuit. His work in the philosophy of nature was a perfect fit with my own views; in fact, it was a godsend. First *The Phenomenon of Life* and then *The Imperative of Responsibility* provided me with a higher-order set of conceptual formulations than I was able to manage on my own, an answer to a prayer asking for the right words that are adequate to the issue. He turned the light up and showed me the way.[4]

I had an earlier title for this book, *Alan Chadwick and the Salvation of Nature,* which I thought of adopting partly because it related to the influence of Tillich on my thought and because he had given a sermon with that title, which elucidates the theme in a compelling way. But the theme turned out to be too difficult and too theological for the purpose of telling the story of Alan's gardens, although the salvation of nature remains an abiding concern even though, from all indications, it is a hope beyond hope.

There Is a Garden in the Mind, the title I have chosen, was inspired by a phrase from Norman O. Brown's meditation on the garden, "My Georgics," in which he speaks of "a garden in the mind." Page Smith repeated the phrase in his eulogy when Alan died. I have had the Chadwick Garden in my mind for more than forty years!

There are too many people to acknowledge and thank who have played a part in the Chadwick adventure and legacy over these four decades. You know who you are and I salute you all with my gratitude and thanks, brother and sister planters and caretakers of vital roots.

I have to mention and acknowledge those who have directly encouraged me over the years and who read the manuscript and gave me helpful comments: Page Stegner edited the first draft and his help was invaluable; Victoria Nelson also gave the first draft a critical read. Likewise, Betty Peck, Eva

Fosselius, Ralph Abraham, the Rev. Herb Schmidt, Sim Van Der Ryn, Richard Baker, Virginia Baker, Bill Davis, Craig Siska, Krys and Steve Crimi, Pat Riley, Eric Thiermann, Lawrence Hershman, Bernard Taper, and the Rev. Peter H. John, whose critical reading of the final draft and especially the bibliography was most helpful. Steve Cross saved me from my block over finishing the book, and Ehren Borg's help with the final draft was invaluable. I am most grateful to him for bringing the book to completion. Evan Schaffer and Nada Miljkovic were instrumental in organizing the final stage of production with their computer support. William Rubel introduced me to the history of the French intensive method in the work by Nicolas de Bonnefons, and its introduction into England by John Evelyn, and I am grateful for our conversations on garden history.

Some years back, my nephew Benjamin Ford opened and ran a superb restaurant, Chadwick's, in Los Angeles, devoted to Alan's memory, featuring an organic menu, which I supported and appreciated. He now runs Ford's Filling Station in Culver City.

Becky Leuning transcribed the tape of Alan's lecture on thyme. George Malloch provided the first grant for the Chadwick Archive through the Herbst Foundation; and Peter Rigg, Richard Senior, and Chris Histed, relatives of Alan, helped with details of his life and ancestry, and with additional funds for the archive. I am grateful to them all, and especially to Richard Senior for solving the mystery of Pudleston, the Chadwick estate in England, and for providing photos of its recent restoration. He has maintained an unflagging interest in the project and has been helpful in every way. It is one of the unaccountable coincidences that he and his wife, Diana, spend their summers in the same small town in northern Wisconsin as we do, Phelps, where we have become good friends.

The book was designed at the Greenwood Press by my old friend Jack Stauffacher, one of the world's great typographers and fine press book designers. Jack has shared the Chadwick experience since our meeting, in 1970, when he heard there was a Goethean gardener in Santa Cruz. He has commemorated our more important garden events with a number of his elegant broadsides reproduced here. His daughter, Francesca, assisted in the production of the book, as did Dennis Letbetter, whose enthusiastic response to an earlier version I much appreciated, and who acted as photo editor, with assistance from Andrew Gaines. Jim Faris helped in the early stages and then again with the cover. I am also grateful to Eric Thiermann, who supplied the photo of me carrying my daughter, Jessica, on the first walk with the chancellor to find a possible garden site before Chadwick arrived. I am deeply grateful to them and to all who have helped in this effort. Last but not least, I want to acknowledge the support of my editor at North Atlantic Books, Jessica Moll, and the copyediting in the final stage given by Jennifer Eastman, whose critical eye was exceptional.

Nicolas Poussin, Et in Arcadia Ego (The Arcadian Shepherds). *The Louvre.* →

Et in Arcadia Ego

A famous painting by Poussin hangs in the Louvre—*The Shepherds of Arcadia.* It depicts four shepherd youths in an abandoned garden, in reflective meditation, looking at the inscription on a neglected tomb, which reads *Et in Arcadia Ego,* "And I am in Arcadia." It is a sepulchral voice from the grave, affirming the goodness and sweetness of life, after it has been lived:[1] I, too, was/am in Arcadia, having lived and enjoyed the fruits of youth, just as you, in your reverie, gaze upon me. Death making its presence known in the midst of life.

The Latin phrase was a popular slogan in Europe in the eighteenth century and was adopted by Goethe for his famous *Italian Journey.*[2]

Chadwick and I, in our Goethean lineage, through Rudolf Steiner, who carried on the Goethean legacy, adopted it for our garden project, in line with this tradition, a tradition that goes back to Virgil and the affirmation of a spiritual landscape.

On various visits to Paris, after gazing upon the Poussin in the Louvre, I have visited the Père Lachaise Cemetery, in the middle of Paris, where I like to think about the Arcadian affirmation amongst the graves—so much death in the midst of so much life. Buried there are Gertrude Stein and Alice B. Toklas, Yves Montand and Simone Signoret, Oscar Wilde, Jim Morrison of the Doors, Chopin, Abelard and Héloïse, to name a few, all crying out from the grave to be remembered for the life they lived.

I have also thought of this Arcadian outcry as the wistful voice of the end of the culture of Old Europe, saying goodbye in the face of the emerging industrial and technological society, the garbage dump and graveyard of Western culture now in the late stage of its self-destruction.

I also think of the Arcadian tomb as the grave of refuted vitalism, representing what had to be sacrificed in the face of the emerging industrial technology—vitalism representing the affirmation of the integrity of organic nature, affirming what was and would be no more—vitalism dead and buried, the vital force impugned and entombed, the bugbear of modern science.

In a chapter in his *Nature, History, and Existentialism* entitled "The Historical Background of European Nihilism," Karl Löwith reflects on the dissolution of Old Europe, identified as "the religious and moral unity of the Christian Occident." He cites the revolutionary movements, beginning with the German Reformation, then the French Revolution, and the Russian, and how they all made a clean sweep of the past. He cites Goethe prophesying the impending barbarism, declaring, "We are already right in it."[3]

In a conversation in 1829 on Europe's plight, Goethe said that the nineteenth century was not simply the continuation of the preceding century, but the beginning of a new period. He saw the time coming when God would no longer be glad of this world and "will have to smash up the whole for a renewed creation."

Poussin and Goethe, in their awareness of the tragedy of culture and the triumph of an ontology of death in the industrial society to come, gave expression, with uncanny prescience, to the end of the Western cultural epoch and the overwhelming success of the view known as physicalism, the materialist-reductionist philosophy of modern scientism.

Chadwick and I took this European slogan as our own in honoring Goethe as one of our spiritual ancestors in the tradition of the organic vitalism we affirmed. In a number of ways it was perfectly appropriate for a garden in California. After adopting the theme of Arcadia for the garden, I found a book on the Santa Cruz Mission and was startled to find a chapter on California Arcadia, describing the interlude between the secularization of the California missions (Santa Cruz was the first to be secularized) and the flowering of Spanish-Mexican culture, illustrated by the romantic portrait of the gay caballeros on their fiery black steeds (Joachim Murietta) and the beautiful, raven-haired senoritas resplendent in their mantillas on the verandas of the haciendas on the great landed estates.

Other themes played into this romantic notion of a California Arcadia: the discovery of gold and the theme of El Dorado; the old legend of black Amazon women warriors, from the Amadis of Gaul legend, written in Portuguese by Vasco de Lobeira, translated into Spanish by Montalvo, with the addition of a description of Calafia, the Amazon Queen of the Island of California, situated close to the Terrestrial Paradise.[4]

In my mind, Chadwick and I dedicated ourselves to the reestablishment of the Santa Cruz Mission, only this time it was a mission devoted to a renewal of the integrity of organic nature. We played our part in the founding mission of the organic movement in California. I credit Chadwick with replanting its vital root.

As a practitioner of biodynamics, Chadwick had been influenced by the horticultural and agricultural vision of Rudolf Steiner, who, inspired by Goethe, a major figure in the history of vitalism, carried on the vitalist affirmation of organic procedures with a spiritual vision unique to his movement of thought, known as anthroposophy.

Findhorn, a garden project in Scotland, became famous as a Steiner inspiration and captured the imagination of the 1960s, a veritable pilgrimage destination for people in search

3

of some meaningful spiritual renewal. We could have become Findhorn West but for the confines of a university community dominated by science preventing us from openly espousing the Steiner worldview. We were lucky to get by just promoting organic.

Steiner is the odd man out in this narrative, difficult to describe and nearly impossible to integrate, as far as what is acceptable or even intelligible to a university-educated audience and readership. The term *far out* could have been coined to describe him. He is the test case for the defeat of vitalism and one of the best examples of the conflict over what counts for knowledge. One hardly knows how to count him, especially if you went to Harvard and taught at MIT, as I did; even so, as difficult and unintelligible as much of his thought is, I don't count him out.

The reader is invited to consult any of the various biographies of Steiner and to enter, as far as possible, the world of thought he represents, contrary as it is to ordinary forms of thought. He represents vitalism in its most radical type and provides the bridge back to Goethe. Goethe was opposed to Newton, the father, along with Galileo and Descartes, of physicalism. My views are defined by this divide and this conflict, best represented by Goethe contra Newton.[5]

To the reader unfamiliar with much of the language I use, taken from the history and philosophy of science, it may sound like code. The concepts constituting the code have a scholarly literature devoted to them. These concepts and themes appeared to me as I pursued the literature and tried to resolve my consternation over why an organic garden should be a force fit at a university rather than a welcome addition, and why scientists should take umbrage over the meaning of the word "organic." It was as though our resuscitation of the old meaning of vitalism was like Jesus raising Lazarus from the grave: it stinketh.

I once visited J. B. Jackson, professor of architecture and design, in his office at Harvard and told him about Chadwick and our garden project and the tradition of biodynamic and French intensive gardening, going back through Rudolf Steiner to Goethe (as well as our slogan adopted from Goethe's *Italian*

Journey), and he told me about the theory that "gardens were planted on gravesites"; hence, the "raised bed."

A garden grave—let my garden be my grave—became our affirmation, Alan's and mine,[6] the retrospective affirmation of the goodness and sweetness of life, the affirmation of the goodness of creation, which gardens represent, so that the garden of Eden and the Arcadian garden are one, unified as twin sources of Western culture, mythical exemplars of a spiritual landscape.[7]

Paul Tillich summed it up perfectly:

The "garden" is the place where the curse upon the land is overcome. In it vegetative nature is liberated from chaos and self-destruction; "weed," there is none. This "garden of the gods," of which every human garden is a symbol and an anticipation, will reappear in the salvation of nature.[8]

I love the theme of creation and the unambiguous affirmation God pronounces when it is seen as good. It is the ground of all hope, but I thought the salvation of nature was more than I could hope for, in spite of the hope Chadwick gave us in what amounted to a second chance. Hope is an important theological theme. Ernst Bloch wrote his three-volume classic, *The Principle of Hope,* on the theme. Hans Jonas followed in his steps with his *Imperative of Responsibility,* which, in its original German title, *Das Prinzip Verantwortung,* echoes Bloch. Gardens are grounds for hope. You sow seed, and it comes up and prospers, and the yield is often enormous. Nature's bounty, exemplifying the principle of plenitude, is a cause for hope. Gardens die and are reborn according to the seasons. "Life into death into life" was a favorite saying of Chadwick, especially when he thought of compost and dead stuff as the material for new life.

In spite of the depressing signs that the earth is endangered, Tillich, in the tradition of St. Paul, never lost his hope for the salvation of nature, even though he knew that when scientists announced the need for a science of survival, they didn't mean the survival of individuals or social groups, of nations and of races, but of life altogether on the surface of this planet. He compared it with the story of the great Flood in the Old Testament and in the myths of many nations. Then the gods or God brought about the destruction of life on earth because

5

of wrath over mankind. God was sorry for making man on the earth, and it grieved him to his heart, so he vowed to blot man out. Noah alone is saved along with a pair of each species of animal. Remember the dove and the olive branch? Now, however, the destruction is in the hands of man himself, as though nature made a mistake in producing this destructive creature. No sign from God may be given, because we have brought the destruction upon ourselves.

Tillich refers to the profound human concern and tormented anxiety over the fate of the earth that is characteristic of this era, and this he said decades before the gloom-and-doom genre of the environmental lament, along with the raft of books announcing nature's "death." He refers to looking deep into the minds of his contemporaries, especially the younger generation, and discovering a dread that permeates their whole being, a dread that was absent a few decades earlier and one he finds hard to describe, although he attempts to do so: "It is the sense of living under a continuous threat; and although it may have many causes, the greatest of these is the imminent danger of a universal and total catastrophe."[9]

This is exactly what I perceived in the students who looked to Chadwick as a way back to the trust in Mother Earth and her protective and preserving power, which, they thought, but for Chadwick, had disappeared. There was no need to tell them that the predicament they shared had been brought about by the scientific and technical development of the twentieth century—the realm created by human beings, which Tillich always called "the world above the given world of nature," because it was beyond the realm given by nature when humanity first emerged from earlier forms of life; a realm now subject to self-destruction.

I remember picking up the theme of the tragedy of culture as a variant of the tragedy of nature in a book by Ernst Cassirer, *The Logic of the Humanities,* and wondering what he meant. Now it is obvious. And the lament of God in the Biblical account reminds us of this theme of judgment, frustration, and tragedy:

There is no theme in Biblical literature, nor in any other, more persistently pursued than this one. The earth has been cursed by man innumer-

able times, because she produced him, together with all life and its misery, which includes the tragedy of human history.[10]

Today it is man who has the power to blot himself out, and often he is so sorry that he has been made man that he desires to withdraw from his humanity altogether.... Can it be that the earth, fully conquered by man, will cease to be a place where man wants to live?[11]

As Hans Jonas puts it in his discussion of humanity's disturbance of the symbiotic balance:

Nature could not have incurred a greater hazard than to produce man: with his emergence, it potentially upset its internal balance and left it to the gathering momentum of his career to do so actually. That actuality has now come to pass.[12]

I found I was more influenced by the despair of the historical period we're in, and the self-destruction that is so prevalent, than the hope for the salvation of nature. Titles such as *Silent Spring* and *The Death of Nature* and *The End of Nature* have superseded *The Greening of America*. How dated Charles Reich's account about the revolutionary aspirations of the 1960s sounds now, even though the garden was at the center of such hopes with the theme of "Flower Power." How can one be sensitive to the plight of organic nature and feel hopeful, especially when the very survival of the earth is threatened and the doomsday clock is ticking?

I remember a television program about the storage dumps (many of them presumably in the hands of the Mafia) leaking chemicals throughout the United States. At the end of the program the list of such dumps *in every state* scrolled down the screen and I sat there thinking *it's all over*—in both senses of the phrase! A series of programs narrated by Walter Cronkite, entitled "Armageddon," details the worldwide prospects for disaster in chemical and biological weapons, *and* nuclear, all beyond anyone's wildest imagination.

I had been obsessed with the smashing of the atom and the feared "wayward reaction." Enrico Fermi, who led the effort, did the math that would determine its feasibility. He was worried that the earth might be destroyed should the experiment go haywire. A "suicide squad" stood by to risk death by intervening if the rods had to be replaced in the pile. The squad had to wear special suits. The "wayward reaction" didn't happen as Fermi feared. The experiment went off without a hitch as Fermi hoped. They even broke for lunch. The atom was smashed, heralding a new era. Then, when the Bomb went off, Oppenheimer quoted the Bhagavad Gita, "We have seen death; we are the destroyers of worlds." He knew that the wayward reaction had happened *in another sense,* and would continue to happen. The earth *was* threatened with destruction. Weapons of mass destruction could lead to a nuclear holocaust.

While writing this book, I was wavering between despair and hope. I had to force myself to think about hope after a friend and colleague read the first draft and complained about the gloom. I had to shift my vision and look at what had been accomplished and what a great legacy Chadwick had bequeathed us, he who knew as well as anyone what a fix we were in. I remembered the words of Martin Luther, "even if the world were to end tomorrow, I would still plant my cherry tree today."

I once gave a talk at a Unitarian church outside of Santa Cruz and spoke about Chadwick, his vision, and what he had accomplished, and I noticed a man in the front row quietly weeping. Afterward, I went up to him and asked what was the matter, and he said, "I didn't know that we had been given a second chance."

That was enough to hold me for a while. I realized it was a mistake to look within myself, where I could only hear hollow reverberations in the void and the sense that nothing could fill it, and instead listen to the message of hope that is held out to us. It is not one we could make up. It does not come from us. It is one for which we are the recipients, as in the sense of "vouchsafed." As St. Paul says about Abraham, "hoping against hope."

I realized I had been unduly influenced by existentialism and the quandary and predicament of human beings at this time in history. It was too easy to give in to the mood of despair and oblivion, as though the image of man as crowned with glory and honor, a little lower than angels, was just what we wanted to get rid of and wished we had never possessed, dispensing, as well, with the testimonies of the Psalmist, or Shakespeare, or Pascal, on the heights and depths of being human. Forget the heights, especially in the wake of the Holocaust and the Bomb, coloring everything having to do with hope. The world was too much with us....

Wasn't the sympathy for native cultures, especially the American Indian, a hidden desire to return to the state of creatures unaware of themselves and their world (in the sense of the burden of rational self-consciousness, characteristic of Europeans and the legacy of ancient Greece), limited to the satisfaction of their animal needs, embedded in the tribe, unburdened by the subject/object split of a science-determined world? This is the questionable side of vitalism and one that has come to the surface, where the mind itself is viewed as a kind of disease, counter to the impulsiveness of vital drives, checking them, suppressing them, transforming them, in order to achieve full rational self-conscious literacy, the aim of education.

This is what Nietzsche meant in his criticism of rational self-consciousness and his affirmation of the will-to-power and his predilection for the heroic might of Achilles over the rational self-consciousness of Socrates. Nostalgia for the archaic, where earliest is best and least contaminated by the evolution of culture to its current decadence; the archaic power of being is what people longed for in their all-pervading sense that something was missing. *Aber etwas fehlt.*[13]

The entire culture of Western self-consciousness, going back to the ancient Greeks and the birth of rationality, is now under attack as eventuating in industrial technocracy and the control and domination and exploitation of nature by the human mind.

I have my hesitations about this attack, although I understand it, especially in the turn from revelatory and receptive reason to instrumental or technical and controlling reason, a turn I associate with Galileo and the rise of modern science and the mathematization not only of nature but of knowledge as well, including the rejection of the human subject understood as the bearer of "secondary" or "occult" qualities.

E. A. Burtt gave me this theme:

Now, in the course of translating this distinction of primary and secondary into terms suited to the new mathematical interpretation of nature, we have the first stage in the reading of man quite out of the real and primary realm. Obviously man was not a subject suited to mathematical study…. The only thing in common between man and this real world was his ability to discover it, a fact which, being necessarily presupposed, was easily neglected, and did not in any case suffice to exalt him to a parity of reality and causal efficiency with that which he was able to know. Quite naturally enough, along with this exaltation of the external world as more primary and more real, went an attribution to it of greater dignity and value. Galileo himself proceeds to this attribution…. The features of the world now classed as secondary, unreal, ignoble, and regarded as dependent on the deceitfulness of sense, are just those features which are most intense to man in all but his purely theoretic activity, and even in that, except where he confines himself to the mathematical method. It was inevitable that in these circumstances man should now appear to be outside of the real world; man is hardly more than a bundle of secondary qualities. Observe that the stage is fully set for the Cartesian dualism—on the one side of primary, the mathematical realm; on the other the realm of man. And the premium of importance and value as well as of independent existence all goes with the former. Man begins to appear for the first time in the history of thought as an irrelevant spectator and insignificant effect of the great mathematical system which is the substance of reality.[14]

Chadwick and I entered this scene in Santa Cruz at the point of a checkmate. The social and cultural order (or disorder) was called into question by the student body of the time. They were listening to the call of the times as formulated by Timothy Leary, "Turn on, tune in, drop out!" Get out of the bourgeois rat race. Don't submit to the training system of servants of industrial technocracy. Go back to basics. Turn on to the natural order and its vital ground and find it in yourselves. Revive the power of being of the archaic past we have lost. See eternity in a grain of sand. "Be here now!"

Chadwick was a prophet for just this time, as he inveighed against the destructive consequences of industrial society upon organic nature as much as he brought a healing hand to the earth. The soils he produced with his composting techniques were as healthy as you could get, but the salvation of nature as a theme was still beyond my reach, even though I knew I could get up from my writing and reflections on these matters at any time and stroll around in my garden and pick a ripe pear or an Arkansas black apple, watch the figs mature, see the borage growing in the path, the Towers of Jewels *(Echium)* looming above the tree dahlias, already twenty feet high, almost laughable in their fecundity and proliferation, ready to grow anywhere, even between the bricks in the patio. I planted a bay tree when it was six inches tall, and now it reminds me of the Burning Bush, so awesome is it, in breadth and height, twenty feet tall and in command of the center of the garden!

I could go on and on about the revelations of mysteries right under my nose in my own backyard—the *Artemisia absinthium* I planted in the place of honor (when I first put in an herb garden and found out Artemis was the first herbalist of the Western tradition in ancient Greece) grew to twenty feet; the volunteer *Eupatoriums* that appeared along the spring at the back of the property almost to the day that I found out about Mithridates Eupator (who was famous for "the mithridate," as it came to be called, which his court physician, Krateuas, concocted to make him invulnerable to poison); the *Silybum marianum,* or milk thistle, which appeared about the time we found out about its properties as a liver restorative and as a cure for *Amanita p.* poisoning, also a volunteer; the Tibetan rose I grew from seed that Adelaide DeMenil gave me after a trip to Tibet: I watched it bloom on Easter Sunday; the thyme and chamomile beds I planted on the slope next to the spring that runs at the back of our property, designed to the shape of the body, so that you could lie down in them and smell their salubrious scents; the Indian peach, which is more like a plum, that I grew from seed provided by Joanne LeBoeuf, now in bloom and ready to fruit, all five of them. All this I ultimately owe to Chadwick and his hope in the bounty of nature and the beauty of creation.

Paul Tillich's sermon, with the theme of the salvation of nature, was a theme I had in mind for years in thinking about Chadwick and a philosophy of gardens. Tillich alerted me to Schelling's statement, "Nature, too, mourns for a lost good," which haunted me in its relation to Alan, who grieved more than anyone I have known over the loss of "nature's good," a saying that came to me when Alan died.

I was aware of the theme of the salvation of nature in the letters of the apostle Paul—the fall of nature, and all creation groaning with eager longing for redemption, with signs too deep for words, bearing witness to the stigma of finitude on

ET IN ARCADIA EGO

Trees, plants, and flowers — of virtuous root:
Gem yielding blossom, yielding fruit,
  Choice gums and precious balm;
Bless ye the nosegay of the vale,
And with the sweetness of the gale
  Enrich the thankful psalm.

Christopher Smart *from A Song To David*

Trial proof for Alan Chadwick & Paul Lee of the
UC Santa Cruz Student Garden Project
22 Jan '72 The Greenwood Press

Broadside for the Chadwick Garden.
The Greenwood Press, 1972.

behalf of all creatures. Tillich alerted me to the meaning of salvation as an act of cosmic healing in his essay "The Relation of Religion and Health." I copied it out in longhand when I found it and then had the pleasure of publishing it with my introduction years later. This is what he says:

What is the place of health in the frame of the idea of salvation? In asking this question, we do not turn to the modern theological doctrines of salvation for an answer. They have mostly lost the original power of the idea of salvation, its cosmic meaning which includes nature, man as a whole, and society…. Salvation is basically a cosmic event: the world is saved.[15]

I was thrilled to find this essay, because I had given up pursuing a medical career (in the footsteps of my physician father) and turned to philosophy after my chemistry professor, judging my clumsiness in the lab, offered me a C if I abandoned premed, since I was sure to flunk. My main interests were philosophy of religion and theology, following, as it were, in the footsteps of my mother, whose family background was made up of Lutheran ministers and a very famous German Old Testament theologian—Otto Eissfeldt.

It was at St. Olaf College that I experienced Arcadia and Eden firsthand, in the example of my philosophy teacher and his wife, Howard and Edna Hong, the great translators of Kierkegaard. They embodied and lived a type of Edenic or Arcadian style that impressed me deeply. Howard had built his home on the edge of the campus in the fieldstone of the place, and it had the warmest and most nurturing character of any home I have known, but more than anything it expressed the spirit that animated them. If anyone set me up for meeting Chadwick, they did. They represented a lifestyle in harmony with organic nature at its best.

Paul Tillich became my mentor when, at the height of his popularity, I heard him give some lectures on existentialism at St. Olaf. I didn't understand a word he said, but I had the sense I had found my teacher. He made it possible for me to articulate the themes the Chadwick Garden revealed to me. I rely on what I have learned from him more than from anyone else, with the exception of Hans Jonas.

My interest in a philosophy of gardening encompasses many themes taken from Western culture. Central is the theme of Eden and Arcadia, the symbolic gardens at the foundation of the cultures of Israel and Greece. This memory of an original garden of culture is the expression of an affirmation of the goodness of creation just as it is a longing for paradise. Eliade has written the classic essay on it, "The Yearning for Paradise in the Ancient Tradition."[16]

If *Et in Arcadia Ego* is the voice from the grave of Western culture saying farewell, then Goethe used it as an expression of his despair over the future. Old Europe was going down. No more the Green Knight (Witiko),[17] no more the song of von der Vogelweider, as it came to fruition in the lieder of Schubert, who set to music the poems of Goethe and whose *Die schöne Müllerin* can be listened to as the swan song of German culture. Goethe took the pulse of this demise. He was the classical author who knew in his heart of hearts that he was the last one to bear witness to what had begun with Homer. The strain was more than he could bear, so he took a two-year hiatus and went south, writing in his journal and painting with watercolors.

He was even initiated into the Arcadian Society in Rome and told about it in his journal, a society of poets with a theme going back through Dante to Virgil's Arcadian poems, the *Eclogues* and *Georgics*.

Goethe realized that the tradition of Western culture had come to an end in him. From Homer, to Virgil, to Dante, to Goethe—throw in Shakespeare and Milton—the epic tradition of the perfect tense: the transmission of cultural substance had run its course. Faust is the epitaph. Sell your soul to the devil and join in the triumphant rise of industrial society after the French Revolution and the placing of Athena on the altar of the Royal Abbey of St. Denis—from rationalism to physicalism—the rise and triumph of the revolutionary bourgeoisie. It is a juggernaut, this modern period we are struggling to call "postmodern" in order to escape from its thrall and put it behind us.

The memory of the Arcadian affirmation, the wistful farewell to the noble youths, the shepherds, who pause in reflection before the inscription on the tomb, lives on as a voice from beyond the grave. "And I, too, am in that garden."

Goethe's Italian Journey *Et In Arcadia Ego*
1786-1787

3 September 'I slipped out of Carlsbad at three in the morning.'

Trento 11 September 1786

Verona 16

Padua 'Here where I am confronted with a great variety of plants, my hypothesis that it might be possible to derive all plant forms (*Urpflanze*) from one original plant becomes clearer to me and more exciting.'

Vicenza 19

Vicenza 'I called upon Scamozzi, an old architect who has brought out a book on Palladio and is himself a competent and dedicated artist.'

Padua 26

VENICE 28

Ferrara 16 October

Venice 'So now, thank god, Venice is no longer a mere word to me, an empty name, a state of mind which has so often alarmed me who am the mortal enemy of mere words.'

Bologna 18

Florence 23

Perugia 25

Terni 27

Rome 'All the dreams of my youth have come to life; the first engravings I remember – my father hung views of Rome in the hall – I now see in reality, and everything I have known for so long through paintings, drawings, etchings, woodcuts, plaster casts and cork models is now assembled before me.'

ROME 1 November

NAPLES 25 February 1787

Naples 'I won't say another word about the beauties of the city and its situation, which have been described and praised so often. As they say here, *Vedi Napoli e poi muori!* – See Naples and die!'

Palermo Sicily 2 April

Girgenti 23

Caltanissetta 28

Catania 2 May

Taormina 7

Messina 10

Returns to Naples May 17

Palermo 'The enchanted garden, the inky waves on the northern horizon, breaking on the curved beaches of the bays, and the peculiar tang of the sea air, all conjured up images of the island of the blessed Phaeacians. I hurried off to buy myself a Homer so that I could read the canto in which he spoke of them.'

100 copies handset & designed by Jack W. Stauffacher of the Greenwood Press, in celebration of the 200th Anniversary of J. W. Goethe's Italian Journey – *lecture, concert & exhibition at Holy Cross Church, 11 March 1987, Santa Cruz, California. Kis, van Dijck & Meridien types. Printed on French BFK Rives paper. *Part 1 and 2. Trans. Auden & Mayer, Schocken Books, 1968. Copy number*

Broadside on Goethe's Italian Journey.
The Greenwood Press, 1987.

Paul Lee and his daughter, Jessica, on a walk with the
chancellor to look for a site for the student garden project, 1967.
Photos by Eric Thiermann.

Chapter One

The English Gardener Arrives

Alan Chadwick arrived one day in 1967, some weeks after I had organized a walk with the chancellor and a group of interested people to look for a possible site for a garden project. It was an irresistible impulse, the source of which I did not know. I thought a garden on the campus would be a good idea, but I wasn't clear about what prompted me to think so, or what I was supposed to do about it. Chadwick was coming, and I must have sensed it. I like thinking that now. It is one of the few experiences in my life in which, in retrospect, I have the feeling that I was guided.[1]

I wasn't interested in gardening; as a typical academic, I was interested in the *idea* of gardening. I thought it would be a good project for the students on the campus of a university that had been a great ranch landscape—the Cowell Ranch— with vistas looking out from redwood groves to Monterey Bay and the Pacific Ocean. The students could do the work. I would watch and oversee and enjoy the asters and the poppies when they bloomed. And, of course, in the mid-1960s, "flower power" was in the air, wafting down from the Haight-Ashbury on a cloud of smoke. We all got a whiff of that. I wanted to put flower power into practice.

George Hunston Williams had been my church history professor at Harvard, and I had helped him with a book he wrote, *Wilderness and Paradise,* describing the history of these motifs in the Bible and throughout Western culture, transposed by analogy as desert and garden. The second half of his book is about the rise of higher education in America. Inspired by desert/wilderness and garden/paradise themes, pioneers from the east headed west to plant gardens in the wilderness, to start schools in accordance with the biblical directives, also reminiscent of the schools of Plato and Aristotle, which included gardens. It was the first time my name appeared in a book, in his list of acknowledgments. I like to think it was a sign of things to come, when I lived out those very motifs after relocating to Santa Cruz.[2]

Before I assumed my Santa Cruz teaching duties at Crown College, I taught for a year at Cowell College, where Page Smith was the provost. My colleague and office partner, Donald Nicholl, a visiting professor of history, had given a speech that affected me deeply, "A Sense of Place," referring to his British friend David Jones, the artist and poet, whose sense of place was acutely attuned to Wales. Donald bemoaned the difficulty of achieving such a sense at a state university, where students were mostly subjected to bureaucratic processing: a secular desert where the spirit was at stake.[3] On one of his last days before returning to England, we had a long talk about his impressions, and he spoke about the "spiritual laceration" he had suffered as a result of his visit, a phrase he borrowed from Dostoyevsky. He also had in mind something like the need for roots at an institution where the life of the spirit and spiritual roots were the last things on anyone's mind.[4]

I had seen a plan for the campus that called for a projected fixed population figure of 27,500, somehow arrived at as the target for each of the campus sites in the system. This meant something like 15,000 parking lots, which conjured up a lot of asphalt. I groaned under this institutional imposition on a great ranch landscape and could hear the redwoods groaning with me.

I thought a student garden would help offset this institutional imposition.

Santa Cruz was supposed to be the new beacon of hope for higher education, a major departure from the established campuses of the University of California, but for the fixed figure of the eventual population. Following the model of British universities, Santa Cruz would be comprised of smaller colleges, each of which would have a theme, a representative faculty, a library, dormitories, all under the aegis of the university, but autonomous units unto themselves. Cowell College, the first to open, in 1965, was devoted to the humanities. Teaching would be honored over publishing, so the promotional propaganda read, a promise that was not kept under the pressure of "publish or perish," the bugbear of academic advancement.

Some of us had the suspicion that the ulterior motive for a network of independent colleges was to disperse the students so they could not easily organize. Santa Cruz was a reaction to Berkeley and the mega-university of industrial technocracy, provocative of student unrest, which eventually erupted nationally in response to the Vietnam War. And erupt it did at Santa Cruz as well. Geographic distance between the colleges deterred no one in acting out their anguish over the war.

A British flavor was injected into the culture of the university by using British academic terminology: *common rooms,* not *lounges; provosts,* not *deans; boards of study,* not *departments;* and a number of British professors were hired to carry through the influence, notable among them Jasper Rose, professor of art history, and Glenn Wilson in political science.

I didn't have an English gardener in mind to further the theme, but I should have.

A few weeks after the walk with the chancellor, the English gardener arrived, as though on schedule. He was told about my interest in a garden project by his friend Freya von Moltke, who was visiting the campus for a quarter. He had stopped off to visit her, returning from a trip to New Zealand, where he had thought of resettling. She had told him he wouldn't like it, and she was right. It was as though he wanted her to tell him what to do next. A week or two before, Freya and her companion, Eugen Rosenstock-Huessy, a visiting professor at Cowell College, had come to our home for lunch, and she told me she had heard about my walk with the chancellor and that I wanted to start a garden. She had a friend coming who would do the garden for me. I said, "Okay, Countess."

Freya was the widow of Count Helmuth von Moltke, one of the great figures in the resistance against Hitler. He was the leader of the Kreisau Circle, named after the estate he inherited as the grandnephew of the famous German General von Moltke, the founder of the modern German army under Bismarck, who was buried at Kreisau, making it a national shrine. For thinking about the future of Germany after Hitler, and holding secret planning sessions at Kreisau, Helmuth was accused of treason and was hanged from a meat hook with piano wire. There is a national memorial devoted to him and others at Plötzensee Prison in Berlin. He was caught up in the net of the Officers' Bomb Plot, an unsuccessful attempt on Hitler's life, and even though he had been *against* assassination, he was executed for his ideas about the future of Germany.[5]

A woman of luminous beauty, with a voice to match, Freya had become the companion of Eugen Rosenstock-Huessy, the great polymath, who fled Germany when Hitler came to power and who had worked with von Moltke in youth work-service camps until Hitler nationalized them. Eugen had been Page Smith's professor at Dartmouth, where, in 1940, they had started Camp William James, a leadership training camp for the Civilian Conservation Corps. They wanted to bring the spirit of William James and the vision of his famous talk at Stanford in 1906, "A Moral Equivalent of War," into what had become a kind of holding tank for welfare youth, due to the so-called means test one had to sign, indicating poverty, in order to be eligible for the corps. They had the blessing of Mrs. Roosevelt and Dorothy Thompson, the famous journalist, to open up the corps to the middle class, and so they started a camp for that purpose at Tunbridge, Vermont. It was short lived, and within months the adventure was over. The war had begun.

Page had invited Rosenstock-Huessy to Santa Cruz to teach at Cowell College as a visiting professor after his retirement, and Freya accompanied him.

I later came to realize that the short-lived effort on a farm in Vermont—Camp William James—was to be reborn in our Chadwick Garden in California, once the confluence of historical forces unfolded. It became clear to me only years later, after Page Smith and I teamed up to start the William James Association, in 1972, and later helped Jerry Brown, when governor of California, inaugurate the California Conservation Corps, with the hope of carrying through the Chadwick legacy.

Freya was Chadwick's muse—everyone could see why—and the love of his life. They met and became friends in South Africa, where Chadwick had gone to act in a traveling theater company and eventually shifted to gardening at the Admiralty Gardens in Capetown.[6]

After the defeat of Germany and the loss of her estate—Kreisau—to the Russians, Freya had fled to Capetown with her sons to join family who had settled there. She met Alan in Capetown. After becoming friends, she told me how Alan had come to see her in her cottage. They had an argument, and Alan had displayed his famous temper and rode off on his bike, and as she was about to jump on her bike and chase after him, she knew that that would be it. It would be construed as a declaration of love with the implication of a possible marriage. Either/or. She stayed home.

I remember Alan talking about the wildlife of Africa and his joy romping with the lions and tigers and the gazelles and whatnot as if he were one of them in his element.[7] Freya's sons have fond memories of Alan and their friendship with Alan, acting as a substitute father and introducing them to nature's mysteries as only he could do.

Who was Alan Chadwick? What were his roots? What was his background? Born on July 27, 1909, he was from landed gentry of considerable means and a family history of distinction going back generations. He often referred to Pudleston Court, the family estate after Swinton Hall, as if he had been brought up there in the lap of luxury, but Pudleston was sold about thirty years before Alan was born, although his grandfather retained the farms for the rental income. These lands could have been Alan's reference. He had china and silverware with the Chadwick crest, which I was led to believe were artifacts from Pudleston. He and his brother, Seddon, were brought up at "Long Coppice," Bournemouth, where there is a stained-glass window bearing the Chadwick arms, so we are clear about his actual home and its location, not to be confused with one of the ancestral homes.

Alan's father, Harry Chadwick, born in 1849, was a graduate of Oxford and a lawyer by profession. He met his second wife, Elizabeth Rarp, Alan's mother, at a hotel near Henley, where he attended the famous rowing races. His first wife, Jane Lane Boxall, was from famous stock; an ancestor, Jane Lane, saved the life of the king of England—Charles II—in an episode that was considered one of the great events of English history. It is one of eight historic incidents com-

21

memorated by eight-by-ten-foot frescoes in the Houses of Parliament. The king decreed that the first-born female in the line from then on should bear the name "Jane Lane."

After Jane died, Harry lived in Eaton Place, London, in the house formerly occupied by Lady Hamilton, the mistress of Lord Nelson, and one of the most fabulous figures of the time, famous for her eccentric tableaux performances where, sitting in a large box for a stage, she would strike a pose. Goethe was delighted by her performance.

Alan's grandfather was Henry Strettell Chadwick (1807–1889), the oldest son of Elias Chadwick, and therefore the first in line to inherit. Later in life, he lived in Kensington Gardens Square, one of the most fashionable districts of London. The "Garden House" is still there and is now a shelter for the homeless. His kinsman was Sir Edwin Chadwick, a social reformer allied with Jeremy Bentham and Florence Nightingale, involved in sanitation reform and sewer systems, earning him the nickname of "Drains" Chadwick. Elias Chadwick was Alan's great-uncle, who sold Swinton Hall and bought Pudleston Court in 1846, a 911-acre estate. He demolished the existing house and built a fine modern stone mansion, with tower and turrets, in the old English castellated style of architecture, pleasantly situated on a sloping eminence in the midst of tastefully laid-out ornamental grounds (Littlebury's Directory of 1876). Alan's father inherited Pudleston from his uncle Elias.

An anecdote about Alan's great-great-grandfather is worth repeating. Elias Chadwick of Wigan (1729–1808), who lived at Swinton Hall, was a cotton manufacturer and is remembered in "Recollections of Old Swinton" (1914):

The following quaint story of old Mr. Chadwick is worth relating as casting light on the doings of those times: "He was in Manchester on one occasion sitting in the old Seven Sisters public house, either drunk or pretending to be asleep, when two gentlemen came in. Supposing him to be asleep they began to talk about a certain ship due to arrive in Liverpool that night, and where they were going the next day to purchase the cargo of cotton the ship had brought. The old man was neither so drunk nor so fast asleep as not to hear all that was said, and to understand the situation.

"Rising up, he made for home and on arrival he said to his coachman

The Chadwick coat of arms.

An example of the Chadwick plate he proudly displayed in the garden, an artifact from Pudleston.

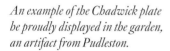

'John, yoke Captain in the gig!' 'Why master, where are you going at this time of night?' John asked. 'We're going to Liverpool,' was the reply. John was amazed but he did as he was told.

   "As they were returning the next day they met the same two gentlemen driving to Liverpool. They remarked to each other, 'We are done!' And so they were, for old Chadwick had bought the cargo of cotton and cleared the sum of £36,000. (£1,500,000 today). Old Mr. Chadwick was referred to as a 'sturdy veteran with £100,000 in each pocket.'"

This was the period when the Chadwicks acquired their wealth, with textile production and with coal production from mines around Winstanley. They played a part in Britain's in-

Chadwick's publicity photo as a professional actor.

dustrial revolution, indicated by the growth of mills from forty in 1780 to eight hundred in 1830. Coal powered the machines that manufactured their textiles.

It is a strange coincidence that Alan's nephew Peter Rigg, one of my sources for the family history, was a patient at Pudleston in 1941, when it had become an officers' convalescent home during World War II.

Although Alan referred to his landed-gentry past and the estates involved, none of this seemed to make any difference, but for his aristocratic bearing, his manners, and his breeding, when he dropped, as though from on high, onto the Santa Cruz campus. He had the habits of an ascetic hermit, living on a meager salary, asking for nothing, subsisting mostly on produce from the garden, devoted absolutely to his gardening, which occupied all of his time. Eventually he would take part in some activities on the campus, such as public lectures, which I arranged, and he starred in a production of Shakespeare—*Love's Labours Lost.* We all showed up to watch Alan strut his stuff. Bernard Taper, in researching Alan's career in the theater in London, obtained many of the press reviews of his performances, now on deposit in the Chadwick

Archive. They bear witness to his considerable talent as an actor, although it is a stretch to think of Alan in *A Streetcar Named Desire*. He played the part of the suitor.

His theatrical training and experience were always in evidence. He was always dramatic, in elocution, in gestures, in deep emotions. He wanted students to follow suit and often tutored them in deportment and speech. We knew it would be important to try to capture him on film and to record the glory of the garden at its most blooming season, so we obtained a grant, and Michael Stusser, a student apprentice devoted to Alan, began shooting film.

I took Alan to the recording studio on campus to help develop a soundtrack for the documentary we were making of the garden. I sat him in front of a microphone, and I guess it was turned on too loud. The feedback sound startled him and infuriated him, and he got up and stormed out. I was going to interview him. So much for Alan's involvement in the film.

An amazing coincidence occurred somewhat later. Michael Stusser was in the sound lab one evening working on the film when he heard Norman O. Brown's voice recording his meditation on the garden, which he immodestly called "My Georgics," after Virgil, no less. Stusser ran around until he found Brown in another studio and asked if he could use it as the voice-over for the film, and Brown consented. It is inimitably Nobby, as we all called him, the premiere professor on the campus, the darling of the New Agers, whose bibles were his *Life against Death* and *Love's Body,* both popular books at the time.[8]

Remarkably, Chadwick's apprentices (especially Craig Siska) carefully preserved more than a hundred tapes of his talks from throughout the course of his gardening career. The tapes, now in the Chadwick Archive at UCSC's McHenry Library, were copied and organized by Krys and Steve Crimi, in collaboration with Margaret Gordon.

I wish I had taken the chance to inquire into Alan's life and background, or taken notes when he reminisced with me about his family history, their great estates and gardens, and how they influenced him and directed his abilities in this regard. I wish I had another chance at the whole process, now that I know something about garden history and the significance of the great English gardens, as well as the Italian and French, in the history of Western culture. It is considerable. We could have developed a course of studies in garden history if for no other reason than to accommodate the humanities in the teaching of Western culture, and then to add this most interesting theme to the university curriculum, now a well-organized scholarly pursuit.

The heritage is so compelling, and the connection between English gardens and Greek and Roman culture so clear. One line of transmission is through Andrea Palladio (1508–1580), one of the key figures of the Italian Renaissance, who restored the antique meaning of architecture, in a line that goes from Vitruvius (fl. first century BCE) to Palladio to Inigo Jones (1573–1652), who introduced the principles of Palladian and Vitruvian architecture into England, along with the principles of classic forms, the classic orders, the columns (Doric, Ionic, and Corinthian), as well as ruins, grottoes, the cave of the nymphs, obelisks, and so forth—all of the features of Italian gardens that were incorporated into British gardens on the great aristocratic and royal estates. It is a glorious tradition.

Palladio, for whom I have inexplicably developed a kind of obsession, was Andrea Gondola, a stone mason and sculptor discovered by Gian Giorgio Trissino (1478–1550), an Italian Renaissance polymath and mentor, who had a villa in Vicenza, where many of Palladio's great villas were to be built. When Trissino met him, he knew this was to be the greatest architect in the history of culture. So he renamed him "Palladio" (after Pallas Athena, the goddess of wisdom) to celebrate his discovery and to anticipate his destiny. I learned the symbolic meaning from Rudolf Steiner studies, going back to the Palladium, the underground chapel in Rome that housed the great figure of Pallas Athena. Aeneas had brought from Troy the statue of the great goddess, symbolizing the transmission of the spirit of ancient culture from Greece to Italy. Palladio's name carried the spiritual transmission of this cultural tradition. And so the principles of Greek and Roman architecture came to flourish in Renaissance Italy.

Just as the great villa gardens expressed one of the high points of Roman culture, and again of Renaissance Italy, so too they did of Georgian England. Lord Burlington was the focal point, coming on the wings of the Grand Tour, in which British aristocrats, like Goethe years later, made their pilgrimage to the sources of the culture, to Virgil's tomb—to Arcadia!

The spiritual landscape of the classical tradition, the garden in the mind, was reborn in England, as the spirit of the place.

Alan brought this spirit of the culture of gardens to Santa Cruz and fulfilled my hope for a sense of place once the garden was established, and though nothing on the scale or grandeur of the great gardens of Europe and England, the garden proved to be a magnetic draw for students, giving them a place to plant themselves.

The English garden was an enormous source of fascination for the founding fathers of our country. Jefferson and Adams were avid gardeners and developed a passionate interest in botany and in seed and plant collecting. They travelled together visiting the popular garden sites in England. George Washington shared this love of gardening and took great pride in the management of his estates.[9]

It is not known when and where Alan was introduced to the system of French intensive gardening. During the years in England when he was growing up, an interest in the French market gardens around Paris was reflected by references in books and magazines. Avid kitchen gardeners would certainly have been aware of the system of raised beds combined with heavy manuring and of the use of cold frames that was the hallmark of the French approach. Garden historians would have been familiar with the approach, since the primacy of the French system for growing vegetables in the kitchen and market gardens was well known in England from at least the second half of the seventeenth century, when, in 1658, John Evelyn, the influential British author, horticulturist, and man about town, published *The French Gardener,* a translation of the first popular work documenting the French raised-bed gardening system, written by Nicolas de Bonnefons. This work was followed by translations of other important French texts on the same subject, notably also by John Evelyn, an abridgment of *The Compleat Gard'ner* (1693) by Jean de la Quintinie, the man who designed the *Potager du Roi* for Louis XIV. By the close of the eighteenth century, the French system was fully absorbed into the English system of vegetable culture. It was practiced on a large scale in London's market gardens and in private gardens—from estates to more modest dwellings, as evidenced, for example, by John Abercrombie's hugely popular *Every Man His Own Gardener* (1769). Abercrombie's work quickly became a standard in the gardening literature and remained in print though various editions for the next hundred years.

George Washington kept a copy of Philip Miller's *Gardener's Dictionary* (1731) on his desk and consulted it for information on American trees and shrubs. He also admired Batty Langley's *New Principles of Gardening;* Langley favored the English approach of natural gardens over French formalism.

The raised-bed gardening system that Chadwick popularized was the standard system of kitchen gardens in the British North American colonies and in the first decades of our national history. At some point, in both Great Britain and the United States, the power of nineteenth-century farming technology overtook the brilliance of the French intensive methods for growing vegetables for the country kitchen and the city market. Increasingly, the home gardener began to ape the systems used in farm fields. Up until modern times, table vegetables weren't grown in open fields. Open fields were for staples like grains and potatoes, not for parsley and lettuce. There was a rigid conceptual divide between the kitchen garden and the field. They each had their separate literature.

Alan Chadwick's extraordinary contribution to American gardening history was to have reintroduced to the United States the all-important distinction between kitchen gardening and farming. Whatever might have been his source, books, visits to France (if he ever travelled there), an inspired British gardener, he modified the French intensive system to work in the modern cultural context.

I think it is important to note that perhaps because he was working in California, where there is a twelve-month growing season, he did not emphasize the season-extending techniques that were, in a sense, at the core of the French system as practiced in northern Europe. As of this writing, we are beginning to see some of these techniques revived, now that there is a widespread interest in reducing the distance produce travels to market. One cannot "buy fresh and buy local" when snow covers fields. The full and complete French intensive system for growing vegetables yields lettuce in January when the snow is heavy on the ground, and had Chadwick been working in Wisconsin rather than in California, he would have offered a modern interpretation of the French intensive system that would have made that possible. Eliot Coleman, author of *Four-Season Harvest,* has blended modern French intensive practice with Dutch gardening methods to develop season-extending practices that don't rely on access to unlimited amounts of horse manure, as did the original French intensive system. I think it is also important to be reminded that Chadwick was working when the time was right for the reintroduction of raised-bed vegetable gardening to American gardeners. In England, also working in the 1970s, John Seymour popularized the same method in his wonderful book, *The Self-Sufficient Gardener.* It was a time of cultural ferment, when we were unusually open to new ideas, and perhaps especially to ones that looked forward by looking backward.[10]

Chadwick double-digging in the UCSC garden, 1970.

Chadwick at UCSC, 1971.

Chapter Two

The English Gardener
Goes to Work

We met at the Cowell Fountain in the middle of the college. He was striking looking—large shock of hair, balletic in demeanor, British in manner, huge hands, dramatic, with the air of a professional actor, which is what he was before he became a gardener. He bore a striking resemblance to Samuel Beckett and Danny Kaye.

After we identified one another and said hello, I said, "Would you do our garden for us?" He said, "Yes." We hardly spoke about anything else, exchanging a few pleasantries, although I do remember mentioning that the garden would probably function as a therapeutic refuge for students on drugs. He looked at me as though I were speaking Chinese.

Alan went out the next day and bought a spade with his own money, picked out a slope at the entrance to the campus and started to dig. Just like that! He spoke neither to me nor to anyone else. He was just there digging away, day after day, week after week. I noticed him the next day when I drove up to class. I glanced over my shoulder, dumbfounded by the image I had caught out of the corner of my eye: it was Chadwick, all by himself—digging! I thought, "Whoa, there he is! Okay! Here we go!" Nobody was informed. He just kept on digging. No one seemed to care or take notice.

I quickly recruited a few students to help, and they fell under his magical spell. Mostly lazy regarding their studies, they learned to work for the first time in their lives. It was a big deal watching these pampered youth walk into Chadwick's maw, hardly knowing what bit them. He gave them a spade and showed them how to use it. He yelled at them if they called soil "dirt." He was ready to replant their vital root.

We gave a welcoming reception for Alan, to introduce him to the university community and to announce the beginning of the student garden project. My wife and I organized a little party at the Cowell College library. She made watercress sandwiches from plants growing in our stream, and I served champagne. Not a lot, just some. We didn't know that watercress is dangerous if the stream is polluted. You can get sick and die. No one did; our stream was clean. We were lucky, but we eschewed watercress from then on. Page Smith, the provost, didn't complain about that, but when he found out about the champagne, he wrote me a nasty reprimand of a letter about what a clever fellow I must think I am and how it was against the college rules to serve alcohol, which was news to me. If anything, he was twice as cordial and friendly in person after that.

Page knew that Alan would do something significant in the project, and we had his complete support, but because the university was such a dense institution with unclear lines of authority, it was difficult for me to figure out what to do. Alan didn't seem to care. He just got on with it, mostly using his own funds in the early months to meet expenses.

As Page Smith tells it:

In an age of "collective leadership" Alan Chadwick was imperious as a King. In a day of carefully modulated and self-conscious "interpersonal relations," he stormed and raged not just at abstractions like laziness or indifference or inattention, but at the poor frail flesh of those who were the destined instruments of his terrible, unflinching will. And then suddenly, the consummate actor for whom all the world was a stage, he would be as sunny, as playful, as irresistible as the prince of a fairy tale.

He was an enigma on the campus, a free spirit, who resisted, by his very nature, an institutional form. We would have to find our own way and develop our own support system. There were so many countervailing aspects, beginning with Buildings and Grounds. They resented that someone could just begin digging on the campus without their sanction and supervision. Who was this wild guy with a spade and what was he up to? And where did he get the spade? It had all the appearances of a hippie plot that had slipped in under their radar.

Alan made himself available to anyone who showed up. There was no fixed schedule. Students could join in with him, and he would show them how to dig a bed, sow flats, prick out, replant, water, and all the while talk to them about what they were doing and what it meant.

Alan initiated the students into the mysteries of nature, something no one at the university knew how to do or had a clue about, let alone care.[1] The nuptial flight of the queen bee was one of his favorites. It became a signature piece. He would act it out. He told me to read Maeterlinck on the bee. We got to know the greatest beekeeper in the world, who lived in Santa Cruz and whose name was Aebee—no kidding—first name, Ormond; and, believe it or not, his father was named Harry. They were a pair. Ormond was in the Guinness Book of Records for the most yield from a hive. He sold beekeeping equipment, and he and Alan got on famously. Alan told me to read Ormond's two-volume *Mastering the Art of Beekeeping*, and eventually I would have hives of my own, after my parents moved next door and a swarm landed in a Duchess Apple tree my father had sent from Wisconsin and planted in the backyard. My father took it to be a divine omen.

Alan was a nut about comportment. He taught his students how to walk. How to enunciate. Diction was extremely important to him, and he had to deal with all the dopey mumblers who stumbled in. It turned out I was right about the garden as a therapeutic refuge for students on drugs. He tried to get them to stand up straight. He made them memorize the Friar's Speech from *Romeo and Juliet*. It was about medicinal herbs. I remember him asking me if I could find a book on elocution and acting by one of his teachers in the theater—Elsie Fogarty, the voice coach for Olivier, Gielgud, Ashcroft, Dench, and others, at the Central School of Speech and Drama in London.

He gave them cooking lessons. He talked about traditional fruits and salads. How dare they concentrate on growing and marketing one apple and call it "Delicious" when it had no flavor at all, and when there were hundreds of varieties of apples to consider, fast disappearing on the endangered species list. This hit home, as we were adjacent to Watsonville, one of the great apple-growing centers in the country.

I received an email today from my colleague, Don Weiss (who is the webmaster for my website, www.ecotopia.org, which features "The Ecology Hall of Fame," which I organized to honor Alan), about a crate of apples that sold in Japan for 200,000 yen, or 7,000 yen each. "It is the ultimate crate of

Ezashi apples based on taste, shape and juices. To be able to say you paid the most at an auction for apples produced in Iwate Prefecture shows enormous respect for the effort and time put in by the farmer."

Alan was the first in our experience to talk about heirloom species and the need to restore the diversity of plants and fruit trees. It was a revelation to learn about all the varieties of lettuce after a steady diet of iceberg. No one I knew had ever heard of or seen arugula. He was especially fond of Alpine strawberries and loved to talk about their electrical-like veins accounting for the flavor.

The Santa Cruz area, extending over to Watsonville, is also a national center for strawberry production, but their methods were a far cry from Alan's, who knew they had to irradiate the soil before they planted and grew the berries through plastic that covered the field in their monocropping effort. He knew they were more interested in shelf life and size than flavor. He worried about the decline in taste as a symptom of the decline in culture and loved to quote Robert Graves on the issue from a talk Graves had given at MIT.

The decline of a true taste for food is the beginning of a decline in a national culture as a whole. When people have lost their authentic, personal taste, they lose their personality and become instruments of other people's wills.

Alan would be delighted by the recent "Slow Food" movement, the widespread reaction to McDonald's and fast food, begun by Carlo Petrini, a northern Italian food journalist who lamented the decline of civilized dining and the corresponding decline in taste. As Patricia Unterman explains:

Slow Food has hit a chord with an international constituency worried about the degradation of the environment, the unknown hazards of genetically modified foods and the loss of handcrafted, labor-intensive, traditional foods in a globalized market place. The growth of Slow Food is a cry against the indignities of modernization—the irresponsible use of technology, the homogenization and standardization of food, and the abandonment of the dinner table. [2]

She reports that 120,000 people attended the third Slow Food *Salone de Gusto* in Turin, including 1,000 journalists. One hundred endangered products were featured in the first

Ark of Taste. When I first read about it some months ago, I thought, "hmm, an existentialism of the palate."[3]

Chadwick understood the union of gastronomy and ecology: one could not exist without the other. He knew that the disappearance of traditionally produced foods meant an impoverishment of the environment, and it was obvious to anyone visiting a supermarket that a decline in variety as well as taste, sacrificed for shelf life, was the obvious case. It took at least a decade after Chadwick for the university to put in an organic salad bar in the dining facilities and for markets to begin to feature organically grown food and varieties, but there was no question that Alan represented the wave of the future.

I remember when I first heard of the Italian immigrant dairies along the coast north of Santa Cruz, each with their own cheese production, and how standardization and pasteurization drove them out of business. They won't return; the dairies are gone, although artisanal cheeses are making a return and are now available from a number of small dairies north of San Francisco, representing a rebirth of the industry. I come from Wisconsin, the Dairy Capital of the United States and known for its cheese. You have to search the entire state for a decent cheese, since Kraft set the standard with Velveeta, a product made from cheese waste. The selection in most stores is abominable, although there, as well, artisanal cheeses are returning. Discovering French cheese was a revelation, one of the highest points of French culture, as far as I'm concerned, along with the classic French botanical garden.[4] As de Gaulle famously said, "How can you govern a country that has over four hundred varieties of cheese?"

Although Alan introduced us to these wonders of the organic world and the culture that went with them, and spoke about them in depth, he had an odd scruple about not being a teacher and reminded everyone of this fact repeatedly. I thought he protested too much, but he meant he wasn't an academic. He worried about words getting in the way of immediate perception and the practical gain from experience, even though he was the first to introduce me to binomials, the Latin terms for genus and species used to identify plants. He was extremely deferential to me and always referred to me in public as Professor Lee. In private, he called me "Sausage," which I loathed. I was led to believe it was a term of endearment from the British theater world. He had charming nicknames for his apprentices. "Cherubim" is one I remember, bestowed on an apprentice who looked like one, or more than one, as it is the plural of cherub. He liked Latinate affectations. One apprentice, Dennis, he called "Denisio" and often would use Latinate endings on words, partly for fun and partly for dramatic effect. He was very affectionate and enjoyed intimacies even to the point of conspiracies, always selecting favorites on whom he would bestow his charms.

Partly to play to Alan's mischievous side, I proposed that we stage a reading of Gary Snyder's "Smokey the Bear Sutra" in the Crown College quad, and Alan agreed to present Smokey with his shovel as part of the stunt. I had my father dress up in a bear costume, and we did it. Alan walked up in a very ceremonial way and, in a stentorian voice, proclaimed, "I do perceive it is Mickey Mouse. No! I do perceive it is Donald Duck. No! Oh, I do perceive it's Smokey the Bear!" and he handed the shovel to my dad.

Chadwick presenting his spade to Smokey the Bear on the occasion of reading Gary Snyder's "Smokey the Bear Sutra," Cowell College courtyard, UCSC.

He worked like a dog, not even resting on weekends. He seemed to have taken on the charge of replanting the vital root of existence in the late stage of the self-destruction of industrial society. At least that was how I thought of it. It was a spiritual calling.

Norman O. Brown called him a wizard.[5] He told John Cage that he had to meet Chadwick when he came to the campus. I had met Cage just before coming to Santa Cruz, in 1965, when we had lunch at Barbetta's, a fancy New York restaurant. I had been introduced to his album on the music of indeterminacy, which I enjoyed immensely. Cage told carefully timed anecdotes to random sounds and made a permanent dent in my acoustic response to sounds of the environment. A train whistle never sounded the same after Cage opened my ears. He told me an anecdote at lunch, which appeared in the *New Yorker* a few weeks later, in the Talk of the Town section. Jake Brackman, a former student of mine from Harvard who wrote for the *New Yorker,* was at the lunch with us. Cage told me about his interest in the design-decade publications of Buckminster Fuller, showed me his copies, and told me I could get them for free from Southern Illinois University Press. He said that I should meet his friend and fellow composer, Lou Harrison, when I got to Santa Cruz. He said his father had recently died and his mother was depressed so he suggested that she visit some relatives in California and have a good time. She responded, "Oh, John, you know I've never enjoyed having a good time!"

Cage's mushroom stories were some of my favorites, so when he visited Santa Cruz I organized a mushroom hunt with Chadwick so he could meet the wizard and see him in action. Robert Duncan, the Bay Area poet of renown, accompanied us, as did a couple of Chadwick apprentices. It was a memorable day. Chadwick was in great form, gamboling across the pastures, jumping in the air and clicking his heels. Cage was charmed.

Chadwick, gardener at Santa Cruz. Nobby'd said, "you must meet our wizard." (Chadwick's back, Nobby told me, had been injured in war, but when we went mushrooming with his student helpers, Chadwick half-naked, leapt and ran like a pony. Catching up with him, it was joy and poetry that I heard him speak. But while I listened he noticed some distant goal across and down the fields and, shouting something I couldn't understand because he'd already turned away, he was gone.) Students had defected from the university or had come especially from afar to work with him like slaves. They slept unsheltered in the woods. After the morning's hunt with him and them, I thought: These people live; others haven't even been born. Chadwick described magnetic effect of moon on tides, on germination of seeds. "Moon inclining draws mushrooms out of Earth." We talked of current disturbance of ecology, agreed man's works no matter how great are pygmy compared with those of nature. Nature, pressed, will respond with grand and shocking adjustment of creation. Out of ourselves with a little o, into ourselves with a big O. My mushroom books and pamphlets (over three hundred items) will go soon to Chadwick (gardener who knows how to hunt and who is surrounded by youth he's inspired).[6]

When we returned to my home after the hunt, during which we had found bushel baskets full of a number of varieties, two of which Cage had not seen before, we had a bottle of wine and he told me how elated he had been by Chadwick and his apprentices and how he had been looking for a place to give his large library of mushroom books. He offered them to us for the Chadwick chalet. This proved to be unwise, for security reasons, and so the books went to Special Collections at the McHenry Library, where they are now part of the Chadwick Archive.

Cage could see that Chadwick was unique; a free spirit who simply alighted on a place where only chaparral and poison oak would grow. His Bulldog spade broke through the crust of the university hardpan and created one of the most productive gardens ever, based on his amalgamation of the French intensive and the biodynamic systems of food and flower production, both strictly organic. It was the first organic garden at a university in the country, to my knowledge, and the only one to conjoin two systems, one developed around Paris and the other an occult and esoteric system developed by one of the strangest figures of the twentieth century—Rudolf Steiner.

At the time, organic was difficult enough to introduce at a university, the Steiner system—impossible! Chadwick mostly kept his mouth shut about Steiner, and used the French intensive system as a kind of screen or shield, as though to protect the biodynamic mysteries from profanation.

Santa Cruz lies on the north shore of Monterey Bay, just miles from Pajaro Valley and the huge, industrial farm fields of California, made famous in Steinbeck's novels. Monocrops are the rule: Brussels sprouts, artichokes, apples and strawberries the main focus. Monsanto is conspicuous as the chemical storage facility serving the farmland with its distribution centers. One drive through the area, bleak and stripped of nature, depressingly illustrates industrial-agricultural monocropping and the economics of agribusiness.[7]

Chadwick was desperately opposed to all that and was intent on a renewed spirit of the land and one's relation to it. He hated the industrialization of farming and gardening and the focus on profit. Working *with* nature, learning its rhythms and mysteries, not *against* it in order to exploit it for profit, were his themes. Give back more than you take was a Chadwick axiom. He was my first example of an exponent of the economy of gift. These are familiar themes now after Earth Day and the development of the environmental and organic movements, coming on the wings of the turbulent 1960s and the concern about right livelihood and a renunciation of bourgeois materialism. But in 1967 they were not as yet popular and were just being introduced. It was the message whose time had come. And he arrived at just the right time to deliver it. He was the Pied Piper of the reaffirmation of the integrity of organic nature and its carefree abundance, and the lifestyle that went with it.

A transmission took place. Students seemed to know instinctively that here was a person on the campus who stood for some wondrous form of renewal. Suddenly it was *not* the case that one had to go to school to become a servant of industrial society as a technical world above nature in its late stage of self-destruction. One could return again to the sowing of seeds and the pricking out into beds and watch enormous yields, as the profligate bounty of nature was allowed to do its thing. It was a spiritual renewal as much as it was an organic one. In fact, they were identical in the sense of natural vitality where spirit, as in "spirited," is abundant life. In the organic gardens of Alan Chadwick, a new biology of the spirit was born.

Although this vision of an organic lifestyle was lived and demonstrated by Chadwick, it was as out of place at the university as religious studies, which the chancellor asked me to organize as a course of studies, now defunct. The university was preparing to become a major research institution, with a disproportionate amount of resources going to the natural sciences. "Follow the money" is a good maxim for identifying the sharing of resources and the exercise of power. It tells the story of what counts for knowledge and who counts. The Chadwick episode lasted about five years, and even though it was part of the effort at innovation, it was never appropriately integrated into the structure of the life of the campus. It always amazed me that Page Smith expressed no regret over the short-lived episode he guided, the first half-decade of the institution, of which he was the initial architect. He was grateful for what it was and had a sense that it would be short lived at best. At least it had been given a chance. He saw the warning signs.

I remember Page speaking about the moment he thought the jig was up when he realized his involvement in higher education had come to an end, when graduate students in the history of consciousness program told him that professors were the antiheroes, just what they hoped *not* to become, after he had spoken about his veneration of Eugen Rosenstock-Huessy, his professor at Dartmouth, with whom he shared a bond that would last a lifetime. Page was horrified. They thought he was a crazy sentimentalist with his Doctor-Vater romanticism. I felt the same way about Tillich as Page did about Rosenstock-Huessy. Once such a relationship is established with a scholar of exceptionally remarkable talents, once such a transmission occurs, from teacher to student, a transmission of spiritual substance, the spiritual substance becomes an integral and crucial part of one's life, the experience and the memory are cherished forever.

Those who flocked around Alan did not share this contempt, although it probably helped that he was not on the faculty. He was a source of veneration because of his communion with nature, so evident in what he could bring about in his garden. It was obvious. The garden spoke for itself, and the gardener and the garden were one. This source of veneration was a bond that many students appreciated and cherished for the rest of their lives. They had met a man who had a

Alan and an apprentice in the Chadwick Garden, 1971.

sacramental view of nature and its powers and knew how to transmit it, as he knew how to commune with it.

As a consequence, Chadwick exposed a fundamental dichotomy in the understanding of nature, what could be called a sacramental view (with an aspect of magic) and a rational-objective view, each of which having their attendant attitudes. Students, by and large, were sick of the rational-objective attitude, especially if they were not pursuing a major in science. They wanted to believe in magic, as one of the popular songs of the day intoned. The natural power in things, the power of being, was what they longed for and had a hard time finding anywhere at the university, unless they went out into the surrounding forest and lived in a redwood tree, as some of them did. They wanted to discover a vitalistic interpretation of nature as opposed to the technical attitude and its merely quantitative analysis and reductionistic methodology. In this opposition, Chadwick was an ally and a model. It was an anomaly that he was there at all. Two things supported his presence: the newness of the campus, where innovation was possible, and the growing consciousness about the environment, which would result in Earth Day, only three years away. It was as though we were prophetically aware of what would be a national wake-up call. We were riding the groundswell of a wave that would soon break over us and confirm what we were doing.

But the university, under the sway of the hard sciences, had made reason instrumental ever since Galileo and Descartes, reducing nature to matter in order to mathematize it. Rational thought, in the sense of controlling or technical reason, had dispelled the "powers" in order to subject them to critical scrutiny and analysis. Descartes expresses this attitude perfectly:

... there are no powers in stones or plants so occult, no sympathies or antipathies so miraculous and stupendous, in short, nothing in nature (provided it proceeds from material causes destitute of mind and cognition) that its reason cannot be deduced from these [i.e., mechanical] principles.[8]

This is practically the battle cry of the sciences and could be inscribed over every experimental lab; students wanted more than anything to expose it for what it was. This raises a theme central to all my thinking about the garden and its meaning at a university devoted to natural science as determining the aim of education, with the social sciences and the humanities as secondary and side issues, on a descending scale, tolerated, but not worthy of what really counts for knowledge. This was not as evident then, at the beginning of the institution, as it is now, but I felt it acutely at my college—Crown College—devoted to the natural sciences as an emphasis and theme, where most of my colleagues were scientists, and I, teaching philosophy and religious studies, was a fish out of water.

I remember having a discussion with Kenneth Thimann, the provost of Crown College, a world-renowned botanist, over his hesitation to even credit philosophy of science with a place in the curriculum, although he could see a place for the history of science. I had mentioned to him my interest in vitalism and its role in the sciences, and he responded by saying, "Oh, yes, what's the name of that woman?" He meant, of course, Agnes Arber, an authority on Goethe's botany and a leading example of what I was getting at. All he could think of was a woman whose name he had forgotten. I could see that there was no room within the college to acknowledge Chadwick's work and the tradition he represented. Science had turned its back on anyone espousing vitalism; the battle had been won in the early part of the nineteenth century, when vitalism was presumed to have been refuted and eliminated. Natural science, since Galileo, had worked its reductionist, physicalist, positivist trend to complete success.

Natural science was really the science of matter. It took me a long time to realize that the reductionist trend in modern science, stripping life of all its salient qualities, ended up with matter as all that matters. I don't know why it took so long, but one day the word turned on like a blinking neon sign: *matter.* It was the bottom line, the fundamental term. Nature didn't matter any more in the reductionist trend. Walking over to the garden from the college was like crossing no-man's-land. The divide was all the more distressing because Thimann, the provost of my college, was a botanist. I came to appreciate how the physicalist/vitalist conflict was personified in the figures of Thimann and Chadwick within the selfsame subject matter, outstanding in their fields, only the fields were lab and garden, with Thimann in the one and Chadwick in the other, representing contending worldviews.

The issue: two antithetical interpretations of nature. Chadwick represented the sacramental view, in which the power and meaning of nature was evident and in which the principle of plenitude was demonstrated. This was why Steiner, the prototypical vitalist in the tradition of Goethe, was so important to Alan, although he mostly kept it to himself. The other was a view of nature that reduced it to matter, as a combination of chemical and physical forces, utterly devoid of sacramental meaning, the rational-objective attitude, represented by Thimann and the natural sciences generally, under the complete command of experimental laboratory procedures.

Only when the latter view of nature is reached may we speak of "things" in the strict sense, that is, as entities completely conditioned. Mathematical physics and the technical control of nature based on it are the most impressive and the most consistent expressions of this view. Nature is brought under control, objectified, and stripped of its qualities. No sacramental conception can find a root in this soil.[9]

So Chadwick created his own soils, digging through the crust and the hardpan of the campus with his Bulldog spade. In the tradition of Steiner, back to Goethe, he was devoted to penetrating into the depth of nature without profaning nature's mysteries.

From the opposite figures of Chadwick and Thimann, representing the vitalist and the physicalist, I found my way back to Goethe and Newton, the two preeminent examples of the divide in former centuries. Goethe, the vitalist, had gone up against Newton, the physicalist, in an effort to refute his theory of color, based on Newton's optics. It was another example of the quarrel of opposing views.

As Paul Tillich comments on the issue:

Goethe was more successful ... in his famous doctrine of colors and in his fight against Newton's quantitative-dynamic theory of light and color. In this controversy (which is not yet decided, even on the level of physics) the quantitative-technical interpretation of nature, represented by Newton, clashed with the qualitative-intuitive attitude toward nature, represented by Goethe. Goethe was passionately interested in what we have called the "power" of colors, their spiritual meaning and effect.[10]

What was remarkable about what Chadwick represented was the reestablishment of a vitalist tradition of Goethe and Steiner on a campus where nothing vitalist was represented and where science had hardened into an ideological cramp of scientistic physicalism that would not allow for a debate. We were like the Marxists in political science and economics—a thorn in the side to be removed as quickly as possible. Tillich describes the situation we faced:

In the nineteenth century, amidst liberalism and the idolization of science, bourgeois class interests succeeded in bringing about a very strictly political selection—mostly without the consciousness that the allegedly purely scientific evaluation was also determined by the ideology of classes and confessional instincts. Consequently, decisive questions, namely, in the human sciences, but also in the natural sciences, could not gain acceptance. They contradicted the interests of the ruling parties and were not allowed. One need only think of the fate of the purely scientific problems raised by Marx and by socialism at the universities. This frame of mind prevails as an aftereffect to this day, so that if a scientifically outstanding scholar were influenced by Marx methodologically or materially, his appointment would be fought as political, whereas the appointment at the same time of a dozen professors of opposing tendency causes no political offense in any way at all. Seldom has the restrictive power of class interests and confessional instincts shown itself more clearly in the midst of free science. Nevertheless, it is better for science that it undertakes this unconscious and unwanted self-imposed restriction of its freedom than that it allow itself and its fundamentally scientific attitude to be violated through any oath or ism.[11]

The crux of the matter is "the unconscious and unwanted self-imposed restriction of its freedom." I balked at this phrase in defense of the repression of Marxists and communists on the faculty. Did Tillich say "in the midst of free science"? Wait a minute. My whole brief on physicalism is just the point. Science sacrificed its freedom in the ruthless elimination of vitalism, except, unlike Marxism, at least in Tillich's odd remark, it was *conscious and wanted,* knowing that it meant the reduction of organic nature to matter in the service of industrial society. Scientific freedom was violated by *this* ism! Hence the physicalist Oath!

It should be remembered that I was of the generation of professors in the period of the Loyalty Oath, which every-

45

one employed by the University of California was forced to sign. One had to swear one's true faith and allegiance to the constitution of the State of California, which struck me as a species of idolatry. And it is worth noting that the physicalists in the Physicalist Society in Berlin took their oath in blood, which not only violated their own position as physicalists (what could loyalty possibly mean or matter to a physicalist, let alone an oath?), it made them look foolish as scientists. It was an indication of how violently vitalism was disdained and disallowed.[12]

All three kept their vow throughout their lives, with spectacular scientific success, which in turn helped to make their proposition an article of faith, and "vitalism" a discredited cause, throughout the life sciences. What escaped them was the fact that by making a pledge, no matter which, they already contradicted or acted counter to the particular content of this pledge. For they did not bind themselves to what is not a matter for decision at all—namely, to let the molecules of their brains now and hereafter take their causally prescribed courses and allow them to determine their thought and speech (if they do that anyway); but they bound themselves to remain faithful in the future to a present insight, thus by implication declaring at least their subjectivity to be master over their conduct. In the mere fact of a vow, they credited something totally non-physical, their relation to truth, with just that power over their overt behavior which the content of their vow on principle denied. Making a promise, with faith in the ability to keep it and the equally implied alternative of not keeping it, does admit into the chart of reality—if not into scientific discourse—a force "other than those found in the interaction of inorganic bodies." "Fidelity" would be such a force....[13]

I could not have been more stunned when I encountered this refutation of the oath by Jonas. I have included it here because it drives a counter-nail into the physicalist coffin and exposes how obtuse they were in their arrogance.

We had no immediate understanding of the tradition we represented in opposition to the physicalists. It was enough to go against the grain and promote an organic approach. It was only after a concentrated study that I began to see the effort as neo-vitalist and the inception of an environmental movement that would take root and change the course of history.

Alan amidst the delphiniums and hollyhocks in his garden, 1971.
Photo by Elizabeth Kennard.

The most amazing restoration of vitality was exactly what everyone witnessed on that slope where the garden took root. It was a place of haunting beauty, especially if one caught Chadwick, his shirt off, sitting among the hydrangeas, the columbine, the foxglove, and the hollyhocks, looking like Nature Boy himself, or the Green Man, talking to students about the properties and effects of the herb thyme *(Thymus vulgaris)* or the significance of old-species roses and their hardy strength compared to disease-prone hybrids, and then see for themselves all the life-forms that sprang into being at the touch of his green thumb.

I was reminded of a remarkable figure of speech from Augustine's *Confessions,* in which he talks about working himself over, as though plowing his psyche, like a farmer working his field, in his self-ruminations, his self like land he cultivated:

Who is to carry the research beyond this point? Who can understand the truth of the matter? O Lord, I am working hard in this field, and the field of my labors is my own self. I have become a problem to myself, like land which a farmer works only with difficulty and at the cost of much sweat.[14]

I thought of the garden as Chadwick's torso, where he worked himself over, which, remarkably, is the definition Sartre gives for existence: what works you over. Double-digging.

He had a peculiar vocabulary unique to him. He talked about *idée,* using the French pronunciation for the Platonic idea, meaning the form of things, in the tradition of Goethe and his "Urplant," exhibiting a particular propensity for morphological structures. He loved the word *oikos,* Greek for the habitable household, as a cultural structure, the basis for economy. He spoke often and admiringly of *clairvoyées* and *avenues,* namely the French way of planting trees and bushes to create a line of vision and atmospheres of enchantment.

I remember, on a trip to France to visit famous botanic gardens, going to the great garden outside of Paris, *Saint-Germain-en-Laye,* and looking down the line of lindens that seemed to lead to infinity. I was undone by the view, quietly weeping, overwhelmed by the beauty of it; it was so spectacular and stunning, a perfect example of what Chadwick loved.[15]

He heaped contempt on what he called "the toys of the nursery," meaning all the stuff people were occupied with, especially anything that guzzled gas—automobiles, tractors, lawnmowers, weed-eaters, as well as electronic gadgets or superfluous hardware. He wanted everything done by hand, introducing Bulldog Tools, guaranteed for life, the predecessor of the Smith and Hawken Tool Company, which became famous for securing the American franchise after Paul Hawken learned about the tool from Alan. He hated the way tractors and heavy farm machinery compacted the soil, treating it with contempt. He preached biological diversity against monocropping and knew all the reasons why. He knew how to guard against pests without using pesticides, knowing which plants to plant—companion planting—so that they would flourish and protect themselves and each other from disease.

I'll never forget running up to the garden upon returning from the first summer interlude, after leaving Alan for three months. We always go to our northern Wisconsin summer home—Cisco Point—every year. Alan thought I had abandoned him, even though I had written a number of letters to him. He was sitting in the garden at a picnic table with his first apprentice, John Powell, when I ran up to greet them on my first day back, eager to see what progress had been made. I thought they looked frazzled, like refugees from a concentration camp. In fact, they looked as though they had had shock treatment. Electric shock. Their hair stood on end. There was a sense of insanity in the air. I was dumbfounded. Alan had his first fit, full force, in my face. I *had* abandoned them. Where the hell had I been, lolling about in northern Wisconsin, at our lake, while they worked their heads off trying to get the garden going. He was furious. It was my introduction to his famous temper that Freya had warned me about when she told me he could be difficult. Difficult? The guy came unglued, completely unhinged, as though all the thespian ability to act half-crazed was at his disposal; he let it all hang out right in my face, smoking up my nose. Well, I thought, it was one way to discharge the id. But why on me? I flicked off psychic vomit for weeks.

Some months later the chancellor called me in and with an irritated tone berated me about the project. Where was the budget? What about Alan's salary? Where was the feasibility study? (A what?) I had never heard of a mission statement; fortunately, neither had the chancellor. How were we going to coordinate it with Buildings and Grounds? I wondered, "where are they located and who are they?" It was all very rhetorical and petulant, prompting me to think, "how the hell should I know about any of it. It's your university, you bully with a head like a small bomb, and an ex-marine to boot." The chancellor held all the power. Why didn't he pitch in and offer answers to his own questions from the resources at his disposal? Why dump it all in my lap just because it was my idea? He took the walk with me when we first looked for a garden site. He seemed to be in favor of it. He was a political scientist and an administrator and knew the ropes as well as his way through the labyrinth of the university bureaucracy. Why intimidate me and complain when he could help? More rhetorical questions with his lower lip protruding. I sat there not knowing what to say, realizing I had gone out on a limb. I heard the sound of a saw.

I walked away from the meeting knowing my goose was cooked. I still remember the palpable black cloud over my head, like the guy in the Li'l Abner comic strip, Joe Btfsplk, meant to be pronounced like a Bronx cheer. I thought of my colleagues on the science faculty of Crown College giving me one—a Bronx cheer—for playing my New Age card in the academic game, where, like the army, you don't volunteer or suggest the Next Big Thing unless you are some naïve schmuck. The jig was up. I was going to go down for starting an organic garden. Stick your neck out, wise guy, and watch the axe fall. So much for your innovative breakthrough on the organic nature front.

Shortly after, the administration called. It was Howard Schontz, vice-chancellor of Buildings and Grounds. He said that he was sorry to tell me Chadwick had to go. He could no longer work as a gardener on the campus. He has to go? Why? Because he was an alien and there was a law on the books. No alien could work on a university campus. I laughed to myself thinking Alan was an alien, all right, but one from outer space, by way of England, South Africa, and Long Island. I asked why there was such a law, and Howard said he thought it was aimed at Japanese gardeners during the Second World War in order to deny them university employment. It was still in force. I said Alan was British. No matter. The law was a law. I hung up, suddenly aware of the triumph of the obtuse bureaucrat as the specter haunting higher education. The ssssystem was beginning to express itself. I could hear the hiss. This refers to a moment when I was still in Cambridge, teaching at MIT, and I had run into a friend who knew I was looking for a job as my next teaching position. He told me about Santa Cruz and then cautioned me when I showed interest and asked me, "do you know anything about the California ssssystem?" He hissed the word like a snake in the grass. I had to admit I knew nothing. Now I was beginning to find out.

50

Days passed. Howard called. He had a solution. I was all ears. Alan could enroll at Cabrillo College, a local community college, and *as a student* he could work in the garden! Wow, I thought, that was creative. I went over to Cabrillo, enrolled Alan, without his knowledge, and paid his fee. It was $75. I should have framed the cancelled check as the first item for the Chadwick Archive, a blood tax paid to the obtuse bureaucrat. I found out later that the law, in fact, was no longer in force, wouldn't you know; they hadn't read it carefully, but the lesson remained with me. And I didn't get my money back.

Then we got a letter from the vice-chancellor of agricultural sciences, responding to a letter of complaint from an agriculturalist emeritus, which I took to mean "Old Fart." He wanted the garden shut down immediately because chemical pesticides and chemical fertilizers were *not* being used, and how could the university support something so antiscience in the approach to agriculture at the Santa Cruz campus. I don't think he knew that Alan planted by the moon, which might have clinched his argument, but he did refer to the project as a cult, although, when you think of it, horticulture, agriculture, culture, cultivate, all include the word. Later, the vice-chancellor wrote back that he thought it would be better for the garden to die its own death, due to the fact that no synthetics were being used. This would be a better learning experience for the students than kicking them off. I thought that was Solomonic.

It took me a while to perceive the significance of that correspondence and why the garden was an insult and an offense to the scientific establishment at the center of power at the university, but it was one of the first warning shots. I had to wait for a dinner at a colleague's home to get the full brunt of the charge when I stepped it off with a chemist on the way to the dinner table. An organic chemist. He turned to me and said, "Paul, do you know that the garden has done more to ruin the cause of science on this campus than anything else?" The remark struck me with the force of a blow. I thought, "what was the 'cause of science' that a garden could ruin it?" And then it dawned on me. He thought it was a hippie plot meant to further embarrass the scientists on the campus. The quarrel was over the meaning of "organic." He thought it meant "artificial synthesis," and he thought I thought it meant some old sentimental and medieval notion of the integrity of organic nature against its chemical reduction. I decided to make an inquiry that would last a lifetime. It was the signal moment for me, as it took me into the physicalist/vitalist conflict, the defeat and refutation and elimination of vitalism and the suborning of organic nature by natural science to the extent it was determined by physicalism.

It was a long time after rehearsing the physicalist/vitalist conflict that I came to read Husserl and his critique of physicalism from the point of view of his newly formed philosophical alternative—phenomenology. I had simply neglected to study Husserl in favor of his student Heidegger, one of the foremost proponents of existentialism, who was all the rage when I was in school. It is Husserl who gave me a background in mathematical physics, prior to chemistry, paving the way, with the significance of Galileo as the scientist who mathematized nature, as the key theme. He was the turning point. The conflict with the church over the Copernican hypothesis and the conflict with the church over the meaning of transubstantiation in the Eucharist are taken into a new context when one sees the significance of Galileo as the representative of the triumph of mathematical physics over what counts for knowledge, and the shift from nature as organic growth to the object of mathematical calculation. The reduction of nature to matter, or what we call "dead things in space," is a slightly nasty metaphor for calculable entities, but an apt one, nevertheless, when one sees the move from the mere indifference of matter, neutral in character, to the critical subtraction—removing the essential features of life—in the historical development of a mechanistic conception of the universe.[16]

Owen Barfield expresses it well:

The new cosmos—a complex of matter and forces proceeding mechanically from spiral nebula to everlasting ice—took such a firm hold on the imagination of Europe that labels like spiritualism, spiritualist, spiritualistic, were employed to describe those who believed it was anything more, and even Vitalism and Vitalist to distinguish those who held that life, as such, had any purpose or significance.[17]

The triumph of mathematical physics comes to its apogee in the conflict between Newton and Goethe over optics, where the physicalist/vitalist confrontation is most acute and assumes a classic form.

Beyond the explicit conflict over color theory and optics as the major contrast between Newton and Goethe, it was as though Goethe, to pursue his vitalist opposition to physicalism, juxtaposed botany to physics, as David to Goliath, a subject matter doomed to subordination, in the determination of what counts for knowledge, in the system of the sciences. He had a sense for it, I'm convinced, obviously dictated by his vitalism. Botany would lose out to the onslaught of mathematical physics over what counts for knowledge. Mathematical physics would be the determining subject matter in the effort to make knowledge exact, technical, and instrumental. The integrity of organic nature would be jeopardized in the triumph of industrial society, which physics and chemistry would assist, especially when it became possible to artificially synthesize organic nature from inorganic sources. Vitalist botany versus physicalist physics and organic chemistry were weighed out in the balance, and eventually the scales would tip.

Alan had worked eighteen hours a day, seven days a week, for two years, when it dawned on me I should propose a weekend off. I took him to Tassajara, the Zen Buddhist monastery and spa in the depths of the Carmel Mountains, south of Santa Cruz, where he could relax, enjoy the waters, and eat Tassajara bread.[18] Before the Zen Center of San Francisco acquired it for their monastic retreat, Tassajara had been an old California Indian hot springs and then a popular spa. My friend Baker-roshi, the abbot, continued the tradition of a vacation retreat for visitors, and it seemed like the perfect place for Alan to get some rest and relaxation. Moreover, they were famous for their vegetarian fare, from fresh ingredients, and especially their bread, which was as good as I remembered from St. Olaf. *The Tassajara Bread Book* would eventually become a best seller and introduce bread bakers to the secret of making good bread: the sponge!

When we arrived, Alan immediately surveyed the area and picked out a site for a garden. His insistence that they begin immediately began a long association between Chadwick and the Zen Center. He would eventually go to Green Gulch, the Zen farm at Muir Beach, north of San Francisco, and develop their garden to supply Greens, the Zen Center restaurant at Fort Mason, one of the most famous vegetarian restaurants in the country, which broke through the brown-rice-and-tofu confines of vegetarianism with an innovative cuisine.[19] In many ways it was a perfect fit: the Buddhists, with their compassion for all sentient beings, and Alan, with his communion with nature and his profligate green thumb.

And he would return there after his contracting cancer and would die there. His grave is on the slope of the farm overlooking his garden and Muir Beach. How appropriate for Alan to be a stone's throw from a beach and a wonderful redwood grove dedicated to the memory of one of the greatest of all environmentalists and a kindred soul in the communion with nature—John Muir. Baker-roshi had a large stone hauled in from Tassajara to mark Alan's grave.

I remember driving out on the mountain road as we said farewell to our mountain Buddhist retreat at Tassajara, and Alan telling me to stop so he could get out. He walked ahead of the car and put his hand down so a tarantula could crawl onto it, and he walked over to the side of the road and put his hand down so it could crawl off. Then he got back into the car. I was impressed. I had never seen anything like that before. We drove on.

I saw birds land on his shoulder. I watched him talk to doves that came to the dovecote he had built in the garden. All forms of life seemed to thrive in his presence. His green thumb was more than profligate; it was generative of the great chain of being in the sphere of organic nature.

And, of course, the university had to have its main electrical generator installation smack dab in the upper side of the garden with a constant infernal hum that was no doubt attuned to Alan's subconscious and assisted in his electrical discharges. I wondered if that wasn't what drove him nuts, that hum, and accounted, in part, for his frequent fits of temper, which were electrical in the extreme. Think of a thunderstorm over a volcano.

He kept a lovely little bird in a cage as his pet. One day I took my six-year-old daughter, Jessica, to an event in the garden, and before I knew it she had opened the cage to hold the bird and had squeezed it too hard, and it was dead. Oh no. The world seemed to come to a halt as we looked at each other, wondering "what now?" And then to confirm our worst fears, Chadwick arrived on the scene. He had a fit. I pretended to be as upset as Alan and yelled at her for what she had done, hoping Chadwick wouldn't hit her. She never went back.

Alan suffered from an old-fashioned form of nervous disorder known as neurasthenia, commonly referred to as "high strung," or exhaustion of the nervous system, a condition that made him prone to fits of ill temper toward any arbitrary provocation like clearing your throat or a baby crying. Harsh noises set him off. You dared not sneeze. A lot of things set him off. It seemed to be a result of his breaking his back while serving aboard a minesweeper during the war. That would have done it to anyone. It was his worst trait—these volcanic explosions of a high-strung neurotic. Freya had warned me about it. "He can be difficult," she said. I had no idea. No one had ever seen anything like it. We sort of forgave him for it, suffering it like bad weather. I learned to make a distinction between idiosyncratic display and institutional process. I think it came to me when John Powell, his first apprentice, sent me a telegram over the summer, after Alan had threatened to quit. The telegram read, "Gardens are grown." I took it to mean that the work went on. No matter what. Forget the idiosyncratic display; tomorrow will be sunny; let the institutional process proceed.

Like the weather, it always blew over, and when it was sunny, it was very sunny indeed. He was fun to be with and loved to tease and play games and fool around, in spite of his ultimate concern—gardening in the classic manner. I would watch fights with clods of soil pitched from afar. One time Rory, one of his apprentices, hit him in the head and forever after earned his respect and became one of his favorites. You either stood up to him or were broken by him. He tested your mettle like no one else I knew, and I marveled at the callow youths, who came in so wet behind the ears, walking out tall and proud, having mastered the art of digging a bed and watching the ranunculi grow. And then there were a few who went away in tears, never to be seen again.

55

He was a force of nature, our gardener, a personification of the vitalist! He knew where the vital root of existence was to be found—it was growing right under our noses—he was keen to show you how to dig it and nurture it. Everything about him was vital. He reminded me of my horse, especially when he misbehaved and reared up and got a wild look in his eye, although no one ever thought of putting a halter on Chadwick! His carriage reminded me of the saying of Heraclitus about the bow of life—he was so highly strung.[20] Marching around the garden beds in his navy shorts and navy top, he cut an unforgettable figure.

One of the apprentices at the time, Beth Benjamin, who went on to start one of the offshoots of the garden—Camp Joy—tells of her experience with Chadwick:

Alan was simply the most fascinating human being on campus for me. Soon nothing else seemed to come into focus but his garden. I was unhappy

Chadwick giving one of his many lectures to UCSC students, around 1971.

and doing poorly in my classes, but in the garden I vibrated with the colors and the smells and the stories Alan told us about the plants and his travels and the new skills I was learning. By April I convinced my counselor that I wanted a leave of absence, and I could finally devote my full time to the world of plants. As an apprentice, I worked from dawn until dusk and was filled with his dreams and our common task of bringing the garden into reality, breaking new ground and tending what we had already planted. He had flaming temper tantrums, told tales, gave us dinner parties, fed us with his own bread and ham and cheese, threw dirt clods at us and laughed as he hid behind the compost piles. He taught us the joy of work, the discipline to persevere in order to make a dream come true, even when we were hot and tired, and the deliciousness of resting and drinking tea after such monumental labors.... I think of Alan almost every day still, 30 years later, and smile with the memories and with gratitude for all he gave me.

He was the personification of the Greek word *thymós,* a particular form of natural vitality, as in the word *spirited,* the sort of spirit a horse has. He had it in spades. I learned the word from my teacher, Paul Tillich, who wrote a book about it, *The Courage To Be,* his astute translation of *thymós.* It is an extraordinarily rich word, as it means

1. the courage to be, or vital self-affirmation,

2. the unreflective striving for what is noble, as in a noble warrior, the embodiment of vital courage (Achilles is a good example),

3. the bridge between reason and desire; relating to both of them, in the middle, between them, the bridge between the head and the groin.

It is a good term to describe the courageous vitality of Chadwick. It is a very good word and it is a pity it is not in common usage. Because it is in the middle, an in-between term, it is represented by the thymus gland, a cognate word, the very organ of courage as the master organ of the immune system, the vital defense against illness and disease. The thymus gland is the bridge, in the middle between reason and desire, as in Plato's construction of consciousness.[21]

Thymós is my favorite word. The name of the herb thyme *(Thymus vulgaris)* is a cognate, which is my favorite herb, considered the herb of courage throughout history, probably because of its germicidal properties. Chadwick was pure *thymós.*

57

I would translate it as "vital root." It is remarkable that it even captures his tempestuous side, as it also means "anger," or "rage," or "wrath," because one of the meanings is "smoke," as in the Latin *fumus*. It also means the ability or courage to say "no," to resist.

Chadwick embodied this meaning against the heady professors on the campus, including myself. He didn't have to talk about it. He could show you how to do it and then have you see for yourself. That's why students flocked to him. Bandy-legged, he could outdo everyone in physical exertion. We boxed a couple of times and he flew at me with his fists like someone possessed. Even so, I knew he was a pushover. We became the best of friends.

He played tennis with Page Smith, who had been wounded in the Second World War by stepping on a land mine, which crippled him for a time, and though he had recovered the use of his legs and could play without much difficulty, he manifested a somewhat laborious gait. Alan would leap the net and retrieve the ball for him, handing it to Page with a bow and a flourish, "your ball, sir," much to Page's stunned delight, mixed with chagrin, as in, "who does this guy think he is?"

When I was most distressed over the prospect of the denial of tenure, and knew that my days were numbered and that I would be deprived of my teaching position, he took me aside and indicated his sympathy for what I was going through, and said to me, "You know, Paul, there is an old saying we had in the navy, 'Fuck you! I'm all right, Jack!'" I thought, "I'll remember that when I need it."

He was completely self-reliant. He never asked for anything. When we finally secured a salary for him—I think it was something of the order of $400 a month—he did not complain, and hardly took an interest in it, as most of the money he made went back into the garden. After all, he mostly wanted to eat what he could grow himself, and after you tried his French beans, you knew why. At the beginning, Mary Holmes, who was a professor of art history and a friend of mine, gave him an apartment at her ranch in the Cave Gulch area off Empire Grade, just a few miles from the campus. She was such a compelling figure, with a charismatic personality exceeding even Chadwick's and a rapier wit on top of it. He mostly behaved himself. She was no one to cross.

He finally was given an apartment at Cowell College. It was a mistake, as he feuded with his neighbors in the building, particularly the family that lived upstairs. If they flushed the toilet after six o'clock, the sound of the water coursing through the pipes in the walls drove him nuts and set him off. He took to breaking wine bottles in the backyard after pounding on the ceiling and yelling his head off. They thought he was crazy. The mother of the two boys who flushed the toilet was the only one I knew who raised her arms in exultation and said "good!" when I told her Chadwick had died.

He cut a striking figure on his Raleigh bicycle, ramrod straight, peddling around the campus and down into town.

He cut a swath wherever he went. We would see him moving through the aisles of Shoppers' Corner, the main grocery store in town, and everyone would take notice of him. His eccentric dress, almost always white shorts and a navy top; his fierce, eagle-like looks; his intensity, as though his purpose was always foremost in his mind; his dedication to restoring organic nature to its rightful place in the production of food. At the

Chadwick on his Raleigh bike, UCSC, 1972.

Chadwick's car. Photo by E. Gaines.

time, there was no mention of organic food anywhere in the distribution chain. Now it is everywhere, and grocery stores in Santa Cruz are organized around the concept, displaying organic varieties, often locally grown.

Finally, someone gave him a car, on the side of which was printed, "THIS TOO CAN BE YOURS!" Everyone laughed and waved when he drove by.

One day he was driving off the campus down Bay Street and was only going a few miles over the speed limit when a cop stopped him to give him a ticket. Chadwick got out of the car, flipped the keys to the cop and pointed to the sign on the door and said, "You can read!" and stalked off. The officer ordered him to stop, and when Alan kept walking, drew his gun. Alan walked over, hit the officer and disarmed him, knocking him down, throwing his gun into the bushes.

I went along for his court appearance, and he showed up in his pale blue Goodwill suit that made him look like some old eccentric fan of Johnny Mathis or Lawrence Welk. He stood and gathered himself up with his most Shakespearian demeanor and addressed the judge with his customary "grrreeet-tinngs!" which he rolled trippingly off the tongue, like sliced ham, accompanied by a theatrical flourish of the arm, as some people winced and others looked astonished. The judge was amused until he heard what happened. Flabbergasted, he called the officer over to him and asked in an outraged tone, "You arrested this gentleman for driving three miles over the speed limit? You drew your revolver on this gentleman? What? This gentleman took your gun away from you? You should be ashamed of yourself! Case dismissed!" We cheered and carried Alan out of the courtroom on our shoulders.

He finally moved downtown and lived modestly in a small apartment. We would have evenings when he played Wagner and we would all go into a trance, quietly weeping together over the sadness of the finite. To my dismay, in his final days in Santa Cruz, he wound up on the floor of the little garden chalet, and I had to bring an old horsehair mattress for him to lie on. There was no toilet or bathing facility, so I had one built. I gave him my grandmother's refrigerator, which we had shipped out from Milwaukee after she died. Why he wound up sleeping on the floor, I don't know and can't remember. It was the end period of his career at the university. He seemed abandoned.

He reminded me of Bartleby, the Scrivener, in that tragic short story by Melville. Bartleby sleeps at his desk and becomes a burden to his employer and finally fades away, disappears, as it were, from existence, winding up in the dead-letter office at the post office, sleeping on the floor over by a wall, where he passes away. It was a spectacle sad to behold: Chadwick reduced to such a state. The dead-letter office? Was this the fate of a vitalist at a secular state university?

Rejected by his main apprentice and the institution that claimed his fame as part of their publicity releases, he became dispirited—the *thymós* had gone out of him, even though his contribution and achievement was documented and acknowledged. *Sunset* magazine, through their garden editor, Joe Williamson, who wrote one of the first appreciative articles on Alan and the garden, was convinced to adopt a strictly organic policy for the magazine, thanks to Alan's example. *Life* magazine featured a two-page photo of the garden in their article on the new campus of the university system.

The farm project, on another site, had begun, but Alan's main apprentice had given up working with him and wanted to develop the UCSC Farm on his own, without Alan. There was an angry standoff. The apprentice bought a small Italian tractor, out of defiance against Alan's contempt for machines, and it continually broke down, as though Alan had cursed it.

There were just too many temper tantrums to endure, and my effort to invoke the distinction between institutional process and idiosyncratic display no longer worked. I thought this distinction was particularly clever and therapeutic when the main apprentice came down to my home to complain about the latest fit and how he couldn't take it any more. I still think it's a good distinction for coping with personality quirks when there is a common task to be accomplished, and when you can overlook the quirks and get on with the work. Meanwhile, Alan was getting ready to leave.

Even though he often spoke about leaving, he had only made actual plans twice before. He spoke repeatedly of the Seychelles, and how he was going to go there and garden in peace, free from industrial society and the plague of the automobile and all the other toys of the nursery. I had to look it up on a map.

Finally he recruited a ragtag group who were going to go off to New Zealand with him, where a relative before him had settled. Richard Seddon (1845–1906) was the longest-serving prime minister of New Zealand. He was born near the Chadwicks; his mother was a Chadwick; Alan's brother was named Seddon. Alan and his group managed to scrape together the cost of the voyage. One woman was leaving her husband. I had this weird hallucination of their stepping off the boat together into the wild blue yonder. No plan. No means. On a wing and a prayer. After all, it wasn't much different from our beginnings at Santa Cruz, but I didn't want him to go. I thought it was preposterous and asked Huey Johnson, who was head of Nature Conservancy (and who would eventually start the Trust for Public Lands and then head of Natural Resources for California under Jerry Brown), to talk Alan out of it.

Richard Baker, my Zen pal, told me he was bringing Johnson to the campus to meet the chancellor. I told Richard to drop Huey off at the garden an hour early so he could talk Chadwick out of going. I walked around in the garden and looked at the poppies and held my breath. Huey rose to the occasion. "California needs you more than New Zealand," reaffirming for Alan the importance of his work at the university and what it meant for a generation of students looking for a second chance. What it meant for California. The nation. The environmental movement. Didn't he understand that he was regarded as one of the leaders of the organic movement in California and a beacon of light in the renewed affirmation of the integrity of organic nature? It worked. It was a calculated risk on my part to have interfered in this way.

He had been a force fit, at best, pun intended, emphasis on fit; the garden, an unintegrated appendage to the university. It was partly my fault. I didn't know how to organize it any better than it did itself. It had its own life and dynamic. We let it take its course.

Rereading the letters and memos from those years surprised me, when I ransacked my boxes of papers and memorabilia looking for anything I could deposit in the Chadwick Archive

Alan with two of his main apprentices, Steve Kaffka and Steven Decatur, around 1970. "These people live; others haven't even been born," said John Cage.

I had started for the university's Special Collections. I found letters of appreciation attesting to the support and generous response from the university community to Alan and his efforts. Many appreciated what he was doing, and its contribution to the life of the place, and said as much. There were the letters attesting to it. Okay, so it wasn't so beleaguered. It made me qualify my own memory, partly because I thought I carried the brunt of the effort as a faculty member. I had to recruit the students. I had to function as a go-between. I had to mediate disputes and smooth ruffled feathers. It was a constant strain, given my other duties, but I was young and full of energy and never complained or even thought of asking for help. "Ve get so soon old und yet so late schmart" was the saying on the wall in Herbel's Meat Market across the street in Milwaukee, where I grew up. Although I knew the adage in my youth, it wasn't until much later that I came to appreciate its meaning, just like it says.

Now and then I have thought about the problem of being involved in a historical process and taking account of it, recording it, keeping track of it while it is going on, and how difficult this is when one is absorbed by it. I'm surprised so much of the process is remembered and accounted for in the documents I was able to retrieve years later from what I had saved, all those boxes stuck away in my garage. I remember Paul Tillich asking me, in a poignant moment, about the future of his legacy. He drew a distinction between "the personal Tillich" and "the archive Tillich" and he wondered aloud what the fate of the archive Tillich would be and how long his influence would last. Now I know what he meant. It takes a certain mentality, a certain ability—call it a certain attribute of self-transcendence—to do it and to account for it and keep a record of it at the same time, all the while it is going on. We're lucky to have preserved what we have.

I used the term *spiritual life* one time at the Penny University, a discussion group that meets every Monday in downtown Santa Cruz. Page Smith and I started it in 1973. A nice woman informed me the following Monday that she had looked up the word *spiritual* in the dictionary, and a religious meaning was only the fourth or fifth definition. That was exactly my point. We don't naturally think of spirituality as grounded in the body. There is almost no sense of a biologically based spirit or spirituality, except, maybe, when we ask compassionately, "What's the matter?"

This expression is my personal joke. We do sense the biological basis when we use the term *spirited* to talk about an especially vital horse or vital person. High spirits are self-evident. I have worked out a biologically based understanding of spirit in my studies on *thymós* and the region of the thymus gland, what I call the *thymic field,* as a bridge between reason and desire and a solution to the mind-body problem. But that's another matter.

When the physicalistic trend in modern science reduced spirit or the vital center to the mind and then eliminated mind or consciousness in favor of brain activity, you ended up with neurophysiology. Here is what Tillich has to say about the issue:

One of the unfortunate consequences of the intellectualization of the spiritual life was that the word "spirit" was lost and replaced by mind or intellect, and that the element of vitality which is present in "spirit" was separated and interpreted as an independent biological force divided into a bloodless intellect and a meaningless vitality. The middle ground between them, the spiritual soul in which vitality and intentionality are united, was dropped. At the end of this development it was easy for a reductive behaviorism to derive self-affirmation and courage from a "merely biological" vitality. But nothing is "merely biological" as nothing is merely spiritual. Every cell participates in freedom and spirituality, and every act of spiritual creativity is nourished by vital dynamics. [22]

It is important to me to make this theme of a lifetime clear to my reader. I am saddled with a dualism that Hans Jonas points to as a major conflict in Western thought. He argues that it was Orphism (and Gnosticism) that was responsible for the turning inward—what is known as the discovery of the soul or the mind, what I call *rational self-consciousness;* Socrates is the reference point. This turning inward, the discovery of human subjectivity, the inwardness of the human spirit, had a curiously polarizing effect on the general picture of reality, according to Jonas: the very possibility of the notion of an "inanimate universe" emerged as the counterpart to the increasingly exclusive stress laid on the human soul, on its inner life and its incommensurability with anything in nature. This is the historical background of the subject/object split.

Cognition took over the function of the human soul, the thinking self: the *cogito* of Descartes was juxtaposed against inanimate nature, namely everything extended in space. You know the drill if you have ever studied philosophy in college. Descartes is as important as Galileo in the turn we call physicalism. Epistemological subjectivity objectified everything by way of mathematizing it in order to reach true and distinct knowledge. What a bind that has been!

Think of the subject/object split as the horns of the dilemma on which we have been impaled.

After Earth Day, the Chadwick Garden brought it home—I now knew firsthand what was meant by the critique of industrial and technological society, in its ideological superiority, under the banner of physicalism. We were up against it; we were in charge of a neo-vitalist revolt. It was a hippie plot after all! I knew what we were up against: "a major research institution," training servants of industrial society, to aid and abet the late stage of self-destruction.

We were just a blip on the radar screen.

Chapter Three

The Garden Plot

We were to learn that a garden plot had a double meaning, at least as far as the word *plot* was concerned. We would also learn that what was regarded as an archaic and obsolete meaning of *organic* was what we proposed and that the linguistic shifts in meaning that had taken place from antiquity to modernity were about to shift back. It was a sea change.

I suppose the biggest eye-opener for me was the shift in meaning of the Greek word for "nature" and "forest," through Latin to English. It tells the tale. *Nature* in Greek is *physis,* meaning "what grows," "living growth," or a "plantation." *Hyle* is the Greek word for *forest*—think of it as the material background of the plantation or what the plantation has been cut out of as in a clearing and the forest as wood on the way to becoming building material.

Aristotle "is the first to give the word its philosophical meaning of 'matter.' But hyle *in Greek does not originally mean* matter, *it means* forest. *Let us repeat that:* hyle *is the Greek word for* forest. *The cognate of* hyle *in Latin is* silva. *The archaic Latin word was* sylua, *phonetically close to* hyle. *It is strange that the Romans should have translated the Aristotelian* hyle *with the word* material *when the Latin language possessed such a cognate. But even the word* material *did not stray very far from the forests.* Materia *means* wood—*the usable wood of a tree as opposed to its bark, fruit, sap, etc. And* materia *has the same root—yes, root—as the word* mater, *or* mother.*"*[1]

This is such an insight I am grateful to a number of sources for giving me the words that tell the story. *Physis* and *hyle,* both Greek, shift to Latin, then to English, under the pressure of the development of science, no question about it. It was our responsibility to rediscover it. We had to recover the original meanings, and Chadwick helped us do it. The history of the transformation of these words tells the story in a nutshell. Organic nature was supplanted by physics and transformed into the science of mathematized nature after Galileo. The background and underlying stuff (forest roots) became the dead stuff of materialism, the dead stuff or material basis of dead things in space. Once this had become common parlance among natural scientists, that is, physical scientists, the actual elimination of vitalism was sure to follow, and its elimination was pursued with a relentless fury, to the point of a blood oath.

Physis meant *"plantation" in Greek; Plato called God a planter or* physis! *The word comes from a verb which means "living growth"! Physics, however, in the Renaissance, became what it is today: the science of dead matter. For the first time in the history of thought, dead matter was held to have preceded living growth. In a living universe, too, we may have to cope with corpses. But the mechanical "natural science" after 1500 tried to explain life out of its corpses by making nature primarily a concept of dead mass in space! Only recently have we discovered that the term "nature" between 1500 and 1900 was used in a sense or with an accent unheard in any other epoch: mass, quantity, space, i.e., dead things, filled the foreground of scientific thought. Physics was held to "explain" chemistry, chemistry biology, biology psychology, psychology philosophy. Dead things were to explain the living; personality by adrenalin in the glands.*[2]

I became interested in the history of these key words when I was involved in the medicinal herb industry, where herbal usage forms an intermediary step to the modern. "Physic" is an herbal preparation more or less synonymous with "tonic." You take a physic, especially if you need a laxative. That's the Greek meaning. And *physician* is the word for a doctor of medicine who, up to seventy-five years ago, dispensed herbal and mineral remedies.

Materia medica is Latin for the organized field of study regarding medicinal herbs. So far so good. Forest herbs, vital roots are the material; the connection with organic nature is intact. The words still carry their original meanings. And then a shift takes place, which, following Hans Jonas and his description of the turn taken in the Renaissance, is a shift from life to death. It sounds extreme, but when you move from the forest and the plantation and vital roots and medicinal herbs to dead things in space and dead matter underlying them, along with artificial synthetics, the point should be clear. It *is* extreme.

Physics takes over as the science of dead matter, dead things in space, reduced to atoms and molecules and divisible parts, the movement of modern science largely associated with Galileo, the mathematical physicist responsible for the mathematization of nature.[3]

Hyle should have gone to *silva,* in Latin, but instead went to *mater,* which, initially, is consistent and okay, as in Mother (*mater*/maternal) Nature.

Like the fate of physics, it ends up as *mater*-ialism, the dead stuff underlying the dead things in space. Forget Mother Nature. She doesn't matter. And *physic,* as in what grows, and herbal remedies, suffered a similar reversal when physicians forsook the botanical basis of medicine for synthetic drugs in the delivery system of industrial society health care.

This is physicalism, the overwhelmingly predominant trend in modern science, responsible for its reductionism, where only physical and chemical forces count for knowledge. After 1828, when the chemical revolution is added to the revolution of mathematical physics, Galileo and Newton, this view increasingly holds sway as the exclusive meaning of the structure of scientific revolutions. Physicalism is the structure! Thomas Kuhn simply assumes the victory in his formalistic and abstract discussion of revolutions in his popular account: *The Structure of Scientific Revolutions*.[4]

It is indicative of the coup that from the point of view of the physicalists, the defeat of vitalism is regarded as small potatoes, a skirmish in the precincts of chemistry rather than the final critical blow of a multiple-century trend. It is indicative, as well, that even the urea experiment, the critical event of 1828, should be pooh-poohed as the smoking gun in the demise of vitalism. A famous chemist named McKie, in *The Journal of Chemical Education*, does his best to downplay the role of urea and derides the issue as a legend; after all, didn't Woehler use some bone; therefore, it wasn't a clean synthesis.[5] The upshot: vitalism wasn't murdered; it committed suicide. The blow was self-inflicted. That's the guilty talk of the victor: don't blame me; they did themselves in.

The garden opened my eyes to this conflict, the conflict between organic gardening and organic chemistry, the conflict between nature and artificial synthesis, between orange juice and Tang, between what is grown in the ground and what is produced in the laboratory of experimental science, the conflict between physicalism and vitalism, only one of a list of classic conflicts, by the way, in the history of ideas: the conflict between the humanities and the sciences; between the ancients and the moderns; between poetry and philosophy; between religion and science; between environmental advocacy and industrial society exploitation, just to name a few.

All these conflicts, largely academic in their conceptual formulations, are symbolic of larger trends in the culture as a whole, representing a split in the culture, the so-called Two Cultures split, whereby they account for a host of quandaries, seemingly insoluble and indefinable, until you get the point.

I got the point. Thinking about the conflict for thirty years, it is the *leitmotif* of my studies—this power struggle at the basis of higher education, dividing the sciences and the humanities and how they are organized over the theme of what counts for knowledge.

I am aware of the fact that the two terms I use to characterize the Two Culture split—physicalism and vitalism—are not familiar to most readers. They are terms from the philosophy and history of science, where they are often lumped with a complex of other terms—materialism, mechanism, determinism, reductionism, empiricism, rationalism on the side of physicalism; and organicism, wholism, systems theory, *Naturphilosophie*, *Lebensphilosophie,* phenomenology, existentialism, romanticism, voluntarism, pragmatism, on the side of vitalism, throw in vegetarianism and homeopathy, just to stretch the point. I use the two terms as generic for these respective lumps. They are the flags I have stuck at the top of the two piles.

Chapter Four

Goethe the Vitalist
contra Newton the Physicalist

Alan usually referred to Kew Gardens and Wisley as two
of his favorite gardens and horticultural training centers in
Great Britain, two places he revered for their professional-
ism, especially when the issue of further training came up
regarding promising students who wanted to enter the profession. He could have also mentioned the network of botanical gardens in most of the great cities of Europe, harking back
to a period when botany was the supreme science and still in
touch with its biblical and classic cultural backgrounds: Eden
and Arcadia.

It is hard to believe that the conflict between physics and
botany begins in the botanical gardens of the Renaissance.

Remarkably, the shift is simple to the point of being simple
minded, from nature to matter. Organic nature is departed
from as industrial society develops as a world above the given
world of nature, and as matter increasingly occupies the foreground, as the focus of scientific interest. Organic nature and
its vital features are associated with secondary qualities, and
secondary qualities are so beside the point when the focus is
on matter that they are called "occult qualities." Organic nature doesn't matter.

I was alerted to the concept of occult qualities in my reading on the theme of matter in the time of Newton, when occult qualities were regarded as a casualty of the mechanical
philosophy, following upon Galileo's rejection of secondary
qualities. Before this I was aware of Newton's alchemical
work, now widely known through the studies of one of my
favorite names in scholarship (she could have been a country singer or a southern evangelist) in the history of science—Billy Jo Teeter Dobbs. This late discovery qualified
everyone's understanding of Newton, the closet alchemist,
working in secrecy on the philosopher's stone on the way

to perfection, a kind of chemical sanctification: in metals (gold), in medicine (a universal panacea), in soul (salvation), in cosmos (the redemption of matter). In a way, alchemy was an answer to Tillich's call for a theology of the inorganic, just as it was an acknowledgement that *salvation* means "to be healed"; it is an act of cosmic healing, in which human beings, nature, and society are healed and made whole. And Newton, of all people, was one of the major adepts in the practice of alchemy, what he called "vegetable" chemistry as opposed to vulgar chemistry. On this score he would be in perfect harmony with Goethe and even with Chadwick, so, knowing this side of Newton, it is not so offbeat after all to call Chadwick a Newton of the grass blades. It is of interest to this approach that all of Newton's alchemical writings were deemed unscientific by the members of the syndicate responsible for editing his papers when they were given to the University of Cambridge by Newton's family, who held onto them until the nineteenth century. The alchemical and theological papers of Newton, what could be called his covert vitalist side, were returned to the family as of no value and were offered at auction in 1936.

Dobbs was one of the first to bring to light the significance of Newton's alchemical work, and she is lucid in her account of the tangled terminology between physics and chemistry on the issue of matter, turning on the difference between particle and substance, with the latter still used in chemistry, because of secondary qualities. Here's the rub: "primary" attributes were extension, shape, impenetrability, motion, and weight. This was true of the mechanical thought of physics. Chemical substance included the so-called occult or secondary qualities: odor, taste, color, crystalline form, and chemical reactivity. Now this may look like a minor issue to you, but it is of paramount significance in the history of science. Dobbs says why in her comment on the program of mechanical philosophy: subjective, sensory qualities did not "really" exist in nature and were to be reduced to quantitative determination of particulate magnitude, figure, configuration, and motion.[1]

Two summary reviews of this issue pinpoint the trend and the consequences of the reductionist methodology:

From the physical sciences there spread over the conception of all existence an ontology whose model entity is pure matter, stripped of all features of life. The tremendously enlarged universe of modern cosmology is conceived as a field of inanimate masses and forces which operate according to the laws of inertia and of quantitative distribution in space. This denuded substratum of all reality could only be arrived at through a progressive expurgation of vital features from the physical record and through the strict abstention from projecting into its image our own felt aliveness. In the process the ban on anthropomorphism was extended to zoomorphism in general. What remained is the residue of the reduction toward the properties of mere extension which submit to measurement and hence to mathematics. These properties alone satisfy the requirements of what is now called exact knowledge.[2]

E. A. Burtt carries through this observation:

The features of the world now classed as secondary, unreal, ignoble, and regarded as dependent on the deceitfulness of sense, are just those features which are most intense to man in all but his purely theoretic activity, and even in that, except where he confines himself strictly to the mathematical method. It was inevitable that in these circumstances man should now appear to be outside of the real world; man is hardly more than a bundle of secondary qualities. Observe that the stage is set for the Cartesian dualisms—on the one side of primary, the mathematical realm; on the other the realm of man. And the premium of importance and value as well as of independent existence all goes with the former. Man begins to appear for the first time in the history of thought as an irrelevant spectator and insignificant effect of the great mathematical system which is the substance of reality.[3]

The issue of organic nature versus mathematical physics hung in the balance during the early period of the European Renaissance, when botany was at its highest point, thanks to the great botanical gardens developed throughout Europe, one of the greatest achievements of Western culture, beginning in Padua and Pisa, although an earlier one is attributed to Germany.[4] These great civic botanical gardens were themselves an expression of the rebirth of Western culture and a celebration of the event. They were also an outgrowth of the medieval herb garden. It jumped the wall. Every city had to have one—a great botanical garden in which to celebrate the rebirth of Western culture; it was Arcadia and Eden all over again. What better place to celebrate the rebirth of culture and the rediscovery of the ancient sources of culture than in a great botanic garden, returning culture to horticulture. From Padua and Pisa the movement swept through Europe.

The Garden of Eden: The Botanic Garden and the Re-Creation of Paradise, by John Prest, tells the story of the effort to locate Eden, in the hope that it had not been swept away by the great Flood. It was hoped that an earthly paradise still existed and could be located. When this effort proved fruitless, the civic botanic gardens became their own Edens and Arcadias, symbolic examples of what had been hoped for but could not be found. Explorers went out to search the world for plants to bring back to these local Edens—the great civic botanic gardens, a re-creation of Eden.[5]

It was these great civic botanic gardens that foreshadowed the future of science, as many of the civic gardens became scientific academies, developing astronomical observatories and chemical laboratories.[6] This is ironic, as though the gardens were the Eden of the Fall, expressed in the second account of the creation story in Genesis, and sowed the seeds of their own demise as far as the fate of botany was concerned, when physics and chemistry would take over the determination of what counts for knowledge after the defeat of vitalism and the victory of physicalism.

Some people fault Christianity as a major player in ecological degradation, man as the ruler over nature, appointed to name everything and dominate it, a distortion of the biblical account of the stewardship of creation given to Adam and ignoring this great Renaissance period of recreating Eden. Faulting Christianity was the accusation of Lynn White in a famous paper on the origins of the environmental crisis.[7] He was ignorant of the sources and tried to make up for badmouthing the Christian tradition as the background for the domination and exploitation of nature by tipping his hat to St. Francis as an exception, because he prayed to birds.

If you would permit me, I would like to shine some light on this issue. The biblical account of creation makes it clear that creation is the original horizon of the unambiguous affirmation of goodness: creation as creation is good! That's the first

74

account. Genesis 1–2:4. No ambiguity there. God creates and *ipse dixit!* It is so because God says so. This account is attributed to the so-called Priestly source (P); it is obviously distinct from the second account, attributed to the Jahwist source (J), where, unlike man created in the image of God of the first account, man is created from the dust of the ground. The name Adam, in fact, is a play on the word for dust or soil *(adamah)*.

Unlike the first account, where each day is unambiguously good and God says so, the second account (Gen. 2:4ff.), which begins on the third day of the first account, introduces the prohibition not to eat of the Tree of the Knowledge that Everything Is Possible (not quite the same as the Knowledge of Good and Evil, as it is usually translated), which arouses the desire to transgress; act on it, and out you go. Toil and suffering accompany the banishment from the garden. And death. No more access to the Tree of Life whose leaves overcame one's natural mortality. And the added curse upon the land. These two accounts are exemplary stories to be kept in balance. Original sin is related to the second account. There is no suggestion of it in the first account, in which everything is unambiguously affirmed as good! The first account is the *more original* affirmation of the goodness of creation, more original than original sin. It takes precedence even though it was most likely written later and then set before the account of the Fall, lest God's creation be compromised.[8]

I bring this up because I don't want the criticism of the biblical tradition and its role in the environmental crisis, misguided as it is, to obscure the significance of the creation account and the symbolism of the garden, albeit the place of the Fall. It is essential that the original affirmation of the unambiguous goodness of creation be held in dialectical tension with the myth of the Fall, where the ambiguity enters, in the prohibition not to eat of the Tree. The symbolic meaning of this narrative is inexhaustible in its depth and eludes attempts to do it justice. As Paul Ricoeur says, the symbol gives rise to thought. One returns to it again and again to look for new meaning. Indicative of this is the following legend, which is one of the most beautiful I have ever read and another reason why I liked the book by Prest, which brought it to my attention.

Some, who were impressed by the symmetry of the Christian religion, and by the way in which Christ had atoned for the Fall, believe(d) that the crucifixion had taken place upon the exact spot where Adam had sinned. This idea found expression in the legend of Seth, who was credited with having made his way back to the Garden, where he begged seeds from the tree of life off the angel on duty at the gate which he planted in the mouth of his father, Adam, when he died. From these seeds, the cedars of Lebanon, were, with a pleasing sense of historical continuity, thought to have been derived, and from the wood of one of the cedars of Lebanon felled for the construction of Solomon's Temple, after many miraculous adventures, the cross itself was supposed to have been hewn. [9]

Now think of the agony of Adam in the garden as that exact spot where the Tree of Life is the Cross and you begin to see the meaning of symbols and their interplay in the biblical symbol system and the tradition of reflection and meditation it inspires.

Eden eventually becomes the paradise of the first account in Genesis without the prohibition. It is conflated with the vision of the Kingdom of God.

The dynamic of plant hunting and the effort to re-create Eden was so strong it has been called the age of the plantocrat, foreshadowing the future technocrat. They wanted to find or re-create a paradise on earth. A plantocracy, Armytage cleverly calls it, who tells the story in his fine study *The Rise of the Technocrats,* is an apt description of the golden age of botany, when the world opened up through exploration and whole new plant families were discovered and brought back to Europe and the network of gardens waiting for them.

Galileo was a contemporary of this profusion of gardens and the passionate interest in botany. He can be credited with the origins of modern science with his dictum, *Il libro della natura e scritto in lingua matematica* (the book of nature is written in mathematical language). He mathematized nature and laid the groundwork for the future victory of mathematical physics in the struggle over what counts for knowledge and who counts, leading to the subordination of botany to physics and chemistry in the system of the sciences.

Descartes followed him and set the stage for the subject/object split in his understanding of the *cogito* ("I think") as the principle of epistemological subjectivity over and against all extended objects, including one's body. Descartes paid increased attention to mechanism, materialism, and mathematics as conceptual tools for the interpretation of nature. He was a reductionist with a vengeance: mathematics was the key to understanding the physical universe and "no other means exists for finding the truth." This exclusive rant perplexes me and leaves me bewildered. It is characteristic of the physicalist animus leading up to the oath.

Get the irony of this. First they tried to *find* the Garden of Eden. They thought it was geographically localized. Sir Walter Raleigh had something to do with it as part of his colonizing efforts in North America. Columbus had Eden in mind in his quest for the New World. Some thought it could be found in Sweden, probably because of Linnaeus, who was thought to be a second Adam, with his ability to name everything according to his Latin binomial system.

Disappointed, they decided to reestablish Eden in the great botanic gardens of Europe. They would re-create it, becoming one of the inspirations for the proliferation of gardens in almost every great city in Europe. In the midst of these gardens, which became the seedbeds of modern science, botany was primary; astronomical observatories and chemical laboratories were added on and developed. Eventually, the scientists in these garden academies would move into the lab altogether and abandon the garden. They eventually found they could reproduce from inorganic sources what nature provided. Under experimental laboratory conditions, they could argue for their identity. A world above the given world of nature was the result, a world where organic nature was reduced to matter.

Organic nature was identified with artificial synthesis and the word *plant* came to mean "factory," both of them dedicated to the making of chemicals, because the chemistry of the living organism was identical to the laboratory and the factory.[10] Plants were little factories; factories were big plants. They both made chemicals. It was only a matter of scale and efficiency and profit.

The shift from life to death, from plantation and forest to factories and laboratories, substituting for nature for purposes of economic gain, happens here, in the evolution of the botanic garden to the triumphant rise of industrial society.

Goethe comes at the decisive moment in this struggle, and in his old age he was contemporary with the chemical experiment that would tip the scales in favor of what he fought against. In his mourning over the passing of Old Europe and the emerging industrial and technological society that would replace it, he suffered a form of nervous breakdown and one day simply dropped out of Weimar society and walked south in search of the vital root he despaired over as endangered. He called it the *Urpflänze*.[11]

To find the root again, to despair over the fate of the vital root, whether the root is part of organic nature or a metaphor for European culture, or the grounding of one's own existence, Goethe had an obsession with this need for roots in the face of the impending uprooting. He sensed it and gave utterance to it. We have already referred to Karl Löwith, in his *Nature, History and Existentialism*, and his discussion of "The dissolution of Old-Europe," how Goethe prophesied the impending barbarism, "We are already right in it." In 1829, the year after the synthesis of urea, he mentions that God will no longer be glad of this world and "will have to smash up the whole for a renewed creation." There were many intellectuals and artists who experienced this crisis and suffered various forms of nervous breakdown because of it. Max Weber and William James are two who come to mind, along with those who suffered a breakdown in the trenches of Verdun in the First World War, like Paul Tillich, who was a chaplain at the front; Max Beckmann, an ambulance driver, also suffering a nervous breakdown; Wittgenstein, who lost his sense of human decency; and Rosenstock-Huessy, who envisaged his magnum opus—*Out of Revolution, Autobiography of Western Man.*

The association of the *Urpflänze* as the vital root—although it is a major issue in Goethe's botanical writings—is fanciful on my part. You probably have to be German to get the drift, especially when it comes to Ur-whatever. It had a lot to do with thinking about fundamental forms. He coined the term *morphology* to discuss the structure of plant form, and he thought of the *Urpflänze,* a prototypical German metaphysical notion, as the form of forms for plant development.

What is at stake in these considerations is an understanding of a ground phenomenon, an idea foreign to most. Heisenberg has a nice sense for it and knows how to formulate the issue. He teases out the Platonic/Kantian conflict in the discussion with Schiller over an Idea. For Schiller an Idea is not empirical, because he operated within a subject/object scheme of inquiry. "How can any experience ever be given which should be appropriate to an Idea? For that is precisely what is characteristic of the latter, that an experience could never be adequate to it."[12] For Goethe an Idea could be embodied in an appearance, so that he could see it with his own eyes. As Heisenberg puts it after quoting Goethe on the point:

A ground phenomenon is not to be equated with a fundamental principle, yielding many kinds of consequences, but is to be regarded as a basic appearance, within which the manifold is to be discerned. Seeing, knowing, sensing, believing and whatever all the feelers may be called, whereby man gropes about in the universe, must then genuinely work together, if we wish to fulfill our important, though difficult, vocation.

Heisenberg, clearly rejecting Galileo's rejection of secondary qualities, knows that Goethe is participatory in his idea of cognition and wants to transcend the subject/object split, as any poet working in the area of scientific research would be expected to do, "Goethe very clearly feels that the basic structures must be of such a kind that it can no longer be determined whether they belong to what we think of as the objective world or to the human soul, since they form the presupposition for both." This reveals an appreciation for the classic meaning of reason as receptive rather than the current view of reason as controlling or technical. Heisenberg corrects my tendency to understand the ground phenomenon as a primary principle from which successive examples are deduced when he states:

This ground phenomenon was not to be a fundamental principle, from which the various phenomena had to be deduced, but a basic appearance within which the manifold was to be discerned.

This is the crux of the famous debate between Goethe and Schiller. Schiller thought the ground phenomenon was an

Idea and Goethe objected that this made it too subjective inasmuch as his Idea was a perceivable structure.

I have thought about this issue in my reading of Plato, for whom the existential ground of the Platonic Ideas was Socrates. He embodied them. They were not to be pushed off into some heavenly realm, the fate they suffered after Plato, who never used the term *heavenly realm.* Aristotle was supposed to have brought them down to earth. This is a superficial reading of Plato. Aristotle never "saw" the forms in the depths of Socrates, for instance, as Plato did. He never got the charismatic power of Socrates, the power that made him a savior (he overcame the anxiety of having-to-die), even though others did. Aristotle played down this veneration. So two types of intellect, two types of cognition, two types of self-understanding are involved here. Call it the *definitional* and *configurational:* analytical logical versus pictorial gestalts.

From the point of view of Platonism, however, what was at issue in this discussion was really not so much what an Idea is but rather by what organ of knowledge the Idea is revealed to us. If Goethe could see the Ideas with his own eyes, they were certainly different eyes from those that we commonly talk about nowadays. At all events they could not be replaced, in this context, by a microscope or a photographic plate.[13]

Or, if you permit me, by synthetic urea.

Goethe was a holistic thinker, one who saw structures rather than analytically reducing them to their component parts according to the subject/object scheme. Goethe stood against this reductionistic epistemology and wanted to transcend the subject/object split and the type of science determined by the so-called natural sciences, with the scales tipped toward physics and chemistry, as the determining pursuits for which we recognize the significance of Galileo and Descartes and Newton and Woehler. Goethe stood opposed to the reduction of organic nature to matter, the trend from life to death.

Goethe, having dropped out of German society, took a two-year walk and went to the oldest botanical garden in the Western world, according to the claim, in Padua, Italy, to look for the Urplant and he found it, or, at least the Italians thought he did. They called the plant, "Goethe's Palm" *(Chaemerops humilis),* to honor his visit. They built a glass case to enshrine it.

I went to see it in 1976 on a trip through Europe in the footsteps of Goethe with my great friend Rolf von Eckartsberg. I stood there and thought, "Well, what do you know? Where else but in the oldest botanical garden in the Western world—would you find the vital root of existence, squirreled away under glass, to wait out the rise, triumph, and self-destruction of industrial society, as a world above the given world of nature, and therefore devoid of vital roots."[14] I have a clipping in a jar in my herbarium.

After his return, Goethe had his famous discussion of the issue with Schiller when they finally met, after avoiding one another for some time, waiting for the reverse magnetism to reverse in order to attract. Reverse it did on one enchanted evening. They spent the night talking about Goethe's *Urpflänze*. Finally Schiller made the mistake of saying, "That's just an idea." It was probably late and he was tired, but it revealed a deep division between them. Goethe was furious. He saw and experienced his ideas! There was no "only" about it! For him seeing the Urplant was like x-ray vision.

I explained to him with great vivacity the Metamorphosis of Plants and, with a few characteristic strokes of the pen, conjured up before his eyes a symbolical plant. He listened, and looked at it with great interest and intelligence; but when I had ended, he shook his head saying: This has nothing to do with experience, it is an idea. I raised my eyebrows, somewhat annoyed. For he had put his finger on precisely the point which separated us.... Well, so much the better; it means that I have ideas without knowing it, and can even see them with my own eyes.

Goethe wanted to see Nature manifesting herself in her wholeness in every single part of her being. For him, it was experiential.[15] As we have mentioned, his Platonism was existential.

Eric Heller, in his essay on "Goethe and the Scientific Truth," in *The Disinherited Mind,* comments:

Goethe's science has contributed nothing substantial to the scientific progress between his time and ours, and nothing whatsoever to the advancement of techniques for the mastery and exploitation of Nature; but he did, by his opposition to contemporary science, lay bare in his time, with remarkable precision, the very roots of that crisis and revolution in scientific method in which the twentieth century scientist finds himself involved.[16]

When I read about Kant recoiling from the unknown root, as Heidegger puts it in his *Kant and the Problem of Metaphysics,*

81

a technical problem in Kantian studies having to do with the transcendental imagination, I thought how it symbolically resonates with Goethe's Urplant. Goethe is trying to overcome "the Kantian recoil" just as Heidegger tries to do with his *dasein analyses,* his inquiry into the meaning of human existence in the face of the oblivion of being. The vital root was at stake in the history of philosophy as well as in the development of modern physicalistic science. The rejection of vitalism was the symbolic battleground for this discussion. Kant, in his effort to accommodate philosophy to science, recoiled from this unknown vital root and left it as a problem for Goethe, Husserl, Heidegger, and others.[17] It can be generalized as a meditation on the fate of the earth as the ground for our existence. It is exactly what I mean when I say that Chadwick replanted our vital root.

If one translates "roots" into "being" and moves to the division of philosophy known as ontology, then a line can be drawn from Kant's denying that existence is a predicate in his debunking arguments for the existence of God, a symptomatic anticipation of the quandary of existence in the centuries to follow, to Husserl's "bracketing" of consciousness in the phenomenological *epoche,* to Heidegger's cancellation of being, and to Derrida's deconstruction of onto-theology. This is often discussed under the theme of the "Death of God" (Nietzsche) and the prevailing trend of nihilism. Is this the legacy of the rejection of Goethe and his visionary defense of vitalism?

I don't know if Goethe had a real plant in mind that would be the exemplar of his search, although he did sketch one for Schiller, and reconstructions of that sketch have been attempted, but the idea of an Urplant is so suggestive of the German search for metaphysical meaning in a period in which forces are unleashed to squash the effort.[18] Scientists, by and large, could care less about "vital roots" or any metaphysical inquiry into the meaning of being any more than they care about the integrity of organic nature. After all, the slogan of the logical positivist school in Vienna, known as the philosophy of physicalism, was "the elimination of metaphysics." They were the ones who threw the baby out with the bathwater.

Wittgenstein, related to the school, said that philosophy is the disease of which it should be the cure. He meant them.[19]

Even though we at the Chadwick Garden occupied only three or four acres on a large campus, the debate was re-enjoined, just about the time the physicalist scientists on the campus thought the issue had been laid to rest, dead and buried. Long gone. They had as much as forgotten about it, although many could still recall the urea experiment and its role in the origins of organic chemistry. They didn't know a new point of departure was coming that would force the issue to a renewed awareness; we were getting ready for Earth Day, April 22, 1970, which brought the debate to a national audience. It was the great check on industrial society, now in the late stage of its self-destruction. I was fascinated by the details of the conflict and began to study the process with a zeal that would not quit.

Actually, the debate was never occasioned within the faculty of the university, nor has it been since. No one talked about it as an academic issue, even though lines were drawn and sides were taken. It was business as usual with the scientists in charge. They probably thought the introduction of environmental studies into the curriculum was a small accommodation to the times, which everyone knew were a changin'. The garden they could ignore, even though they were eager to pick up flowers on their way to the lab.

I had been a student of Paul Tillich at Harvard, and he had taught me the phrase "the late stage of the self-destruction of industrial society, as a world above the given world of nature." I had a vague notion of what was meant and now I have taken it on as a kind of mantra. If I repeat it too often in this account, it is due to my inability to edit it out. It functions for me as a drumbeat. I read Tillich's essays on technology, on existentialism as the philosophical protest against industrial society, on the fate of the person in industrial society, on what it meant to be turned into a thing on the assembly line, on daylight saving time, a cog in the machinery of production and consumption. All of this came into poignant focus when I found out that MIT students called themselves "tools."[20] However sad, it was a rare moment of self-appraisal.

It was a proud moment when I accompanied Tillich to MIT, where he gave a major address on the occasion of the centenary of the institute, along with Aldous Huxley and Robert Oppenheimer. The title: "How Has Science in the Last Century Changed Man's View of Himself?" I thought he was prophetically uttering the word of God. It is one of the best talks he ever gave, and I must say he rose to the occasion, even though it mostly fell on deaf ears. At the end he said this:

May I conclude with the hope that the ever-increasing protest against the dehumanization of man in the latest stages, not of science and technology, but of scientism and technicism may soon become more than a protest, but a support for a view of man that takes into consideration all dimensions of the multidimensional unity that man is.[21]

This is a critical statement, which will also fall on deaf ears, inasmuch as any criticism of science evokes a defensive reaction. What is at stake here has to be emphasized: it is the criticism of scientism, an ideological stance taken by science, beginning with Galileo and Descartes, culminating in the nineteenth century with the philosophy of physicalism. This is the ideological core of modern science and it spreads its wings from the center and acts as an organizing principle for a fundamental attitude. It has three major components that make up the scientistic creed, as formulated by Eric Voegelin:

1. That the mathematical science of natural phenomenon is a model science to which all other sciences ought to conform.

2. That all realms of being are accessible to the methods of the science of phenomenon.

3. That all reality that is not accessible to the sciences of phenomena is either irrelevant or illusionary.[22]

When one looks at Saint-Simon, for example, the exponent of a quasi-religion, or pseudo-religion, where modern science shows itself in the most absurdist light, the Physicalist Oath becomes a pseudo-religious vow, a comical extension of the "So Help Me, Helmholtz!" I was alerted to Saint-Simon's role by the critique of Eric Voegelin and his use of Frederick Hayek's discussion of the scientistic creed and its bearing on the formation of a new type of man.[23]

It is demonstrably clear why the French engineer became the model for the new type of man needed in the development of industrial society. The curriculum for training such a man was developed at the École Polytechnique as the implementation of the scientistic creed, with technocracy as the outcome of the plantocracy and the garden academies of the Renaissance. The garden engineer became the technocrat of industrial society once the training was in place.[24]

It is not much of a stretch to move to the tradition represented by Helmholtz, who inspired the Physicalist Oath, formulated by his colleagues Brücke and DuBois-Reymond.

"The new medicine," declared the twenty-four-year-old Virchow, "has a mechanistic approach and its object is the establishment of a physics of the organism. It has shown that life is nothing more than the sum of phenomena which proceed from general physical and chemical (that is to say mechanical) laws. It denies the existence of an autocratic Life or Healing Force."[25]

Mendelsohn describes how Helmholtz and his gang deliberately set out to alter the philosophy of biology as expressed in the manifesto of 1847:

"We four imagined [they said, looking back] that we should constitute physiology on a chemical-physical foundation and give it equal scientific rank with physics." This is clearly an attempt to create a new field and to consciously establish for it a "central dogma." Brücke, DuBois-Reymond, Helmholtz, and Ludwig are the four who, working together, set out to propagate a new philosophy for physiology. Each became a statesman for a program—really for a radical scientific policy not unconnected, as far as I have indicated, with the other radicalism of the 1840s.

The task of science, as he [Helmholtz] sets it out, is clear—all phenomena are to be reduced to attractive and repulsive central forces, the intensity dependent solely upon the intervening distance. Analytical mechanics then, particles in motion, became the paradigm for the sciences. They are all assumed to be reducible to a material base. Helmholtz had taken on the job of providing the theoretical underpinning for an outlook in physiology (and now all the sciences) that was being enunciated programmatically by his Berlin compatriots.[26]

"To be a mechanist meant to be on the attack!" And the object of the attack was vitalism. In order to promote his view,

85

he, along with two other physiologists, Brücke and DuBois-Reymond, founded the Berlin Physicalist Society, where physiology would be a simple extension of physics into another realm. The Physicalist Society is a continuation of the academies developed in botanic gardens throughout Europe.

Armytage describes how the stage was set for the beginning of scientific academies in the proliferation of botanic gardens throughout Europe, setting the stage for the Physicalist Society.

Technology had found its clerisy in the academies—220 of them by 1790.... Collecting, measuring and examining everything they could see or lay hands on, these academicians devised telescopes and microscopes, experimented, travelled and wrote. Though such groups appeared at the same time and in the same places as the botanic gardens, they were, in every sense, discrete. And they became more discrete as they wrote about, as well as to, each other. In the eighteenth century theirs was truly a commanding worldview ... an international general staff endowed with a strong esprit de corps.[27]

Get the military metaphors. They meant business. It was warfare.[28] Now add the development in France, where the scientific intellectual appeared as a new type of man of the emerging technology, with the training of the École Polytechnique, a school set up to produce and train the new type.[29]

Here is what it took to produce such a human being in service to such a machine, as Mumford calls it, the Pentagon of Power:

Its physico-centric curriculum (students studied mathematics, physics, and chemistry exclusively) produced a new type of man, "appearing," according to Professor Hayek, "for the first time in history." Having never learned to interpret human life or growth in terms of mankind's literary past (since their training did not include history, literature, or languages), they tended to see life in scientific terms. As its self-appointed spokesman, Count Henri Saint-Simon (1760–1825), expressed it: "We must examine and co-ordinate it all from the point of view of Physicism."

Physicism according to Saint-Simon would need a new physical "clergy" to both interpret and organize society on scientific lines.

Thus a whole generation grew up to whom that great storehouse of social wisdom, the only form indeed in which an understanding of the social processes achieved by the greatest minds is transmitted, the great literature of all ages, was a closed book. For the first time in history that new type appeared which as the product of the German Realschule and of similar institutions was to become so important and influential in the later nineteenth and the twentieth century: the technical specialist was regarded as educated because he had passed through difficult schools but who had little or no knowledge of society, its life, growth, problems and values, which only the study of history, literature and languages can give....

It has been well described how the whole of the teaching at the École Polytechnique was penetrated with the positivist spirit. The very type of engineer with his characteristic outlook, ambitions, and limitations was here created. That synthetic spirit which would not recognize sense in anything that had not been deliberately constructed, that love of organization that springs from the twin sources of military and engineering practices, the aesthetic predilection for everything that had been consciously constructed over anything that had "just grown," was a strong new element which was added to—and in the course of time even began to replace—the revolutionary ardor of the young polytechnicians.[30]

Lewis Mumford refers to the contradictory workings of mechanism and vitalism as profound religious influences and predicts that one day a book will be written that will expose their contradictory workings from the sixteenth century onward:

This book will show that even while the mechanical complex was consolidating its control, it was being modified willy-nilly by the growing appreciation of organic nature in every aspect: witness the better regimen of child-care, hygiene, and diet introduced by the Romantic movement, mainly through Rousseau's writings, if not his practice; witness the growing interest in play and sport which modified the harsh attitude toward such relaxation introduced by Calvinism and utilitarianism: witness the kindly teaching practices introduced by Froebel's Children's Garden (Kindergarten)—the precise antithesis of Comenius' mass-organized drill-school; while at the same time the growing love of nature expressed itself in zealous amateur gardening, in landscape design, in rural sports, and outdoor exercises—hunting, fishing, rambling, mountain-climbing. In some degree these activities cushioned the impact of mechanization, and for over a century they have been opening the way for a more organic culture.

When that book is written it will show how this growing appreciation of all that distinguishes the world of organisms from the world of machines gave rise, at a given point in the nineteenth century, to a fresh vision of the entire cosmic process. This vision was profoundly different from the one offered by those who left out of their world picture the essential qualitative attribute of life: its expectancy, its inner impetus, its insurgency, its creativity, its ability at singular points to transcend either physical or organic limitations.

The name given to this new vision of life was bestowed belatedly, only when it began to be systematically pursued: it is now known as ecology.[31]

Sir Albert Howard is usually credited with espousing growing plants without synthetic chemicals in his work as an agricultural advisor in India, in the state of Indore, where people were so poor they had to devise inexpensive means of maintaining soil fertility, through composting. Howard taught farmers to combine rough weeds and crop wastes in layers with high-nitrogen manure and a little soil, making a pile that soon heated up to over 150 degrees as a result of the multiplication of bacteria and fungi. He was hostile to the trend to use chemicals, fostered by Liebig, as an application of organic chemistry to farming, who thought nitrogen (synthetic urea), phosphorous, and potash—N, P, and K—were all the soil needed, thus disturbing the life cycle of the plant and nature.[32]

F. H. King, the head of USDA's Bureau of Soils, took a trip to China and was impressed with the system of agriculture practiced there and wrote a book about it: *Farmers of Forty Centuries.* J. I. Rodale, after visiting India, with an experience like King's, picked up the Howard philosophy in the late 1930s, with the Dust Bowl experience of the Depression on his mind. He restored the term *organic* as the name for the natural method of farming and gardening, emphasizing the need for compost and humus for soil fertility. He cautioned against factory-processed food and synthetic additives and procedures, and called attention to standards of taste and flavor in his publications from Emmaus, Pennsylvania. His son, Robert Rodale, almost took me to China with him on a trip he made with Ernst Winter, whom I had met and had become friends with, another exponent of biodynamics, famous for running a training center at a castle in Austria. When the school closed and he shut down the castle, all he took were his compost piles. Rodale sent me a postcard and exclaimed that the entire method of gardening in China was the French intensive.

Mumford could have had the Rodales in mind, as well as Steiner, as well as Frank Lloyd Wright, as the "author" in question, all advocates of an organic approach to culture and critics of industrial technology and its machines. Michael Pollan is probably the best candidate, with his *Omnivore's Dilemma*.

Hans Jonas, my favorite author on the subject, didn't write the book Mumford predicts, but his single essay (and then only sections of it) are fragments of that book that extend the issue back to the ancient world in contrast to the modern, with Galileo as the turning point, with his mathematization of nature. He puts it better than anyone, and even though it sounds overstated or exaggerated, once you get the drift, once you have taken up the subject matter and made it a matter of intensive study, there are no formulations I know of that grasp the inner meaning of the theme as well as his. In six pages he tells the story of how life and death characterize the split between the ancient and modern worlds, and how the cosmos once was alive, and how this has been forgotten since physicalistic reductionism set in as a trend in modern science, characterized by a relentless stripping of life's features and attributes.

…And its more recent lifeless image was built up, or left over, in a continuous process of critical subtraction from its fuller original content: at least in this historical sense the mechanistic conception of the universe does contain an antithetic element and is not simply neutral. Moreover, that "subtraction" was set in motion and for long sustained, not by the critical understanding but by dualistic metaphysics which has demonstrable roots in the experience of mortality. Dualism is the link that historically mediated between the two extremes which so far we have opposed to each other unhistorically: it was indeed the vehicle of the movement which carried the mind of man from the vitalistic monism of early times to the materialistic monism of our own as to its unpremeditated, even paradoxical result; and it is difficult to imagine how the one could have been reached from the other without this gigantic "detour." [33]

I quote Jonas here simply for the point of the two monisms—vitalistic and materialistic—and their contrast. Jonas helped me lift off from a focus on chemical materialism in the development of organic chemistry and artificial synthesis, reducing entities found in organic nature to their most simple physical and chemical constituents and then synthesizing these chemicals from inorganic sources. I traced this development from 1828 and then began to appreciate how it was added to the revolution that had already occurred in physics, thanks to Copernicus and Galileo. It was Husserl who described Galileo as the turning point from the ancient world in his mathematization of nature, and this line of thought Jonas carried back into the ancient world, in order to show the transition from life to death. It was Jonas who provided the widest view and had the ability to formulate its meaning.

Is there a figure we can point to through whom the physicalist/vitalist conflict goes in a way that dramatically illuminates the issues? Yes, his name is Sigmund Freud.

In his *Autobiography,* Freud mentions how he went to a public lecture when he was a young man and heard Goethe's "Ode to Nature" read out loud. He was so moved, so he says, he decided right then and there to enter the medical sciences, in order to unveil nature's mysteries, another kind of Freudian slip. Can't you see him rather hesitantly and somewhat indelicately pulling it up on the old girl—the goddess—*Natura?* And where does he end up? Our young Freud? In Brücke's laboratory taking the Physicalist Oath and dissecting the nervous system of a certain order of fish in search of neurones. Freud is important to me not only because I did my doctoral thesis on his concept of guilt but because he is a seminal figure in the physicalist/vitalist conflict. From Vitalist Ode to Physicalist Oath! He was inspired by one and took the other. The physicalist/vitalist conflict, call it a split, goes through him.[34] He suffered a nervous breakdown over it, when he was told to leave the lab, partly because he had cocaine on his nose, and go back and get his medical degree. Cocaine wasn't the only reason. He was Jewish.

Poor Freud. How was he to know that Goethe's ode wasn't by Goethe, when even Goethe didn't know it. Goethe accepted it into his canon late in life, forgetting that he hadn't written it, even though it was good enough for him to claim authorship. It was an old Orphic hymn, and who should have found that out, working at the Goethe Archive in Weimar, but Rudolf Steiner, who did the textual/critical work.

Freud was moved, anyhow.

Over eighty predicates of the goddess are compressed into its thirty hex-
ameters. She is the age-old Mother of All; father, mother, nurse, sustainer,
all-wise, all-bestowing, all-ruling; regulator of the gods; creator; first-
born; eternal life and immortal providence. This universal goddess is not
the personification of an intellectual concept. She is one of the last religious
experiences of the late-pagan world. She possesses inexhaustible vitality.
Natura is cosmic power.[35]

The hymn is dedicated to *Physis.*

It is the nostalgic remnant of Old European culture when
such powers were somewhat intact and able to inspire. I remember seeing a torso of the goddess *Fortuna* at a Roman
antiquities museum in Germany and, when the guard wasn't
looking, I kissed it and asked for its blessing.

Goethe's "Fragment on Nature," which first appeared anon-
ymously in 1782 or 1783, was circulated in manuscript. Goethe
wrote to Knebel that he was not the author. No matter, it came
to be known as "Goethe's Ode." Years later, he saw the ode
again and wrote to Chancellor von Muller, "Although I cannot
remember composing these observations, they are quite in
accord with the conceptions to which my mind then soared."[36]
The year was 1828, the year of the artificial synthesis of urea.
The main point to make here is to juxtapose the Vitalist Ode
to the Physicalist Oath.

Chapter Five

Urea! I Found It!

The origin of organic chemistry is usually credited to Friedrich Woehler and the artificial synthesis of urea. The urea experiment in 1828 was decisive for the decision to reject vitalism. Vitalism was regarded as refuted thanks to a given experiment in a given year. Take it as the move from the garden into the lab, the lab of industrial and technical society, the world above the given world of nature. The lab in the plant-become-factory. This date gave me a specific historical reference I found instrumental in telling the story, when *organic* took on a new meaning, ostensibly contradictory, but so what? *Artificial* and *synthetic* can mean *organic,* if we—the organic chemists—say so! This swindle was the beginning of all confusion.[1] From then on, the meaning of reality would become more and more confused, as *simulation* and *virtual* would take hold of human intelligence as substitute "realities," once *artificial* and *synthetic* were indistinguishable from *organic.*[2]

Artificial intelligence is symptomatic of this trend, which knows no end in the encroachment of computers and the hope held out by techno-geeks that eventually, sooner than you think, no one will be able to tell the difference between a computer and the human mind. Synthetic human beings will be the result: clones. We won't know the difference. Organic nature will fade more and more into the woodwork.

In former times a special force was assumed—the force of life. More recently, when many phenomena of plant life had been successfully reduced to simple chemical and mechanical process, this vital force was derided and effaced from the list of natural agencies.[3]

You might ask: how come everyone doesn't know this— the physicalist/vitalist split as the deepest split within the culture? Why isn't it common knowledge? I don't know. It should be. I guess no one has organized the literature and described the historical trends and themes in exactly the way I see it. And who has had the experience of starting an organic garden while teaching at a college devoted to the natural sciences, to open up the themes in just this way? Many might find this a wild oversimplification of very complicated themes much discussed in the history and philosophy of science, where there is little regard for vitalism—a sentimental, romantic, religious, if you will, sympathy for organic nature, a view that was refuted in 1828, a minor episode in the full scheme of things. But I see it as crucial. Symbolic. It has great heuristic power as an explanatory point of view. Things fell in place for me once I found the key in the date and the experiment; the victorious Archimedean shout went up, "Urea! I found it!"

I had to find the moment after which it was no longer possible to defend the integrity of organic nature. I had to find the moment when organic nature was collapsed into the inorganic, because everything was reduced to physical and chemical forces. It is the moment when the hard sciences lined up against the soft ones no longer deserving the name science. The industrial society engineer became the model of what counted for knowledge. He did the counting. I was stunned to find a loyalty oath, formulated by physicalists, taken in blood—raise your right hand—reading in part, "not to take into account any forces operating in any entity but the physical and chemical forces, or other forces equal in dignity." So help me, Helmholtz.

The "equal in dignity" was a direct slap at vitalism. No vital force was equal in dignity to a physical or chemical force because a vital force was a metaphysical ghost. Eliminate it. There is no physics for it and therefore no math. Eventually, logical positivism would make it their slogan, "the elimination of metaphysics" as well as every other kind of nonsense that could not stand the test of laboratory verification and mathematical determination.

What should enter the gap left by vitalism as a movement of thought but existentialism, the outcry against the trend, against industrial society as a technical world above organic nature, and against the reduction of human beings to things in that technical world, where alienation and estrangement become the catchwords. Now this is when I realized I could put two and two together. A new understanding of existentialism was accorded to me as a result of discovering the physicalist/vitalist conflict.

The argument that the urea experiment refuted vitalism and lead to its elimination, thus removing the defender of the integrity of organic nature, gave me a new appreciation for existentialism as the heir of this refutation and elimination. I use the metaphor "Chief Mourner," to describe the role existentialism played in the aftermath of refuted vitalism, which explains why it seems to be a council of despair. I borrowed the term from the children's nursery song "The Ballad of Cock Robin." Cock Robin gave me the association with Rachel Carson, who sang the ballad, so to speak, in her lament over the effect of DDT on robin populations, thereby initiating the environmental movement, at least in one of its signal events, when she wrote the articles for the *New Yorker* that were later published as *Silent Spring.*

Who killed Cock Robin? "I," said the Sparrow, "with my bow and arrow." Who'll be Chief Mourner? "I," said the Dove, "because of my love."

For Cock Robin, read vitalism; for the bow and arrow, read the artificial synthesis of urea; for the Sparrow, read physicalism; for the Dove, read existentialism, as Chief Mourner. And all the birds of the sky fell to sighing and sobbing, when they heard of the death of poor Cock Robin, when they heard of the death of poor Cock Robin.

Earth Day, April 22, 1970, was the crowning moment of this neo-vitalist reawakening and the historic end of existentialism.

A pervasive sense that "something is missing" became an all-encompassing mood at the outset of the twentieth century. I was startled by the phrase, in German, in the midst of Brecht and Weill's *The Rise and Fall of the City Mahagonny:* "Aber etwas fehlt," repeated, with a note of sad melancholy, by Jimmy Mahoney.[4] Mahagonny is industrial society in the late stage of self-destruction. "Oh show us the way to the next whiskey bar. Oh don't ask why. Oh don't ask why. I tell you we must die."

The shift was made from the fate of organic nature to the fate of existence itself in the predicament of industrial society as a world above the given world of nature.

The crowning blow in the struggle over what counts for knowledge was the artificial synthesis of urea, an experiment credited with the defeat of vitalism. As we never tire of repeating, the date was 1828. Goethe died in 1832. Existentialism begins in 1841–42, in the Berlin lectures of Schelling. They are all tied together in an inextricable knot of historical forces.

Believe it or not, Goethe had met the scientist, the future chemist, Friedrich Woehler, when Woehler was a boy, in a mineral shop in Frankfurt. Faust in the flesh. The Faust-to-be. I would like to think that even though they may not have exchanged a word, they may have bumped elbows, a nod, maybe—and, intuiting who this young man was to become, Goethe went home and finished his poem.

I remember the thrill when I picked up a book at an outdoor bookstore in Kensington, a suburb of London, *Crucibles: The Lives of Great Chemists,* by Bernard Jaffe, thinking there may be a chapter on Woehler, and opened to the very page describing his meeting with Goethe:

He received his early education from his father, who interested him in nature and encouraged him in drawing and in his hobby of mineral collecting. Friedrich carried on a brisk exchange of minerals with his boyhood friends, which he continued even in later life. On one occasion he met the old poet Goethe, who was examining specimens in the shop of a mineral dealer in Frankfurt.[5]

So the line began to disclose itself, from Goethe to Steiner to Chadwick, a line, insofar as it represented vitalism, completely denounced and rejected by modern science in its physicalist mode. I read about how vitalism, the argument for the integrity of organic nature, was considered by physicalism to be the most despised point of view, along with German *Naturphilosophie,* represented by Schelling. I began to see how industrial society was part and parcel of this rejection of organic nature in the development of a world above it, where factories were plants. I began to collect quotes from both sides to illustrate the conflict.

For the chemistry of the living organism is fundamentally identical with that of the laboratory and the factory.[6]

Now this is almost stupefying to entertain and yet it has become a commonplace. It would be my candidate for the

95

dumbest thing anyone has ever said in the history of the human race. It is the perfect expression of the triumph of technical reason and the protest it engenders, which is the central purpose of existentialism. Here is Tillich's account of the broader historical features of the triumph of technical reason that eventually brought about the existentialist protest after the defeat of vitalism:

> The present world situation is the outcome—directly in the West and indirectly elsewhere—of the rise, the triumph, and the crisis of what we may term "bourgeois society." This development has occurred in three distinguishable though overlapping phases. In the first, the new society struggled to establish itself over the remnants of a disintegrating feudal society—the period of bourgeois revolutions. In the second, mainly through the creation of a world mechanism of production and exchange, the new society came to triumphant power—the period of victorious bourgeoisie. In the third, mankind struggles to regain control over the self-destructive forces loosed by a regnant industrial society—the present crisis in civilization. The disintegration and transformation of bourgeois society is the dynamic center of the present world situation.[7]

Our story comes out of the second period, the period of the victorious bourgeoisie.

> Reason was supposed to control nature, in man and beyond man, because nature and reason were held to be in essential harmony. But in the measure in which the bourgeois revolution succeeded, the revolutionary impetus disappeared, and the character of reason as the guiding principle was transformed. They sacrificed reason as the principle of truth and justice, and employed it mainly as a tool in the service of the technical society they were bent upon perfecting. "Technical reason" became the instrument of a new system of production and exchange.[8]

This technical reason, controlling nature, the Cartesian *cogito*, is overlooked in efforts to account for the environmental crisis when it is read back into the biblical sources in order to blame Christianity, where it does not belong. *Logos* in the biblical account is revelatory reason, about as far from technical reason as you can get, especially when the Logos becomes flesh, full of grace and truth, as in the opening hymn of the Gospel of John.

> Technical reason provides means for ends, but offers no guidance in the determination of ends. Reason in the first period had been concerned

96

with ends beyond the existing order. Technical reason became concerned with means to stabilize the existing order. Revolutionary reason had been conservative with respect to means but "utopian" with respect to ends. Technical reason is conservative with respect to ends and revolutionary with respect to means. It can be used for any purposes dictated by the will, including those that deny reason in the sense of truth and justice. The transformation of revolutionary reason into technical reason was the decisive feature of the transition from the first to the second period of modern society.

This displacement of revolutionary reason by technical reason was accompanied by far-reaching changes in the structure of human society. Man became increasingly able to control physical nature. Through the tools placed at his disposal by technical reason, he created a worldwide mechanism of large-scale production and competitive economy that began to take shape as a kind of "second nature," a Frankenstein, above physical nature and subjecting man to itself. While he was increasingly able to control and manipulate physical nature, man became less and less able to control his "second nature." He was swallowed up by his own creation. Step by step the whole of human life was subordinated to the demands of the new worldwide economy. Men became units of working power. The profit of the few and the poverty of the many were driving forces of the system. Hidden and irresponsible powers controlled some parts of it, but no one the whole. The movements of the mechanism of production and consumption were irrational and incalculable. So it became for the masses a dark and incomprehensible fate, determining their destiny, lifting them today to a higher standard of life than they had ever known, throwing them down tomorrow into utter misery and the abyss of chronic unemployment. The decisive feature of the period of victorious bourgeoisie is the loss of control by human reason over man's historical existence. This situation became manifest in the two world wars and their psychological and sociological consequences. The self-destruction of bourgeois society and its elaborate scheme of automatic harmony is the characteristic of the present period of transition.[9]

This, of course, is the content of Tillich's Marxist-influenced existentialism, where Marx more than anyone understood the effect of technical reason in the dehumanization of men and women. He could not follow Kierkegaard's classical Protestantism, because, for Tillich, it was over.[10] Technical society had finished it. Everyone was being drawn into an all-embracing mechanism of production and consumption and insofar as one is enslaved to it one loses his or her character as person and becomes a thing. Another dead, or as good as dead, thing, in space.

Hans Jonas descries how salient features of life were stripped off, one after another, in the reduction that characterizes this trend. I read Hans Jonas years ago and wrote to Chadwick about his views. The formulations I now consider to be the axiomatic ones for my theme are embedded in an essay with a very odd title, "Life, Death, and the Body in the Theory of Being," the first essay in his *The Phenomenon of Life*, *Toward a Philosophical Biology.*

My friend and colleague Rolf von Eckartsberg first brought it to my attention and then urged me to read it again in the light of my thinking about physicalism and vitalism. I knew of Jonas's seminal work on Gnosticism, but the first time I read *The Phenomenon of Life,* I didn't get it. I read it again and it clicked. I think I had read Husserl by then and knew that Jonas had been his student and was carrying through Husserl's critique of physicalism. He had a distinguished career at the New School in New York. He formulates the issues at a very high level of abstraction, taking in the entire history of Western thought, beginning with the ancient Greeks. I had carried my studies back from the urea experiment and the chemical blow to vitalism to Galileo and the mathematical, physical blow in the Renaissance, when mechanism began to take command. I was aware of the history of mathematics and the role it played thanks to Husserl and Derrida and their work on the origins of geometry and the turn taken by Galileo in the mathematization of nature. Voegelin contributed to this line in his essay on the historical origins of scientism, as did the attendant discussion by Hayek on the formation of the French engineer and the curriculum for training the new type of human being as the bearer of technical reason. But Jonas said it all in the most stunningly concise form.

He characterizes the two historical periods of Western thought as an ontology of life and an ontology of death, and he describes their reversal when modern science took off in the Renaissance and became reductionistic by removing from consideration one aspect of life after another. In the ancient world, "panpsychism" (everything is alive), animism, and hylozoism—"soul flooded the whole of existence and encountered itself in all things"—summed up as "panvitalism," was the primary view. Death was the big mystery. "To the extent that life is accepted as the primary state of things, death looms as the disturbing mystery."

Modern thought which began with the Renaissance is placed in exactly the opposite theoretic situation. Death is the natural thing, life the problem. From the physical sciences there spread over the conception of all existence an ontology whose model entity is pure matter, stripped of all features of life. The tremendously enlarged universe of modern cosmology is conceived as a field of inanimate masses and forces which operate according to the laws of inertia and of quantitative distribution in space. This denuded substratum of all reality could only be arrived at through a progressive expurgation of vital features from the physical record and through strict abstention from projecting into its image our own felt aliveness.[11]

I have a number of like-minded formulations I could give but for the fact that the point is made. What Jonas is describing is the movement toward exact knowledge, what is known as the hard sciences, where what counts for knowledge is determined. It is a sliding scale away from there and it took the logical positivists under Carnap and Neurath to say that the slide was into nonsense, and it starts almost as soon as you leave the laboratory of experimental science, where the protocols are clear, objective, and full of sense.

Woe unto anyone who argues otherwise. They have no place in the ranks of science, where physicalistic positivism reigns. I know as well as you that there are departures from this norm. I have colleagues who are even willing to extend the term *research* to scholarship in order to keep the fraternity open. They might even entertain the definition of *science* as any ruled cognition in the pursuit of knowledge, where science is the cognitive approach to the whole of finite objects, their interrelations, and their processes. They might generously agree that science should not be restricted to natural science and laboratory procedure but should include every methodologically disciplined scholarly research. Usually, such generosity is hard to come by.

This is what makes for a university, not a "major research institution," as a former chancellor of UCSC repeatedly stated in describing the institution, which suspiciously sounds like a place of restrictive positivism based on the experimental method of the mathematized sciences. It is characteristic of the trend that UCSC has added an engineering school.[12]

Well, you go where the money is. Follow the money and you find out what has happened to the organization of knowledge and who gets to organize it. Materialism is the handmaiden of physicalistic positivism. So the cocktail party discussion among colleagues, in the relaxed mode of a few martinis, might loosen things up to include some aspects or vision of the old game, inasmuch as there are still a lot of loose players around who like to teach subjects that have nothing to do with the natural sciences. One generously might find room for them—over the weekend. Then one returns on Monday to the reality of budgets and the cutting of the pie.[13]

The tail end of the process described by Jonas certainly seems to me to be the state of affairs as I see it actualized in the modern institution of the university and higher education in America, although this is primarily true of secular state institutions such as the University of California and certainly less so of liberal arts colleges, some of which still sustain even religious traditions at the center of their foundation, such that the humanities are still valued.

What are we left with? As Jonas says:

In the process the ban on anthropomorphism was extended to zoomorphism in general. What remained is the residue of the reduction toward the properties of mere extension which submit to measurement and hence to mathematics. These properties alone satisfy the requirements of what is now called exact knowledge: and representing the only knowable aspect of nature they, by a tempting substitution, came to be regarded as its essential aspect too: and if this, then as the only real in reality.

This means that the lifeless has become the knowable par excellence and is for that reason also considered the true and only foundation of reality. It is the "natural" as well as the original state of things. Not only in terms of relative quantity but also in terms of ontological genuineness, nonlife is the rule, life the puzzling exception in physical existence.[14]

Physicalism is simply the triumph of technical reason as stated in this sketch and vitalism is the name for what had to be suppressed, dismissed and discarded as the price paid for the need to sharpen the instrument, as though to cut its own throat. Do you see why I gravitated to vitalism as a way of understanding the endpoint of this trend toward reducing the features of life from the purview of modern science and the interest in mechanisms? Vitalism is my grab bag for this wholesale discussion encompassing first of all the development of rational self-consciousness in ancient Greece and then the development of scientific, technical, and instrumental rational self-consciousness from Galileo on, where, finally, the existence of life within a mechanical universe calls for an explanation in terms of the lifeless. My favorite example of this is the definition of life by Oparin, a leading theoretician in the biological sciences: "Life is a qualification of dead matter." But you have to kick it to qualify.

Jonas continues:

Quantitatively infinitesimal in the immensity of cosmic matter, qualitatively an exception from the rule of its properties, cognitively the unexplained in the general plainness of physical things, it has become the stumbling block of theory. That there is life at all, and how such a thing is possible in a world of mere matter, is now the problem posed to thought. The very fact that we have nowadays to deal with the theoretical problem of life, instead of the problem of death, testifies to the status of death as the natural and intelligible condition.[15]

Jonas reveals in these trenchant formulations, unequalled as far as I know in their expressive power, the exchange of panmechanism for panvitalism, which saves me from turning blue in the face over defending my use of vitalism beyond the urea example as a generalized term and organizing principle for describing major trends in the history of Western thought.

To take life as a problem is here to acknowledge its strangeness in the mechanical world which is the world; to explain it is—in this climate of a universal ontology of death—to negate it by making it one of the possible variants of the lifeless. Such a negation is the mechanistic theory of the organism, as the funeral rites of prehistory were a negation of death. L'homme machine signifies in the modern scheme what conversely hylozoism signified in the ancient scheme: the usurpation of one, dissembled

realm by the other which enjoys an ontological monopoly. Vitalistic mo-
nism is replaced by mechanistic monism, in whose rules of evidence the
standard of life is exchanged for that of death.[16]

Jonas actually interprets for me why vitalism is the scapegoat of modern science, and why they had to get rid of it. It
stood for the holdout of the old view, that life itself was self-
evident and, so to speak, *in your face!* Vitalism was the residue
of the old view, now reduced to the fate of organic nature at
the hands of organic chemistry and the experimental laboratory, and to the fate of the organism: "a problematical specialty
in the configurations of extended substance."

Today the living, feeling, striving organism has taken over this role
(namely, the role of the corpse in the ancient world as the primal exhibi-
tion of "dead" matter) and is being unmasked as a ludibrium materiae,
a subtle hoax of matter.[17]

I wish I knew the provenance of that term. It is too good to
be true. Life is a subtle hoax of matter: a *ludibrium materiae*.

I have added this phrase to my vocabulary. Vitalism was the
defender of this "subtle hoax" and therefore had to go. I distill
from Jonas the reasons I have tried to adduce for the rejection of vitalism. He gives the cues. When life was stripped
of its features, there was nothing left to defend. I thought for
a while that vitalism was the definition of a defeated point of
view. It was defeated as defined! I had a comeuppance on this
that I have never forgotten. I gave a talk at Barnard College in
New York on this theme, and Heinz Pagels, a famous physicist, sat in the front row. He was very tall and very German
and imposing. He raised his hand for the first question. I
thought, "uh oh, here I go," and I meant out the door. In a
very loud voice he said, "The reason vitalism lost, Paul, is that
vitalism was WRONG!" What do you say to that? Out the door I
went. I still have a ringing in my ears.

In other words, most scientists think of vitalism as the name
of a point of view that is already refuted. In advance. It is a
kind of booby-prize term in the taxonomy of ideas. Oh yeah,
there is one Big Idea that was already over when it began, it
was so contrary to the trend of modern science. It defended
the integrity of organic nature as the basis of life. Vitalism was
the subtle or not-so-subtle hoax. You might as well believe in

magic. Or occult qualities. Go back to school and take math.

In *The Destruction Of Reason,* George Lukacs gives a penetrating account of the rise and influence of vitalism in Germany from a sociopolitical point of view, determined by his Marxism. He notes that the crisis of the imperialist system, represented by Bismarck's "Bonapartist monarchy," was indicative of bourgeois self-confidence and an imperturbable trust in the "everlastingness" of capitalist growth, leading to the rejection of universal questions and the confining of philosophy to logic, epistemology, and psychology. Vitalism arose to satisfy the need for a worldview. Dilthey, Simmel, Spengler, Scheler, Husserl, Heidegger, and Jaspers were associated with this effort, and the pre-Fascist and Fascist vitalism was represented by Klages, Jünger, Baeumler, Krieck, and Rosenberg.

So the triumph of technical reason became the object of attack on the part of those who saw its truncated form, and existentialism (Schelling and Kierkegaard), and Philosophy of Life (Nietzsche), and phenomenology (Husserl), were three of the leading attacks. As a student of Paul Tillich, I inherited this view and attack. Tillich was associated with the leaders of the Frankfurt School who were the great critics of instrumental or technical reason, foremost among them Horkheimer and Adorno. They were trained in the classical meaning of reason, as was Tillich, and they could see what reason was becoming in the service of industrial society.

The gargantuan mechanism of an industrial civilization was swelling to the height of its power and bringing every aspect of thought as well as life under its sway, thus radically transforming the guiding principles of the human mind as well as the actual conditions of human existence. Reacting against the revolutionary rationalism of the eighteenth century, the spirit of the times became skeptical, positivistic, and conservative in every respect with the single exception of technical science. The natural sciences furnished the pattern for all knowledge, and also for practical life and religion. Science itself became positivistic: reality must simply be accepted as it is; no rational criticism of it is permissible. The so-called fact and its adoration replaced the "meaning" and its interpretation. Statistics replaced norms. Material replaced nature. Logical possibilities replaced existential experience. The quest for truth became a method of foreseeing the future instead of creating it. Rational truth was replaced by

*instincts and pragmatic beliefs. And the instincts and beliefs were those of
the ruling classes and their conventions. Philosophy was largely restricted
to epistemology. It became the servant of technical progress, its scientific
foundations and its economic control. Following the breakdown of belief
in rational truth as the determining factor in life, "technical reason"—not
aspiring to provide truth but merely to furnish means toward the realization of ends determined by instincts and will—became decisive throughout
the world as far as the dominance of Western influences reaches.... The
tremendous success of natural and technical sciences doomed every theoretical protest against their universal applicability to futility.*[18]

This is how I saw the fate of vitalism as the defender of
organic integrity. It fit in like a piece of a puzzle when I discovered the refutation of vitalism as a theme in the history of
the chemical sciences. Granted, I have extrapolated from that
history to make it a major term in the conflict in the larger
historical context, even though vitalism as a concept is very
ambiguous. I am aware of that.

Adolf Meyer, in 1934, saw physicalism and vitalism as merely "worthy old ideologies" that no longer have any real theoretical vitality or validity.

*One cannot escape the impression that these highly respected ideologies
have fallen behind in the development of the special biological disciplines;
in any case they have nothing more to teach those who pursue them.
Vitalism negates the modern Galilean-Newtonian-Kantian ideal of a
mathematical natural science and thereby robs biology of unquestionably
fruitful possibilities of knowledge, while mechanism degrades it to a special and meaningless appendage of theoretical physics.*[19]

The Galilean-Newtonian-Kantian tradition, call it a
paradigm, is exactly what we juxtapose to Goethe-Steiner-
Chadwick, inasmuch as they represent the integrity of botany
against the subjection to the mathematized sciences. Kant's
estimation of Newton is expressed in his elevation of physics and mathematics as the primary science, with biology un-
equal in status.[20] According to Kant, there was no hope for a
"Newton of the grass blades." What a nice term for Chadwick,
except he was a Goethe of the grass blades.

I remember discussing these views with a professor of the
philosophy of science, and when I mentioned vitalism, she
said, "Oh, you're interested in Nazi science!"[21] I went slightly

weak in the knees. And stomach. That association had never occurred to me. Nazism was a pseudo-vitalist reaction to the breakdown of bourgeois society, as Tillich describes it. It was vitalism gone haywire, a demonic, self-destructive effort to affirm native roots, blood, and idolatrous allegiance to a monster parading as a savior: Heil Hitler![22]

The only way in which the original emphasis on life was maintained was the unrestricted realization of formerly repressed drives toward power, pleasure, and destruction. This was done in the name of vitality, against rationality. But the result was mutilated, self-destroying vitality united with bestiality and absurdity.[23]

On the other hand, I like to stress the positive side of vitalism more in line with the forces evoked in reaction to technical reason. Vital forces

…arose and made themselves manifest in both theory and practice. Whether called "instinct" or "passion" or "libido" or "interest" or "urge" or "will to power" or "élan vital" or "unconscious ground," they cannot be denied. They make it impossible to transform man into a psychological mechanism with intelligence and adjustability. They revolt against control by merely utilitarian reason. The conventional veil concealing the dynamic center of living man has been torn aside. Élan vital displaced the rational center of early humanism.[24]

If élan vital is associated with subjectivity, my favorite word, *thymós,* the thymic center, as the vital root of humanity and our sense of ourselves as persons, comes into play. Then Tillich, the great interpreter of the courage to be, points to the subjectivity of the scientist, the bearer of technical and controlling reason, as the one point that cannot be annihilated, even though they annihilate it in others. "Science cannot reduce into mere objects the bearers of science and its application. And this exception undercuts any view of man that is based on reductive behaviorism."[25]

I wonder what he would think now.

Tillich threw me when he called for a theology of the inorganic precisely because it is rarely considered by theology.[26] There are some weighty problems involved here that we hesitate to pursue, even though they help illuminate the terms of the discussion and the complexities involved. His formulations remind me of my penchant for the organic and for slighting the inorganic or the material realm due to overwrought vitalist sympathies. I am happy to stand corrected.

If, in agreement with tradition, we start by calling the inorganic the first dimension, the very use of the negative term "inorganic" points to the indefiniteness of the field which this term covers.

Traditionally, the problem of the inorganic has been discussed as the problem of matter. The term "matter" has an ontological and a scientific meaning. In the second sense, it is usually identified with that which underlies the inorganic processes. If the whole of reality is reduced to inorganic processes, the result is the non-scientific ontological theory which is called materialism or reductionistic naturalism. Its peculiar contention is not that there is matter in everything that exists—every ontology must say this including all forms of positivism—but that the matter we encounter under the dimension of the inorganic is the only matter.[27]

You know the old argument between the materialist and the idealist after they had worn one another out: "Never mind." "No matter."

Now for the corrective:

…The organic has a preferred position among the dimensions in so far as it is the first condition for the actualization of every dimension. This is why all realms of being would dissolve were the basic condition provided by the constellation of inorganic structures to disappear. Biblically speaking: "You return to the ground, for out of it you were taken" (Genesis 3:19). This is also the reason for the above-mentioned "reductionist naturalism," or materialism, which identifies matter with inorganic matter. Materialism, in this definition, is an ontology of death.[28]

Hence his complete agreement with Jonas. And Steiner.

Tillich makes a great point in clarifying the discussion by distinguishing between levels and dimensions of reality.

The valuation of organic over inorganic and the negative use of "in" in *inorganic* is reminiscent of the valuation of rational literacy over native consciousness, in the past referred to as savage, primitive, or illiterate. The evolution of inorganic matter to organic nature and the evolution of human consciousness from native orality to rational literacy is difficult to regard in a neutral mode, as higher implies better. Add gender to the mix and it is time to reevaluate one's terminology. The Greeks thought everyone who spoke a different language was a barbarian.

I had a similar frisson when I read about the need for a theology of the inorganic, when I read George Washington Carver crediting God with the creation of the synthetic realm. I almost threw in the towel. A synthetic theology sounded like an oxymoron to me, but he means something similar to what Tillich means about the inorganic, allowing for the different logical structures or dimensions involved. I don't care. I still balk, even though I wish I had the spiritual sensibility to see God's power in the development of synthetics. God looked upon plastics and saw them as good?[29]

Nevertheless, I cannot suppress my reaction to the stupidity of the physicalist point of view in its arrogance and near-moronic hostility to vitalism, and the self-defeating efforts to describe within its own terminology what it had eliminated— life, consciousness, soul, organic nature, human existence, and so on. All you have to know to get the drift is the definition of life by Oparin—life is a qualification of dead matter. What? Did he think it would get up by itself and walk? Watch it somersault? Is that what's meant by "qualification"? A leap in being by virtue of the absurd?

We are still told that "in accepting a mechanical conception," we must not "fall into the very common mistake of trying to explain vital processes as being due directly to mechanical causes." It has been quite as impossible to banish the word "life" from the biological vocabulary as it has been to banish the word "ought" from the ethical. Biological knowledge has become purely chemical, physical, and mechanical, but not so biological thought. The question, "What is life?" still haunts us.[30]

All the talk about self-organizing systems doesn't help much either. Here's an example:

The origin of life, rather than having been vastly improbable, is instead an expected collective property of complex systems of catalytic polymers and the molecules on which they act. Life, in a deep sense, crystallized as a collective self-reproducing metabolism in a space of possible organic reactions.[31]

This effort at formulation can be extended indefinitely in the miscarried attempt to describe life after the elimination of vitalism and the stripping of life of its qualities, partly as a consequence of distinguishing between primary and secondary qualities. Or the definition of consciousness, for that matter, as in Freud's contribution to the nonsense in his physicalist period, when he was working in the lab under Brücke, dissecting the nervous system of a certain order of fish and defined consciousness as a *qualitative leap* in the neurone. Another somersault? You'd think he would have called it a flip-flop. Might as well start a flea circus to demonstrate the leap as dissect a fish. No wonder Freud walked away from the so-called Project for a Scientific Psychology, the draft of which he sent to his correspondent, Fliess, and never got back, even though the effort to remain respectably scientific continued to haunt him, an effort that failed miserably.[32] No wonder behaviorism eliminates consciousness altogether as indefinable, resistant to scientific inquiry.

One of my favorites is Sir Francis Crick, remarking that, in his estimation, life is *almost* a miracle. It still makes me laugh. I wonder what Sir Francis thinks a miracle is. It is reminiscent of his dumbed down book on the mind, which, of course, according to him, is nothing but some random firings in the wiring, even though he has the nerve to use the word *soul* in the course of talking about the wiring. What could he possibly think *soul* means? A spark? An aberrant spark, at best.[33] It is reminiscent of Jonas's reference to *ludibrium materiae,* the subtle hoax of matter.

It is indicative of physicalists that, after throwing the baby out with the bath, they try to smuggle it back in as if no one is looking.[34]

Logical positivism, as the philosophy of physicalism, the philosophical movement responsible for throwing the baby out with the bath, made the effort to consolidate the hard sciences on a firm and secure foundation, namely, mathematical logic, or symbolic logic, to properly organize a system of the sciences, rejecting metaphysics, ethics, aesthetics, religious language, and all other "theses devoid of sense." The door to the experimental lab was slammed shut and locked. Anything that smelled vitalist was not to be admitted in the determination of what counts for knowledge. In fact, to the extent that this grudge is exercised in the ranks of science, it is antiscience. Science is the pursuit of truth in the name of reason, not the venting of an ideology. Scratch a scientist and you get a physicalist ready to denounce vitalism. Go ahead and try it. I once told students to go up to any of the scientists on the campus and ask them what they thought of vitalism just to register the look on their faces. They found one botanist who admitted to being a closet vitalist. They wanted to "out" him.

This would be funny if it weren't a matter of life and death.

The humanities and the social sciences, to the extent they harbor any vitalist or "soft" sympathies, at a distance from mathematical physics and laboratory chemistry, are only grudgingly tolerated, as they are expected to die on their own, due to neglect and lack of support, just like a garden that eschewed the use of chemical fertilizers and pesticides.

You can see how entangled the discussion gets when you try to think about the difference between the inorganic and organic, and the transition from one to the other, let alone the tendency to identify "life" with organic life because of self-organizing structures or gestalts.

The garden opened up this conflict for me. We had a vitalist gardener out of a tradition that no university would allow on the campus, nervously protected by a chancellor who was nostalgic for the family farm and who had to beat off the complaint of scientists on the campus over the use of an outmoded and discredited meaning of *organic*. After all, everyone ought to know that *organic* meant a combination of physical and chemical forces. Any organic chemist could tell you about it, not some loony gardener stalking about in navy shorts and planting by the moon, bemoaning reductionism when it pertained to apples.

The chancellor was proud to say to anyone who wanted to register their protest regarding the garden and Chadwick's foibles, especially when they complained that Chadwick planted by the moon, "Well, my father was a farmer and he planted by the moon!" That made them pull in their horns.

The chairman of the board of studies in philosophy called me in one day and sat me down and looked at me steadily, until I thought, "uh oh, he is going to ask me if I ever took a course in logic; if not, I would have to do a make-up." Instead, he said, "Paul, what does philosophy have to do with gardening?" That was a defining moment in my professional career. There was a certain rhetorical edge to his voice, tinged with a weary pathos, so I knew I didn't have to answer. It was more of a complaint than a question. If only I had known it at the time I could have quoted Latin in a remark made by Alexander Pope, "gardening is akin to philosophy, as Cicero says, *Agricultura proxima sapientiae.*"

The episode reminded me of the first question they threw at me at my doctoral orals at Harvard, "Mr. Lee, what is the central feature of natural law?" I didn't know what natural law was let alone the central feature. After it was over and I had dug my grave with my mouth, I went home and drank a half pint of bourbon and went to bed and pulled the covers over my head. I suppose this book is a belated effort to answer the chairman's question. The natural law one still draws a blank; it never occurred to me to say, "I don't know."

Eventually I would find the key to the conflict and the basis for a philosophical investigation into the issues. I don't remember when it happened, but I found the date that provided the historical reference for the conflict and the presumed victory of physicalism over vitalism—1828—when Friedrich Woehler artificially synthesized urea. I have friends who tease me about my fixation on this date, but it serves the purpose well. It is mentioned in the texts on the history of chemistry I have read, as well as many of the works on the history and philosophy of science.

There is a running debate in the *Journal of Chemical Education.* I have begun to collect the articles, along with other sources, in order to publish *A Urea Reader,* to provide the interested student with the corroborating material. The debate is a superb source for the struggle to define what was defeated and how it was accomplished. It all turns on the experiment of Woehler and the synthesis of urea from ammonium cyanate; on the one hand the legendary story centering on urea and on the other hand the effort to debunk the legend as merely a legend in order to remove the smoking gun. What was clear to me was that synthetic urea was the smoking gun in the elimination of vitalism.

All Woehler did was heat up some ammonium cyanate (inorganic) and at one hundred degrees centigrade he got urea (organic). Up until that moment it was thought that only an organ, in this case, a kidney, could produce an organic product, urea, the nitrogen part of urine. Not anymore. For this reason,

Woehler is esteemed as one of the founding fathers of organic chemistry, the chemistry of artificial synthesis.

I like the story about students in his lab, on Christmas Eve, when the old man enters, with his nightcap on, singing "Stille Nacht" to him, and he gets tears in his eyes.

There is a point to be caught right here, and it is only in writing this now that I get it—there is a reduction to take into account—from urine to urea. This portends the subsequent story of the defeat of vitalism. It is done on the basis of reduction and reduction only. There was no thought to simulating urine from inorganic sources. It is probably too complicated, given the idiosyncrasy of the chemistry of any given sample. Maybe it takes an organ, only the kidney, to produce urine. I don't know. But the critical step is made in the reduction from urine to urea, a given chemical in the composition of urine. Urea was replicable from inorganic sources once the chemical structure was known, and ammonium cyanate proved to be identical in chemical structure when it was heated to one hundred degrees centigrade. On this reduction the game was lost.

Vitalism argued for some indefinable "life force" or "vital force" to distinguish inorganic from organic entities, against the reduction. It was a feeble defense of the integrity of organic nature, as there was no science or physics for the definition of life and hardly any metaphysics, unless one had recourse to "power of being," which meant nothing to an experimental laboratory chemist.

Steiner, in his lectures on the origins of natural science, alerted me to the founder of vitalism as a specific movement—Georg Ernst Stahl (1650–1734), a Berlin physician and chemist, the exponent of Animism and vitalism and the hypothesis of the Life Force in his *Theoria Medica Vera*. It sounds like a return to Homer, who thought of the Greek heroes as bags of blood, so that when punctured, the *psyche* ("life-breath" or "life-force") was blown away as the last gasp. This is all *psyche,* our word for consciousness, meant in Homer—the last gasp! In the seventeenth and eighteenth century, man again had become an empty bag (forget the blood) and so a machine. Stahl wanted to introduce a vital force to offset the physical mechanics of the day, so he founded the dynamic school and invented the "vital force." "The Nineteenth Century had great difficulty in getting rid of this concept. It was really only an invention, but it was very hard to rid science of this 'life force.'"[35]

Until Woehler there had been a basic misconception in scientific thinking that the chemical changes undergone by substances in living organisms were not governed by the same laws as were inanimate substances; it was thought that these "vital" phenomena could not be described in ordinary chemical or physical terms. This theory gave rise to the original division between inorganic (nonvital) and organic (vital) chemistry, and its supporters were known as vitalists, who maintained that natural products formed by living organisms could never be synthesized by ordinary chemical means. Woehler's synthesis of urea was a bitter blow to the vitalists and did much to overthrow their doctrine.

Another reason this experiment is a signal one is that synthetic urea gave rise to artificial fertilizers, in order to make the soil of industrial farming fertile. And to add insult to injury, urea is the basis for plastics, as in poly-"ure"-thane, one of the operative metaphors—plastic—for industrial society, if you don't like "tools." Synthetic fertilizers and plastic! How appropriate for the world above the given world of nature.

Descartes anticipated this loss of meaning in the distinction between natural and artificial in the seventeenth century:

I do not recognize any difference between the machines made by craftsmen and the diverse bodies put together by nature alone ... all the rules of mechanics belong to physics, so that all things which are artificial, are thereby natural. Give me matter and motion, and I shall make the world once more.[36]

It is a world known as industrial society.

Chapter Six

University Services Agency (USA) and Earth Day

A colleague of mine committed suicide. He was a fellow philosopher. I was the only one to care for him when he suffered a nervous breakdown before his suicide. I thought he was trying to tell me my career was over by putting a pistol to his head and pulling the trigger. I took it personally. I didn't know if it was his blood or mine. If I thought I could ignore the handwriting on the wall, or if I held out any hope that my career would be saved by some miracle, it stopped there and then. I gave up and died with him. In the late summer of 1969, I had to return to Santa Cruz from northern Wisconsin, where we were on a six-month sabbatical, to conduct his funeral. At the service, I quoted Dylan Thomas, "oh you who could not cry on to the ground ... now break a giant tear for this little known fall...."

Before the funeral, I went up to the garden to see Alan. He didn't know I had returned. He saw me coming up the garden path and ran down pell-mell and jumped into my arms, full force, locking his legs around my waist. I don't know how I stayed upright. I just managed to keep my balance, assisted, I guess, by our friendship, as if it were a kind of prop. When I told him what I had come back for, he gazed at me for a long time—a very long time. I have never forgotten that long moment of silent communion and shared comradeship, as he penetrated my depth with his gaze. It was one of the few times when I thought someone had looked into my soul.

After the funeral I returned to northern Wisconsin to lick my wounds, suffering a mild nervous breakdown, exacerbated by a call from the philosophy chairman saying it was too late to turn anything in. So why bother? My goose was cooked. I thought the sabbatical was my chance to do some writing, but I was wrong.

Little did I know that in my despair there were historical forces at work that would renew hope in the human spirit and its ability to resist the forces of destruction on a national and even an international level. Earth Day One was being planned, and our garden would be a place of celebration, when the entire country would be seized by an agony of despair over the ravages of industrial society and by the hope for a renewed affirmation of organic nature and even the environment as such.

It amazes me even now that during that summer I had the opportunity to take a wilderness canoe trip in northern Wisconsin with Senator Gaylord Nelson as part of his wild river legislative efforts and then that months later I watched him on the *Today Show* announce the plan for the first Earth Day the following April. I jumped in my seat.

Nothing else could have confirmed what we had done in our university garden. Earth Day was the big breakthrough. It was another wake-up call after the one issued in the previous decade by Rachel Carson with *Silent Spring.* It was as though the one had brought about the other as a response. For a weekend the nation would stop and think about the late stage of the self-destruction of industrial society. A sense of the need to reaffirm the integrity of organic nature would go out through the land like a call to rally everyone to the cause. A spark was ignited and flamed forth as the environmental movement.

Aside from writing to Alan, I sat around and wove muskie weeds, which grow in our lake, pretending I was an Indian, thinking it was occupational therapy. I had played the part of Chief Black Hawk in the celebration of the centennial of the statehood of Wisconsin. I was the only one in my school that could memorize the name: *Ma ka tai me she ke kiak.* Ironically, the school was Custer High School, as in General George Armstrong. I walked out on the stage of the Civic Auditorium in Milwaukee dressed as an Indian with a fright wig cut like a Mohawk. So it was easy to lapse into my Indian persona.

I figured I had to plan a future without relying on my university position, so after hearing the Rev. Ike, a black prosperity preacher from New York, on midnight radio—"You can't lose with the stuff I use" and "The *lack* of money is the root of all evil"—and writing in for his prayer cloth, a small piece of red material cut with a serrated scissors, which I fingered in my pocket, I dreamed up a nonprofit corporation. I called it

"USA." I was going to start over by reconstituting the country in myself. I would begin organizing it upon my return: a new beginning for the New Year and for the new decade that I anticipated with one big sigh of relief. We were going to exit from the 1960s. I was tired of the tyranny of being hip. And Earth Day was coming.

I wrote to a former Harvard student of mine, Bill Russell, who was a freshman dean at Harvard; he sent me the paper on the Harvard Student Agencies, which began when I had taught there. I thought it would make a good model. They were famous for their bartenders' school. I knew the crunch was coming and a recession was in the offing, so I thought a nonprofit would help in developing student employment, which would make the effort worthwhile whether it helped me or not.

Days after my return to Santa Cruz and the beginning of the new school quarter and the new decade, I ran into my old friend, the Lutheran chaplain to the university, Herb Schmidt, who told me he was on his way to get the available franchise on the only public restaurant on campus. Chadwick and I had tried before to get the restaurant franchise for the garden to supply. I had tried earlier to get Chadwick produce into the Cowell College kitchen, but they were hamstrung by the national franchised food services called SAGA, and although they tried it out for a few weeks and bought lettuce, once they found a snail, or whatever, that was that. No more contaminated produce from an organic garden.

A year or two before, when Chadwick and I had gone in together to see Charles Gilbert, who was in charge of such things, we were told that the contract for the restaurant had just been signed and it was unavailable; we should go and try the hamburgers, as they were terrific. It was called "The Kite" and was famous not for its hamburgers, but for a sign on the cigarette machine as you entered: *No Bare Feet*. Not exactly a version of a welcome mat for students. Now that effort had failed, and Herb was on his way to negotiate.

I told Herb we should start a nonprofit called USA, and the restaurant would be our first project. Lo and behold! He said fine; he had had a similar idea about starting a nonprofit as an extension of the campus ministry. We filled out the acronym

Apprentices at lunch at the Garden Chalet, UCSC, 1970.

with "University Services Agency" and decided to name the restaurant the Whole Earth Restaurant, as it would be supplied by Chadwick produce. I knew Stewart Brand, editor of the *Whole Earth Catalog*. I had performed his wedding ceremony on the beach at Rio del Mar, so I figured he would give us his blessings as a favor in return.

We eventually invited him to come to speak on the occasion of the founding of the restaurant, and he gave a talk about the hip subeconomy spilling over from the 1960s, from the psychedelic subculture, and how it would prosper in Santa Cruz. He was involved with such an enterprise with Dick Raymond and the Brier Patch Trust and figured we would experience the same success. The woman we hired to manage the restaurant, Sharon Cadwallader, went on to become a famous author of cookbooks and food columnist, and her *Whole Earth Cook Book* sold over a million copies. I wrote the preface.

The theme of "right livelihood" was in the air, and Stewart turned out to be right on the money. We became the nonprofit umbrella for the Santa Cruz subeconomy and eventually sponsored over twenty affiliate projects and agencies. When we hit over a million dollars in annual cash flow, I thought of writing it up with the title: *How to Become a Spiritual Millionaire, Where Money Is No Object.* I was going to dedicate it to the Rev. Ike and his little red prayer cloth.

The religious inspiration may seem like an odd resource, going back to the Rev. Ike prayer cloth, but I had been a student of James Luther Adams at Harvard Divinity School, the translator of Tillich and a professor of social ethics. He extolled the significance of the nonprofit corporation as the legal form of voluntary association. I was to learn of the historic occasion for the inception of the principle of voluntary association from my professor of church history, George Hunston Williams, in his magisterial study *The Radical Reformation:* on a night in 1525, a Roman Catholic priest, George Blaurock, was rebaptised.[1] Thus began the Anabaptist movement, establishing the principle of the freedom of assembly and the freedom of worship, in pursuit of which so many dissenters left Europe to come to America. This voluntarism, leading to volunteerism, is basic to the American character and the number and variety of nonprofit corporations is its expression. The fact that my two colleagues in USA were the Protestant and Roman Catholic chaplains at the university and that we explicitly saw this effort as a secular ministry, confirmed, for me, in a personal way, the meaning of this tradition.

Paul Tillich points to something like the nonprofit corporation as a successor to the conventional church when he writes:

The third way requires that Protestantism appear as the prophetic spirit which lists where it will, without ecclesiastical conditions, organization, and traditions. But this imperative would remain a very idealistic demand if there were no living group which could be bearer of this spirit. Such a group could not be described adequately as a sect. It would approximate more closely an order or fellowship and would constitute an active group, aiming to realize, first, in itself that transformation of Protestantism which cannot be realized either by the present churches or by the movements of retreat and defense.[2]

Although we didn't think about it at the time, we were in the tradition of the social gospel and the application of the Golden Rule to business practices. I would eventually meet the granddaughter of J. C. Penney, Cynthia Guyer, a student in one of my classes, whose grandfather was one of the great practitioners of the Golden Rule in business. The J. C. Penney Stores originally were called Golden Rule Stores. Some years later I would receive the Golden Rule Award for my work with the Homeless Garden Project.

When we opened the Whole Earth, the first affiliate of USA, for the garden to supply; it was the only public restaurant on the campus; we had a party. My friend Page Stegner was lead singer for a bluegrass group called the Red Mountain Boys, so I asked them to play. We danced. We drank. Red Mountain wine, a jug wine, was cheaper by the gallon. Calling "good night" from the balcony, as people drove out of the parking lot in the wee hours of the morning, we forgot Alan lived across the road in his apartment at Cowell College.

As my wife and I drove out of the parking lot, this frightening spectral figure descended on us from the road above, looking like a crazy banshee owl flying low. My wife and I were startled. It was Alan in his pajamas, with his bathrobe open, his arms outstretched. He jumped up on the hood of the car with his face on the other side of the windshield and when he saw me he yelled, "I knew it was you! You are under arrest! Remain here until the police arrive!"

I thought, are you kidding, you mad actor! You ought to be on the stage all right, but the one leaving for the loony bin. I sped up; he slid off unharmed, fortunately. The next day nothing was said, and he was, if anything, more than ever, his usual, mostly charming self.

There were times of great festivity in the garden: Easter, weddings, celebrations just for the sake of it, receptions for special guests—like Francis Edmunds, principal of Emerson College, the Rudolf Steiner college in England, who paid a number of visits and was gratified to find a Steiner project at an American university, albeit under partial wraps.

Alan always put on the dog. He would spend the day cooking and preparing, making his unique layered pots of food: fish, meats and vegetables all piled up on top of one another, a unique way of doing it, always supremely delicious. He was a master chef, and, of course, the produce—picked fresh from the garden—was the best anyone ever had. But when the candles were lit and the wine was poured and it came time to sit down, something seemingly trivial would annoy him or in-furiate him, and he would be gone, and we would have to carry on without him. Oddly, it didn't seriously diminish our enjoy-ment; we were just sorry Alan wasn't there to share it, and we accepted his fits for what they were, although there were times when I thought of using his navy saying on him.

I organized an Easter celebration to receive the first dona-tion of money from an admirer from downtown, Mr. Putney. Norman O. Brown showed up and awkwardly embraced everyone in a flash, exclaiming, "He is risen!" and releasing as fast as he hugged, as if he wanted to launch you into space, which struck me as a trick he had taught himself, so reluctant did he seem to be caught in an embrace—an odd response for the author of *Love's Body*.

"Do you see these hands…?"

It hailed. Hail the size of golf balls; hard projectiles descending from the heavens to destroy tender plants. Alan thought the hail was God's wrath visited upon the university with his garden as the scapegoat. He ran and hid, he was so upset. I had to send Jasper Rose, another Brit, professor of the history of art and provost of Cowell College, to look for him and persuade him to come in for the presentation. When I gave my little spiel of grateful acceptance to Mr. Putney, he held out the check for Alan to take.

Alan stood slightly apart and ceremoniously opened his hands very slowly, as if disclosing an unfathomable mystery. As he showed them to the assembled group he asked, "Do you see these hands?" We all were pretty sure we did. "Do they look like hands that would touch money?" I groaned and thought, "oh boy, here we go again" and quickly reached for the check, which was more quickly withdrawn.

We eventually got it, but the point had been made. Alan was certifiable.

These episodes were eclipsed by Alan's talent for growing things and creating atmospheres of breathtaking beauty. His beds were a wonder to behold, exemplifying his techniques: the famous amalgamation of the French intensive and the biodynamic method. There was a method to his madness.

Chapter Seven

The Method

The French intensive system was developed around Paris to supply the Paris market, especially the restaurant market, with the highest quality produce.[1] Raised beds, companion planting, and immense yields characterized the system. Alan used this as his overt approach, allied to the biodynamic system, his mysterious and, for the most part, secret system, about which he said little until the garden was well established, as if he knew it was too bizarre for a university to comprehend, which, of course, it was, even for a hip California university in the late 1960s.

You have to remember that not even *organic* was a term in common usage then. There were no organic sections in the stores. Hardly anyone thought "organic." If you knew of the Rodale publications and the argument on behalf of organic produce, you knew about the criticism of industrial agriculture and monocropping and the extreme use of chemical fertilizers and pesticides. But the Rodale witness to the integrity of organic nature was like a small sect, a voice crying in the wilderness. Hardly anyone was listening. No one could have guessed that a form of food and flower production developed by Rudolf Steiner would take root on the newest campus of the University of California. No one.

Biodynamics, as a strictly organic form of flower and food production, was developed by Rudolf Steiner, the famous Austrian clairvoyant and man of many parts, who founded the anthroposophical movement after his split with Madame Blavatsky and Annie Besant, the notorious promoters of theosophy. They were advocates of an occult and esoteric movement devoted to the wisdom tradition, predominantly of Eastern origin, generally rejected by Europeans under the influence of modern science and in the wake of the French Revolution what was called the "Enlightenment," namely, the rejection of what Steiner stood for—the spiritual world of revelation and miracle. It was definitely a clash between two diametrically opposed meanings of Enlightenment—call it technical rational enlightenment and spiritual enlightenment, one proceeding at the expense of the other.

When these two powerful ladies were told that the re-incarnation of the Christ had been found in the young boy, Krishnamurti, in India, it was too much for Steiner. He took a hike, ending up in Dornach, Switzerland, making it the center for his breakaway movement, anthroposophy—a term of unfortunate coinage, ridiculed in the speech of Lucky in *Waiting for Godot,* where it is mockingly spelled and pronounced "anthropopopometry."

It was in Dornach that Steiner built his Goetheanum and began his own brand of the esoteric and the occult, stigmatizing him as another candidate for the asylum. It was unfair; he was mostly buried, as far as his influence was concerned, although he made a considerable impact in his time and continues to have one in a circumscribed way in the continuation of social institutions he began. It is where vitalism went underground, but for Bergson and a handful of others.[2]

Steiner was a Renaissance man, with immense talent and ability in a variety of pursuits—adult education, then in its infancy, aimed at the industrial working class; dance (eurythmy); art and architecture (innovative in the use of organic forms and illustrated in his remarkable Goetheanum); biblical studies; philosophy (Steiner wrote an excellent history of philosophy, as well as a book on Nietzsche);[3] herbalism and health care (Weleda herbal products carry on the Steiner tradition); an innovative institutional approach for the handicapped (CampHill); education (the Waldorf system); and, of course, a unique approach to the earth and its spiritual forces, incorporated in a method of food production (the biodynamic method represented by the Demeter Association), and others.[4] But when you tack on the spiritual science stuff, for most an oxymoron; the etheric forces, Lucifer and Ahriman; and the whole stew of *Gott und Himmel,* most people throw up their hands, as would, clearly, *all* of my university colleagues! Steiner's hoo-hah was exactly what the physicalists aimed

Alan Chadwick with Francis Edmunds, principal of Emerson College, the Rudolf Steiner college in Forest Row, England, around 1970.

their guns at, whereas he was a calculated response to their crude reductionism, letting out all the stops.

It was at this point that I discovered the scientific side of Goethe as Steiner's anchor. He thought of himself as the heir of the Goethean legacy, and why not? As a young man he distinguished himself as the editor of the scientific writings of Goethe in the Weimar Archive and he wrote extensively and insightfully on Goethean science. Thus, Goethe, as Steiner's major point of influence and model for his life, became, for me, the great exemplar of vitalism, especially in his opposition to Newtonian mechanism. But the trend was so dominantly in favor of Newton, Goethe didn't have a chance. Nor did Steiner, who carved out his own world while the mainstream passed him by.

Steiner fascinates me because he is an index of how bad it got for the vitalists and what a cul-de-sac the effort to affirm organic nature and the meaning of spirituality one winds up with in anthroposophy and theosophy. It is indicative of a spasm of the spirit in the throes of being choked to death by the opposing trend. Steiner was clairvoyant. He manifested extraordinary powers, which his disciples beheld, were in awe of, and stunned by. There was some suspicion that he was the incarnation of a bodhisattva (a messenger from God), although the Eastern religious term is inappropriate.

This apprehension regarding Eastern religions is indicated in the dispute over Krishnamurti. Steiner was worried about Buddhist and Hindu avatars entering the West, as though he anticipated, by some decades, the mad march of gurus in the psychedelic 1960s, some of them destructive charlatans amply demonstrating Steiner's worst fears. The theosophists had picked Krishnamurti as the one to come, Christ all over again; Steiner demurred. It led to the break and the beginning of anthroposophy, partly because Steiner wanted to keep the spiritual movement from going East, to the exclusion of Christianity, which was the direction taken by the theosophists.

One of the best stories about Steiner is his interception of Hitler's séances with his astrologers (through astral projection on Steiner's part) to denounce Hitler as the Antichrist, provoking Hitler to burn down the Goetheanum, which Steiner promptly rebuilt. They make a great antithetical pair in the spiritual torment of the times.

Steiner was concerned about the quality of food and the techniques of food production. He had an acute understanding of the spiritual forces involved, amounting to a unique metaphysical system of thought regarding etheric forces and who knows what, as well as special teas and preparations for making compost in order to develop the most fertile and productive soils. Steiner developed biodynamics as a response to the emerging development of industrial farming and the use of chemicals to sustain soil fertility and to control pests.

Steiner knew that the world above the given world of nature, meaning industrial technocracy, would try to take the world of food production with it, and organic nature would suffer in the uprooting. It may be that because of his resistance to the industrialization of food production, medicinal herbs, as vital roots, were so central to Steiner's understanding of compost for soil fertility and his understanding of health care. It seems appropriate that he was initiated into his clairvoyant powers by an herbalist.

That got my attention! I had entered the herbal industry as a second career after my dismissal from the university and had been hired to represent the herbal industry nationally as executive director of the Herb Trade Association. I knew about Steiner's interest in herbs, both medicinal and culinary, through Alan and his knowledge of Steiner's herbalism and the use of herbs in the making of compost. I knew that Steiner had an affinity for the herbal tradition as part of his affirmation of the integrity of organic nature. Nothing was clearer to me than that American medicine had forsaken its own botanical basis in the shift to synthetic drugs, comparable to the shift to industrial agriculture.

Stinging nettle, a classic medicinal herb, is a key ingredient in the biodynamic preparations for compost, as are a number of other medicinal herbs: yarrow *(Achillea millefolium)*, chamomile *(Matricaria chamomilla)*, oak bark *(Quercus robur)*, dandelion *(Taraxacum officinalis)*, valerian *(Valeriana officinalis)*, horsetail *(Equisetum arvense)*. Check it out! But first you have to bury a stag horn filled with manure in a field for a season and then, when you dig it up, you have the basis for making your preparations out of herbal tea for your compost pile. I bought a cow horn one time at a biodynamic conference, but I have as yet to get the cow manure. You'd think if a cow can substitute for a stag by way of the horn, I could use my Scotties—Willy and Lilly—as a source for manure. You also have to be in tune with the autumn equinox for the burial time.

Then, you guessed it, you dig it up—the horn—on the spring equinox and you start to stir. At sunrise. The stirring creates a vortex, first this way and then that way, for an hour. You probably need to have someone show you, because the stirring is somehow related to the cosmos and cosmic energy. This is the basis for your compost tea, the famous preparations. I think, whatever you make of the spiritual-forces worldview involved, it gets you acutely attuned to what you're doing. When was the last time you saw a sunrise?

I recently read an article in the *San Jose Mercury News* about biodynamics and the attempt on the part of soil scientists to put it to the test. John Reganold, a professor of soil science at Washington State University, it is reported, gives a qualified yes. He mentions how colleagues said, when he began to take an interest, "Why do you want to jeopardize your career by getting mixed up in this crazy biodynamic stuff?"

Last week (September 24, 2009), the *New York Times* reported that Harvard was going green, "The Grass *Is* Greener at Harvard," and—what do you know—making tea for the compost for their lawns. No mention of Steiner, however. I wonder if they know the historical background for what they have adopted. They are pleased with the composition of their lawn, the effect on the soils, the conservation of water and the expense saved by eschewing chemical fertilizers and pesticides. The article mentions that an organic approach requires a radical change in thinking. Harvard has a website that tells you how to do it, simple directions for building a compost pile hot enough to eat weed seeds; building a compost-tea brewer, and brewing teas particularly suited for grass, perennials, or woody plants (www.uos.harvard.edu/fmo/landscape/organiclandscaping).

A former apprentice of Chadwick's, Alan York, is now making a name for himself consulting on biodynamics with various wineries in the Napa Valley. Jim Fetzer, of Fetzer Vineyards, was an early convert, and the Demeter Association, which certifies biodynamics, estimates that thousands of acres of vineyards in California are certified or about to be. My former student and old friend in Santa Cruz, Randall Grahm, of Bonny Doon Vineyards and Winery, has made the switch and hopes to make the finest pinot noir using biodynamic methods.

Still a young man, but already an accomplished scholar, Steiner was recruited to edit Goethe's scientific writings at the Weimar Archive. I see this as the background for the development of biodynamic agriculture, as much of Goethe's scientific writings dealt with botany.[5] I like to think that Goethe understood the consequences of the triumph of mathematical physics in the form of Newtonian determined science and that he threw his weight toward botany as the subject matter to suffer from the victory of physics in the struggle over what counts for knowledge. He was also a devoted herbalist, hiring a family of experienced herbal foragers to go out into the surrounding countryside to collect for him when he was visiting a spa and taking the waters.

126

Goethe was Steiner's hero, and he took his point of departure from Goethe as a universal figure of German culture.
When Alan started to talk to me about Steiner and his influence on his work and the significance of biodynamics, I started
reading Steiner's works, beginning with his book *Goethe, the
Scientist*. It was one of the lines of thought that directed me to
the vitalist tradition, which Goethe represented in his conflict
with Newton over a theory of color. Aha, I thought, when
I stumbled on it—here is the paradigm case of a physicalist
against a vitalist in the debate over the physics of color! How
interesting that Goethe should take on Newton and develop
experiments to illustrate an opposing theory. There is an ex-
tensive literature on the topic, some of it very technical and
therefore difficult for a nonspecialist to follow, as far as the
science of optics is concerned. I was surprised to hear that Dr.
Edwin Land of Polaroid sided with Goethe against Newton
in the debate, now that it is re-enjoined, acknowledging the
substance of the Goethean critique: Goethe, the poet, versus
Newton, the mathematical physicist! The vitalist versus the
physicalist! Goethe didn't stand a chance. At least for over a
century and a half.[6]

This has become a huge topic for me, and I have pursued it
with unflagging zeal for forty years or more. The physicalist/
vitalist conflict in the system of the sciences is indicative of the
deepest conflict in our culture: industrial technocracy versus
organic nature. I realized one day that almost every thought that
crosses my mind has ten to twenty books tied to it. This is why
my repeated efforts to tell this story have miscarried. There was
too much freight. And there was always more to learn.

I was surprised to learn of Steiner's appreciation (rather
than condemnation) of the history of materialism and physicalism, and that he considered it the fate of Western culture
to take just that path beginning in the ninth century. It is clear
that he would have agreed with Husserl's discussion of the
mathematization of nature on the part of Galileo and the dismissal of secondary (or occult) qualities. He spoke of modern
science mastering natural phenomena through mathematics
applicable to the inanimate. And he understood and appreciated that the direction taken, the overwhelming trend, was fated

and had to run its course. *Therefore, owing to this mathematical approach, modern science is directed exclusively to the sphere of death.*[7]

In the stretch from Goethe to Chadwick, if you permit me the line, Steiner was the underground interim, with his occult movement in Switzerland. He tried to withstand the inroads of physicalism and reductionist science in his defense of vitalism. It was a heroic stand, because he had to develop his own world in which to carry the cause. It was a mistake on his part to speak of spiritual science—not to be confused with Christian Science—although it was a courageous attempt to rescue the word from the control of physicalists and their laboratory protocols.

He was perfectly aware of what he was up against, even to the point of the urea experiment, as indicated in this excellent summary of the issues involved:

An example that shows how the results of natural science influenced the conception of the world is given in Wohler's discovery of 1828. This scientist succeeded in producing the substance synthetically outside the living organism that had previously only been known to be formed by an organ. This experiment seemed to supply the proof that the former belief—material compounds could only be formed under the influence of a special vital force contained in the organ was incorrect. If it was possible to produce such compounds outside the living body, then one could draw the conclusion that the organism was also working only with the forces with which chemistry deals. The thought arose for the materialists that if the living organism does not need a special life force to produce what formerly had been attributed to such a force, why should this organism then need special spiritual energies in order to produce the processes to which mental experiences are bound.[8]

It is a pity Steiner was outside of the existentialist movement. He would have made a good ally, if the occult hadn't swallowed him up and removed him from the mainstream of European thought. Existentialism fits perfectly as the protest against the defeat and elimination of vitalism, acting as its ostensible successor, as though existence in industrial society becomes a quandary, a thing among things, another dead thing in space, with life itself understood as a subtle hoax of matter.

Existentialism began in the Berlin Lectures of Schelling in 1841–42, when he took his famous turn against Hegel, with Kierkegaard in the class taking notes, along with Bakunin,

Engels, and Jacob Burckhardt. Some class. Kierkegaard was disappointed and went home to carry through the more radical wing in his remarkable authorship, which resurfaced decades later, in Germany and France, when he was rediscovered.

It is the movement of thought I studied under Howard Hong at St. Olaf, with Paul Holmer at the University of Minnesota, and Paul Tillich at Harvard, who was one of the great proponents of the movement. He made it clear to me that existentialism is the protest in the name of human existence against the dehumanizing trends of modern industrial society as a world above the given world of nature. Existentialism had its play from 1841, ten years after the death of Goethe and more than a decade after the artificial synthesis of urea and the defeat of vitalism, until 1970, when the Earth Day movement took place as a neo-vitalist event on behalf of endangered organic nature. Suddenly I saw it: existentialism is chief mourner for defeated vitalism! Historically and conceptually it fell right into place.[9]

Existentialism lasts until 1970 and the arrival of Earth Day on the weekend of April 22, a convenient date for its termination as a historical movement, once neo-vitalism re-enjoins the debate and moves beyond protest and outcry to the militant defense of the environment against its degradation—a reaffirmation of the integrity of organic nature and a restoration of the old meaning of "organic." The plight of human existence in industrial society is wedded to the plight of organic nature. Both are at risk together.

That's where we came in. Right there! We didn't even have to talk about it. We could show it! Chadwick's garden was the living, vital, testimonial to it. The great chain of being was let down from heaven on that slope and radiated the goodness and abundance of creation to anyone who wanted to come and look, especially at sunrise, when we picked flowers to set out in a kiosk across from the garden, for members of the university community to collect on their way to work or for their dorm room or office. The great chain of being had let down a ladder one could mount if one wanted to climb out of the university, the knowledge-production factory of industrial society. It was an oasis.

We were ready for Earth Day when it hit, three years after the founding of the garden, as if we had created the garden for the sake of having an appropriate place for celebrating it. It became a focal point, and Chadwick acted like he was the second chance no one expected in the late stage of the self-destruction of industrial society.

Earth Day was a turning point. A door opened. Not the door slammed shut on the civic gardens by the experimental laboratory. That stayed slammed. A new door, albeit a back one, was opened at institutions of higher education across the nation. Environmental studies, with a sympathy for endangered organic nature, was newly organized as a major for students who wanted to study the subject matter under a new meaning of ecology: one inspired by the example of Rachel Carson and other great figures of American environmentalism. Neo-vitalism was the name for this new mentality, even though no one thought of the term, or wanted to use it, so burdened was it by its historic rejection and presumed refutation. But the debate was renewed even though no one from the other side wanted to step up to the plate.

What follows is one of the strangest features of this story. I had the opportunity to work under one of the great bota-

A Chadwick lecture in the Quarry,
UCSC, 1970.
Photos by Mario Stauffacher.

nists in the world, the man who hired me to teach at UCSC, the provost of Crown College, Kenneth Thimann. We knew one another when I was giving seminars at a Radcliffe House, where he was the master. The day his appointment as the new provost of Crown College at UCSC was announced in the *New York Times,* a college to be devoted to the natural sciences, I went to the phone and asked him for a teaching position.

I was at MIT at the time and therefore knew about the Two Cultures firsthand: the split between the sciences and the humanities. I remember Erik Erikson, my thesis adviser at Harvard, telling me how he envied my position when I was hired to fill in for Huston Smith, a friend of mine, who was going on sabbatical. Erikson told me MIT was the wave of the future. I thought he was just trying to console me. My students at MIT

131

thought I was hired to give them something to say at the cocktail parties to which they would never be invited. We were to supply a little frosting on the nerd. The humanities were a chocolate offered to the Sorcerer's Apprentices for their hard work in the lab. They could read Homer and think about the fact that the Homeric gods were only known by their trace—like neutrinos.

So it didn't bother me that I was hired by Thimann to teach humanities and philosophy and relocate to a college devoted to the natural sciences, in spite of not knowing anything about the California ssssystem.[10]

The provost of Crown College was the archetypical physicalist, even though he was a botanist, the consequence of the scientific revolution represented in the way he did science, with botany subordinated to physics and chemistry, fulfilling Goethe's worst fears. We all gulped when we heard that Thimann had played a part, albeit indirectly, in the development of Agent Orange, the Vietnam defoliant. It was more than I could bear as the stigma of the physicalist.

And then Chadwick arrived.

The vitalist gardener versus the physicalist botanist: like a Homeric hero in a Trojan Horse with a bulldog spade instead of Achilles's spear, under the noses of the physicalists, who were asleep at the switch, we sneaked him in to inaugurate an organic garden in our prophetic anticipation of Earth Day. A neo-vitalist revolution was the last thing in the world for them to worry about. What? Almost a century and a half later! Who could breathe life into that corpse, dead and buried long ago?

Please remember: this was not a plot, although it was a garden plot. Going in, I had none of this conflict clearly in mind. I didn't care about "organic" and the fate of organic nature, because I hadn't thought much about it, even though I knew about the Rodales and organic wheat from Montana for baking the best bread. Rachel Carson had only recently published *Silent Spring* to issue the clarion call of the environmental movement. We were just beginning to wake up. The implications of her work on ecosystems were still to be worked out and made known.

It was Chadwick who fully awakened us to the issue. I was devoted to teaching philosophy, religious studies (which course of studies I founded at the request of the chancellor), and the history of consciousness (an innovative graduate program), as well as humanities courses within the college. We read about the structure of scientific revolutions without any mention whatsoever of the physicalist/vitalist conflict, as the illustrative historical example, because the victory of physicalism was assumed and vitalism was left out of account as unworthy of mention, refuted and defeated long ago.

Thomas Kuhn, the author of the seminal work on the structure as it turned out, was in cahoots with Carnap and the Vienna Circle and operating under their tutelage, part of the effort of the *Encyclopedia for a Unified Science*.[11] It took me a while to target them as the camp of the enemy.

I slowly began to catch on.

I began to develop my case. After returning from my sabbatical, during which I had worked out the outlines of the physicalist/vitalist conflict, partly in letters to Chadwick, I organized a series of lectures for Chadwick in the UCSC Quarry, where commencement exercises or rallies are held and where notable personages come to speak. I remember hearing and meeting César Chávez there and presented him with a portfolio of my figures representing the moral equivalent of war, of which he was one. It was the perfect venue for Chadwick—a great natural amphitheater, almost Greek in its seating arrangement. I kicked it off with a talk entitled "Up with Goethe; Down with Newton!" I thought it was particularly bold of me and I remember the electric charge when I wrote the title on the blackboard, afraid some scientist might run out from behind a rock and try to muzzle me.

I organized the material I had written to Alan, detailed the physicalist/vitalist conflict, and described where Alan came in after Goethe and Steiner.

And then on came Alan, with his nuptial flight of the queen bee, his plea on behalf of organic nature and the need to take thought of our violations and degradations. He was an Old Testament prophet.

We had lunches following Alan's lectures at the Whole Earth Restaurant. It was a veritable salon, and it reminded Alan of his time in the theater in England and the cultured

Josephine Stauffacher and Alan Chadwick, 1972.

company he kept. He was ecstatic. People from the opera, the arts, all recruited for the purpose by Jack Stauffacher, the dean of fine printers and typographers, and director of the Greenwood Press in San Francisco, joined by his wife, Josephine, flocked down to Santa Cruz for the talks.

Goethe was Stauffacher's hero, and when he heard we had a Goethean gardener at Santa Cruz, he had driven down to take a look. I'd invited the Stauffachers to lunch to meet Chadwick, and we became great friends. Jack commemorated the garden in a series of wonderful broadsides, the first one establishing the theme: *Et in Arcadia Ego,* taken from Goethe's *Italian Journey.*

Gordon Onslow Ford, the painter, and his wife, Jacqueline, also a painter, were part of the entourage. Gordon was an aristocratic Englishman with a strange waterfall effect that seemed to fall across the front of his body like a veil. It was a unique personality trait. I was fascinated by it. He had been one of the members of the group in France around André Breton and Roberto Matta. Jacqueline, a woman of exquisite high spirits, thought Chadwick was the prophet to come. She knew. He had arrived.

That was the high point of our university experience. Chadwick was at his most eloquent. The tapes are on file in Special Collections at UCSC's McHenry Library, in the Chadwick Archive, along with over a hundred other talks he gave in the course of his career.

Here is what his successor, Orin Martin, has to say in describing Alan and his component parts:

A mixture of diverse elements from Chadwick's personal experience, as well as his studies, also contributed to the amalgam he entitled biodynamic, French intensive horticulture. The principal determinants were:

1. the techniques of the French market garden phenomenon in and around Paris starting in the 1500s and peaking in the late 1800s and the early 1900s (French intensive);

2. traditional European garden-scale cultivation techniques, which had always been more intensive than their U.S. counterparts;

3. his own apprenticeships in English and French market garden operations;

4. tutelage under Rudolf Steiner, his spiritual philosophy as well as biodynamics—an attempt to look at a farm or garden as a living organism while studying cosmic rhythms and their effect on plant growth, soil, quality, and nutritious food; and

5. a strong personal infatuation with art, attention to detail, and beauty. Chadwick was an aesthete, having sensitivity to all that was beautiful and a disdain for that which was ugly and dehumanizing. As he said, "The reason for all of it is simply that I love beauty ... I adore beauty and I absolutely detest ugliness."[12]

He spoke of cosmic cycles. He tried to get you to think of sunrise and sunset as cosmic events not tied to the alarm clock or daylight saving time. He took infinite pains to describe and enact everything waking up when the sun came up, juxtaposing that to looking at your watch or having the alarm go off hours later. He spoke of the seasons: the moon in inclination and declination. He spoke about the toys of the nursery, which occupied so much space in our lives. He denounced the materialism that made you go to the beach in your car and sit with the motor running while the sun went down, the evening news on the radio, or the supermarket where you had dozens and dozens of packaged breakfast foods and potato chips and other snacks to choose from. Everyone got the point. Industrial technocracy had estranged us from nature. We were out of touch with vital roots. We needed to take stock

135

and transform our lives and look at what we were doing to ourselves and to our environment. We had to look beyond our own little rut and the lives we lived and open up to the cosmic processes going on around us, where—behold!—everything was new every moment. Behold, I make all things new!

His lectures had the quality of a revivalist meeting. Chadwick was the preacher. The one who called you back to your own nature and the nature surrounding you that was under such radical attack and subject to such forces of destruction.

I thought I should go around and have people sign a pledge just to get some closure on what had opened, a conversion, a rededication and renewal of one's relation to the natural order, rather than just let them go back to their old habits after having heard the Wizard. Commit to it! Seize the moment! Be transformed by a renewal of your minds!

One day I realized to my horror that, even though my wife and I were growing salads and vegetables in our backyard garden (under Chadwick's influence, I finally dug beds in our backyard lawn), we were still buying stuff from the store instead of harvesting what we had on hand. I was horrified to think I needed a supermarket cart and a check-out stand at the edge of the garden in order to go into my own backyard and pick what we needed for the evening dinner, so ingrained were the programs of the consumer mentality. I wasn't horrified enough!

Alan talking to an apprentice, around 1972.

Chapter Eight

Chadwick Departs

The university was an interesting testing ground for the neo-vitalist movement sparked by Earth Day. Across the nation environmental studies programs were organized and added to the university and college curriculum. They had to walk a fine line. Ecology was already a physicalist science. How was it possible to stick a neo-vitalist-inspired course of studies back into the physicalist stronghold and expect to pass it off under the banner of science? It wasn't easy. UC Santa Cruz hired a new faculty member, who came down from Alaska to head up environmental studies. His name was Richard Cooley. I called him Alaska-wolf Joe. Within days of his arrival, I asked to meet with him to tell him about Chadwick and our little toehold on the campus. I think I scared him. He looked completely bewildered and mystified. Steiner biodynamics? Goethe? Double-digging? French intensive? Clairvoyée? I don't think he knew what I was talking about and wanted to say something about how it wasn't in his job description, namely, taking on and sponsoring a mad English gardener and his troop of devotees. He was there to start an academic department and develop a new major, not to coddle a wild man who planted by the moon and hid away an esoteric and occult form of food and flower production that was best kept secret, because it would blow the lid off everything if the word got out.

We might as well have been polygamous Mormons.

Who cared about a buried tradition that went back through Steiner (whom you hardly knew what to make of and couldn't even talk about, given the spook factor of clairvoyance and the occult) to Goethe (who was "only" a poet)? What did poetry (Goethe) have to do with science (Newton)? I could see the handwriting on the wall. After all, Cooley had to protect his position, as precarious as it was, in the effort to make ecology respectable. The revival of a little neo-vitalism goes a long way, especially in the stronghold of the physicalists, who held the reins of power, much of it determined by government grants, who thought the garden was a hippie plot and, in spite of Earth Day, just another insult to the advance of science and demeaning to the reputation of the university. They thought we were there to embarrass them, and we were perplexed by the grudge. Why encourage middle-class dropouts who wanted to grub around in the dirt because they had dropped acid and wanted to get back to their vital roots and grow their own weed? Was that the recruitment message the university wanted to support?

It was already too much for the straight guys on the faculty. UC Santa Cruz was thought of as a school for hippies on drugs. Now they thought we wanted to demonstrate it in a garden, where we were probably growing dope behind the tool shed or anyhow smoking it when we thought no one was looking, having lost our sense of smell, and acting surprised if anyone sniffed. I could see that our unintegrated appendage was going to remain unintegrated, even though environmental studies eventually and reluctantly took the garden under its wing and tried to cope with Chadwick and his interest in starting a farm on another part of the campus. It was, at best, an angry standoff. Chadwick's main apprentice had broken with him, and Professor Cooley was caught in the middle. Let the apprentice start the farm and keep Alan contained in the garden. Cooley finally wearied of the dispute. Chadwick was insupportable. Let him go. We can keep the project going under conventional mainstream means.

Organic, okay; French intensive, maybe; biodynamic eecchh...

Eventually, the agroecology program would develop as an apprentice-training program in organic horticulture and agriculture. To this day it's still going strong as a national center.

It was just about at this time, when the standoff had occurred, Robert Rodale and Wendell Berry came for a visit. I knew about Rodale because I had a friend at St. Olaf College, Les Larson, whose mother, Mrs. Julius Larson, bless her heart, was the one who got wheat from a Rodale-recommended organic farm in Montana and made the best bread I ever had. Another baker was Edna Hong, the cotranslator of Kierkegaard with her husband, Howard, my beloved professor of philosophy. She served comparable bread from the same source for wheat when we had philosophy discussions at their home once a week. It was my inaugural experience with organic bread—first the aroma, which filled the house, and then the taste. I was used to Wonder Bread, and now I *wondered* how they could call that compressed cotton "bread."

My friend Les Larson, inspired by Frank Lloyd Wright, had designed his parent's home. It was called "Wheatledge." There was this large glass bowl of wheat up on the light shelf suspended from the ceiling in the front room making the statement, spilling out over your head. Mrs. Larson told me about *Organic Farming and Gardening,* a Rodale magazine. A copy was on the coffee table. I understood how the Rodales had maintained the meaning of organic vitalism when *organic* had gone over to laboratory chemistry. The critical link goes through Rodale. He carried the torch and was a voice crying in the wilderness.

Lo and behold, Heidi, the Rodale granddaughter, showed up as a Chadwick apprentice.

In a recent editorial in *Organic Style,* a magazine in the Rodale tradition, Maria Rodale reviews the history of her grandfather saving the word *organic* in 1940 as a chemical-free method of farming and gardening:

"My grandfather," Maria said, "was called a quack by the American Medical Association, sued by the Federal Trade Commission, and barely welcomed in polite society (he certainly wasn't invited to join the local country club). After all, establishment types said, what could a Jewish certified public accountant from the Lower East Side of Manhattan know about agriculture and science? He had no university degrees and no special expertise in these fields.

"But J. I. believed in organic with all his heart and his self-educated brain. Rather than bend to the pressures of his detractors, he did what many obsessed entrepreneurs do: launched a magazine (Organic Farming and Gardening) *to get his ideas out there."*[1]

Robert Rodale, who had inherited the dynasty, was coming for a visit, accompanied by Wendell Berry, and I somehow heard about it. I ran up and found them at the farm and asked them to come down for a chat and a cup of coffee. I had no idea who Wendell Berry was, but there he was, the successor to Robert Frost, as well as the great advocate of the family farm and the renewal of the land, who understood, better than anyone else, the meaning of the need for roots, sitting at our dining room table along with Rodale.[2]

I gave Rodale and Berry my talk on the physicalist/vitalist conflict, and where Rodale's father came in, much like I did for the students and faculty at Emerson College, on Steiner, some years later, and his place within the physicalist/vitalist conflict.

I told them about 1828 and the smoking gun—the artificial synthesis of urea—and the presumed refutation and defeat of vitalism and the victory of physicalism. I told them how this chemical blow had subverted the term *organic* to mean "artificial synthesis," the aim of organic chemistry, and how this blow added to that other blow of some hundreds of years before, when Galileo mathematized nature, the blow of mathematical physics, the beginning of the reduction of organic nature to matter.

Physicalism was the name for the ideological takeover of what counted for knowledge, the inner core of the scientific revolution and the content of the new paradigm. I told them about the Physicalist Society in Berlin and the oath taken in blood to drive out any closet vitalists, as they closed ranks behind Helmholtz and Müller and DuBois-Reymond and Brücke. Then came the mopping up operation of the logical positivists in Vienna and the circle around Carnap and Neurath and their theme of "the elimination of metaphysics" and anything suggestive of vitalist sympathies, and how religious language, ethical language, and aesthetic language was regarded as nonsense, strictly nonsense, literally nonsense. No wonder old man Rodale had to recover and reaffirm the integrity of organic nature against the takeover of industrial society and reductive, physicalistic scientism.

Robert Rodale liked it. Years later, he wrote an appreciative eulogy on the occasion of Alan's death; a generous response, given Alan's refusal to talk to him, because, unsuspectingly, Rodale and Berry had gone to the farm first to have lunch with Chadwick's alienated apprentice. Alan found out about it when they went to meet him in the garden, and he walked out on them in a huff.

Soon after, Chadwick walked out of the university as well, leaving undone his dream of a Roman road at the entrance to the farm using stone brought from the adjacent limestone quarry by student slaves—something so bizarre even I thought he was kidding. The farm became the center for the agroecology program, which is now over thirty years old and graduating apprentices every year in the Chadwick tradition, albeit diluted to a plain old organic way of doing things. But who could keep it up after his departure?

Nobody.

I never saw the magic depart from a place as when Chadwick left. This is not to fault the heroic effort made to continue the garden and to make it a showcase for all to behold. Orin Martin, who has been there for years, has dedicated himself to maintaining the Chadwick legacy. For example, he has collected hundreds of species of apples, an achievement Chadwick would have applauded, bringing back the heirloom species Chadwick mourned when he heaped scorn on the Delicious. I marvel at the fact the Chadwick Garden is still there, after all these years, when I drive up to take a look or to escort a visitor who wants to go see.

Alan took a hike. He finally had had it and packed his bags and left. He went to Saratoga, just over the hill, on the way to San Jose. Although he tried to establish a garden there, the support was wanting. After less than a year, he went from Saratoga to the Zen Center farm at Green Gulch, only to return to Saratoga after his sojourn at Green Gulch at the bequest of his sponsor, Betty Peck, who wanted an organic garden for her kindergarten students. They founded the Old Oak Farm and started the garden there, where the children celebrated the seasons and harvested the vegetables, helped by the apprentices (there were always apprentices) in the care of compost and the animals.

At the end of the fifteen years of the Saratoga garden, six thousand children were visiting the garden each year.

Between the two episodes in Saratoga, in his time at the Zen Center farm at Green Gulch, Alan established the garden that would be carried on by Wendy Johnson and Peter Krupnick, to supply the Zen community with organic food, and which would eventually supply two of their projects—the Green Grocer, near the Zen Center; and the Greens restaurant, at Fort Mason in San Francisco.[3]

The Green Gulch Farm seemed like a perfect realization of his work. Juxtaposed to Muir Beach, named after John Muir, one of the greatest environmentalists in our national tradition, a name worthy of the Ecology Hall of Fame,[4] Chadwick labored away to develop a garden of great beauty and productive abundance. Although he left a major imprint on the land and the people who came under his influence, it was another force fit. He thought the Buddhists sat too much. Excuse me. It's called *zazen,* and they do it a lot as the focus of their spiritual practice. In fact, they got up very early every day to do it. Chadwick thought they could become better Buddhists if they gardened more and sat less. Garden zen.

As Wendy Johnson, who became head gardener at Green Gulch, remembers:

Alan's techniques were theatrical, rough, and memorably vivid. One moment he upbraided us by quoting long passages of reverent plant tribute drawn from his memory of Shakespeare, and in the next, he strangled and strung up a marauding blue jay whom he caught bare-handed while the brassy bird was pecking apart flats of newly sown "Ailsa Craig" tomatoes. Alan hung the murdered bird at the entrance gate to our peaceful Zen meditation center as a macabre and ominous warning to all transgressors of the true Garden Way.

That was Alan all right.

After less than a year it was clear that Alan Chadwick could not fully develop his vision of Eden at Green Gulch. He wailed at top volume each time the wooden sounding block was struck for meditation and faithful Zen students mindfully put down their tools and headed calmly for the meditation hall. "Look at this—look at this!" Alan ranted and seethed. "Perfectly able-bodied young men and women running to the atavistic sound of wood beating on wood. Running without shame, and leaving an old man like me to work alone in the garden!"[5]

And they drove around too much in their cars—back and forth—between the Zen Center in San Francisco and Green Gulch, over the Golden Gate Bridge, to Muir Beach, and

Tassajara, miles away in the Carmel Valley. He wanted to take away the keys to Baker-roshi's new BMW. Maybe Chadwick would relent on sitting if they drove less. On and on. He became an irritant. They finally wearied of it—Chadwick's chadwickying them—and they kicked him out.

From Green Gulch he went back to Saratoga. He started a garden again at the invitation of Betty Peck to serve the schoolchildren of the area, a garden of great charm and enchantment. It became one of my favorites, behind the Odd Fellows Hall, an appropriately named location, if you think about it. Chadwick seemed to have his best time in Saratoga. He had passionate supporters and benefactors and the garden he developed thrived on the attention it received from the community and from Alan's extraordinary devotion to gardening. As was mentioned, his sponsor was Betty Peck, an exquisitely beautiful woman with a flair for an eccentric and enchanting lifestyle, who had a small train to ride around her property. She developed a curriculum for schoolchildren with the garden as a major resource. She was one of those who appreciated in the deepest sense what Alan stood for and represented, and she was willing to sacrifice anything to make the garden work. Across the street were Louis and Virginia Saso and their commercial herb garden; they also became great Chadwick supporters. Louis would tease me about having more varieties of thyme than I had, and about who had introduced whom to the properties of the herb, my favorite. I think his count hit twenty. Mine never went beyond fifteen.

I include here a letter I received during the final stage of completing this book from an apprentice of Alan's who worked in the garden at Saratoga:

I was an apprentice at the Saratoga Community Gardens 1977–1979. I think I have vague memories of meeting you or at least being in your presence. Last night I was speaking with my 14-year-old daughter who has an interest in gardening. Instead of heading off to college after high school she wants to do something interesting and adventurous before settling into the career/education mode. I thought of the apprentice program at UC Santa Cruz. I googled it and one thing led to another and I ended up reading a lengthy interview you had done concerning Alan Chadwick and the garden at Santa Cruz. Anyway, here are my Chadwickian musings and meditations.

Some background: I am from a Midwestern farm background. My folks are still alive and live on a farm in Green County, Wisconsin, very close to Dane County. Gardening and closeness to the soil go back generations on both sides of my family. My uncle still lives on a farm that was homesteaded by my great-great-grandfather in the 1840s.

I graduated from the University of Wisconsin in Madison with no particular goals except to advance the coming New Age and get enlightened. During this time I read an article about Alan Chadwick in the New Age Journal. *I was electrified. I had a life long passion for gardening and now I could infuse it with the highest ideals. During this time I began a conversion process to Christianity—which extended over a period of several years. I was reading the Bible, talking to some lovely Baptists and Pentecostals, and had a series of spiritual experiences.*

I went to Covelo to look into the apprentice program by spending a week there. I found a flyer there about the Saratoga program and decided to go there as I felt and saw that Chadwick treated dogs better than people. I still remember, though, his precise technique he displayed in the proper mixing of sifted materials to make soil for seedling flats, along with a few of his gardening injunctions. He had a peculiar force as a teacher.

He visited Saratoga once to give a lecture. He was on his best behavior, but still was a terrible old man and terrifying except to stout and free souls. During the lecture, given outdoors in our little amphitheatre, he was tormented by a horsefly.

I next saw him with a group of his disciples in Napa. I had accompanied Betty Peck and a few others from Saratoga to reconnoiter with Chadwick a truly fantastic property featuring the ruins of a turn of the century spa featuring naturally carbonated and flavored springs on a dramatic hillside. It would have been a wonderful aerie for him. [This was Lemon Soda Springs in the Napa Valley.]

My final experience of Chadwick was seeing him shortly before his death at Green Gulch. There was a gathering of apprentices for a final visit and teaching. I went with a fellow gardener from Saratoga. At his final talk I sat uncomfortably right by him as he spoke in a crowded room. His visage in his final illness had an eagle ferocity. He spoke about the four archangels. As a now evangelical Pentecostal Christian I passed a note to his caretaker to give him. I was exhorting him to turn

144

simply to Christ who was higher than the archangels he spoke of. I'm sure he didn't receive the note and I certainly didn't have the courage to speak directly to him even though I was only a few feet from him. I well remember the stricken looks on his apprentices, so young, seeing death on their master's face. After the talk we had a meal provided by Green Gulch. And my friend and I were given a tour of the grounds and garden by Wendy Johnson.

I think Chadwick was promoting Art—a vision of human hands and skill bringing nature to a level of fertility and beauty it can't do unassisted. I love his teaching on fertility I read years ago. This type of Art is by nature aristocratic, a luxury item, like the great renaissance art, that needs to be subsidized. I have had glimpses of this art in his gardens, also in a small garden done in Saratoga (not the Community Garden, but a private one done by his principles)—it was an intense experience of fertility, plants effortlessly springing out of the ground—you felt it as soon as you entered the garden gate, the fruit of extravagant oceans of organic soil amendments;...my parents' garden after decades of tending has that feeling.

I was ravished by the vision—but I am a farm boy nurtured in economic realities and efficiencies, and I always had a nagging feeling of the dreamlike quality of it all. I knew that hard work and onerous labor even when sanctified by ideals is still onerous. Perhaps nature one day will rebel against short-term efficiencies as being the guiding principle of agriculture and we'll be forced to embrace Art and fertility as the ultimate economy and efficiency—but I have doubts this will ever happen. Perhaps this garden Chadwick was promoting was an artistic and transient glimpse of the New Heaven and New Earth I'm looking forward to—I am still a believer in Jesus and God at times visits my soul with little down payments of the New Heaven and New Earth. As Art for art's sake, Chadwick's garden is more than worthwhile and I am saddened we couldn't have had more complete expressions of it done by the master's hand as an ideal to ponder and to inspire as we do any great art in this imperfect world.

I hope Chadwick found his final and everlasting garden and I hope you will also.

Sincerely,
Jeff Nichols

This letter was a strange gift at the point of finishing this book. Expressions of appreciation are rare as are human contacts carried into friendships that last a lifetime.

I can't remember if the closing of the Saratoga garden, due to development of the Odd Fellows property, prompted Alan to leave, or whether it was the delay on the part of the school authorities to enter into a contractual relationship with Alan and his garden. From Saratoga, he went to Covelo, in Round Valley, under the auspices of Richard Wilson. There he founded a community of apprentices. Again, if I remember correctly, it was Huey Johnson, riding on a plane with Richard Wilson, telling him he should bring Chadwick to Covelo and help him start a garden there. So Chadwick arrived with a couple of dutiful apprentices, and they started to dig. The first year was tough. They were in a flood area and did not realize it until the rains came and they were flooded out, after months of hard work. Wilson moved them to a small farm and that became the site for the grand scheme.

Looking back on it, I am amazed how Alan rolled with the punches. He had terrible setbacks, but he just kept going. He had a mission that history had conferred on him, and he rose to the challenge and did everything in his power to bear witness to it. I liked referring to his arrival as divinely ordained from on high, because he appeared out of the blue and was the answer to a hope and a promise—to start a garden. He was providentially appointed, I want to say. There was some implicit plan that came with Alan, and it was the restoration of the organic integrity of nature, as simple as that. Repair the breach. Make good on the vital flow and its renewal. What's the poem about the sap rising by John Donne?

Covelo is a version of Shangri-La in its geography. It is called Round Valley and one drops into it from above, a basin about thirty miles in diameter, reminiscent of Ojai, outside of Los Angeles, where Krishnamurti lived and had a center, and where *Lost Horizons* was filmed, the movie about Shangri-La. I saw it as a boy, and when the beautiful woman suddenly ages as they leave Shangri-La, and she turns into an old crone, stumbling down the snowy slope, at the end of the movie, the hair on the back of my neck stiffened up and I had one of my first encounters with the uncanny.

Alan arrived in Covelo shortly after it was scheduled to become a dam and be flooded, but Wilson and his cohorts had stopped it. Now it would be a site for a famous garden project under Wilson's patronage. He had a development plan for the town in mind, a kind of ecotopian vision.[6]

Covelo is known for its mixed-tribe Indian reservation; the whites in the valley were mostly redneck cowboys and farmers. Tough guys! The town was like a movie set from an old Western. Chadwick and his apprentices were regarded as hippie incursions. They had to watch out. There were stories about rednecks punching hippies at local football games just to make a statement and to raise a cheer. On our frequent trips to Covelo, Page and I would stay at a funky little motel, and when it was time to have one, saunter into a bar on the main street. Everyone would look up, wondering who were these refugees from a university. The image was hard to shake even in overalls, partly because we knew saunter came from *saint terre,* holy earth, and referred to pilgrims on the way to the holy land. We wanted to walk like that on our way to Alan's new garden. Page routinely ordered a double bourbon. On the rocks. He's the only one I ever knew who did. They might have picked on me, but Page was very tall and very strong, a wrestler in college and a major in the army, the 10th Mountain Division. They left us alone.

Wilson struck the pose of a cowboy in his Levi's and greasy hat, but everyone knew he had gone to Dartmouth and was a wealthy son of a wealthy father and one of the largest landowners in the valley. One time at dinner at his home, he nonchalantly handed me a vintage bottle of Haut Brion that he'd inherited from his father's cellar and asked me if I liked wine. I blinked hard. We tasted it, and it had gone bad, but we drank it anyhow. I still have the bottle.

Richard Wilson was perpetually amused by Chadwick's eccentricities. He thought his temper tantrums and fits displayed his acting ability; he seemed to be energized by the electrical charge. As the Covelo entrepreneur, he had opened a restaurant, which was run by his wife, bought a beautiful

Richard Wilson, 1973.

old granary where he meant to grind wheat for a bakery, and obtained other buildings he meant to develop. He had a plan to put Covelo on the map, and Chadwick was part of the plan. Apprentices slowly arrived and settled in; eventually Chadwick had a devoted and disciplined group.

He gave talks. They were all recorded and now make up the centerpiece of the Chadwick Archive at UCSC, including the talks he gave in West Virginia. Craig Siska (Alan's apprentice at the time) carefully collected and preserved the tapes as a precious legacy for the archive. Siska was assisted by Steve Crimi, who helped with copying and organizing them.

Having played a central part in saving Round Valley from the proposed dam, then governor Ronald Reagan was invited to come and see what Wilson had accomplished and to meet another professional actor, now a horticulturist—Alan Chadwick.

It was one of those moments of elective affinity.

Chadwick had prepared himself for the encounter with great care. He wore an immaculate blue, doubled-breasted blazer over a pair of pure white Bermuda shorts, blue socks and shoes. It was, in effect, a tropical version of full-dress, appropriate for official ceremonies. The British Navy's

148

Chadwick with Richard Wilson and Gov. Ronald Reagan, 1974.

Steven Decatur watched as Reagan and Chadwick separated themselves from the rest of the group. The two men walked down the path toward the soft fruit beds. They were equally tall and distinguished in their different ways: two professional spellbinders at work. Chadwick was bristling with his sense of the importance of the occasion while Reagan, the accomplished performer, relaxed as he presented himself for the cameras. They stopped among the raspberries, as planned—Reagan with his hand to his chin, looking judicious. Chadwick with an arm flung wide in a grand gesture and a visionary gleam in his eye. It was a tableau: The Governor meets The Genius.[7]

It was always a great adventure to drive up to Covelo with Page Smith, who, at the time, was working on his magisterial history of the United States. We would talk about his work on the way. He was one of the few great narrative historians of the time, a style of historiography that had gone out of style in favor of monographic efforts like the "History of the Wisconsin Dairy Industry from 1889 to 1900." Page was notorious for saying there is nothing as contemptible as a fact, which is as funny and audacious as any historian can get. But he had studied and practically worshipped a historian (Rosenstock-Huessy) whose writings had insights on almost every page, in a field where insights were few and far between. Insights, not facts, were what Page wanted.

149

Page was bent upon telling the people's history using first-hand sources. It would go to eight volumes, double volumes in length, one of the most industrious efforts in over a hundred years, each volume a Book of the Month Club selection. He always surprised me: he had no regrets regarding his departure from the university, crediting me with having "sprung" him, even though it placed him in a kind of professional limbo. We thought of it as an exodus from institutional bondage. He was freed up to apply himself to his work as one of the great contributions to American historiography in the twentieth century.[8] Unfortunately, his effort did not receive the acclaim it deserved, especially from historians who disdained narrative history.

Page was a man of infinite grace and charm, from whom I learned the meaning of devotion. It was a quality he unselfconsciously referred to when he spoke of friends he shared with his wife, Eloise. It meant the relationship was unconditional—for life. I heard them say it in an offhanded way, as they told us about friends of theirs whom we had as yet to meet, "Oh,

Richard Wilson, Page Smith, the author, and Alan Chadwick, 1974.
Photo by Jim Hair.

we're devoted to them!" It made an indelible impression. We thought it was providential to be included in their devotion.

He prided himself on being a chicken farmer, with a flock of about one hundred chickens, and he always brought us eggs. He heard about an old Indian woman in Round Valley who had some special bantams he wanted, so we went to visit her; that was an encounter to behold. They spoke as one chicken connoisseur to another, discussing the qualities of chickens they prized. He bought a few, and we brought them back to Santa Cruz to add to his collection.

Page and a colleague, Charles Daniel, a biologist, wrote a book about chickens, after teaching a popular course on them, much to the embarrassment of some of their fellow faculty members, who thought chickens were beneath academic interest. [9] I took Page's interest in the plight of chicken production as an indictment of industrial society and another example of mechanization taking command. He mourned their plight.

Partly inspired by Page, my wife and I have kept chickens for some years and have reveled in their company as well as their egg production. Their vitality and intense strength and demeanor are a never-ending delight.

One year we went up to Covelo at Easter time and had an Easter egg hunt with Alan. I brought along colored eggs and we had a picnic on an old dried-up streambed. Page proudly held up an egg he found to be photographed; the chicken farmer in one of his best poses!

Page Smith was most supportive of the garden at UCSC and valued Alan's work not only because he was the occasion for Alan's visit to the campus, having invited Rosenstock-Huessy and Freya von Moltke to be in residence, but because he was sympathetic to everything Alan stood for and represented. When Alan died, his eulogy went right to the heart of the matter. No one could have put it better.

As already mentioned, Alan's friend and muse, Freya von Moltke, was visiting Santa Cruz with Page's old teacher, the polymath Eugen Rosenstock-Huessy, a unique academic figure of the twentieth century and Page's professor at Dartmouth. Now here is where the story takes on a kind of mystical character, at least in terms of a subtext that I never figured out until after it was all over. Experience, I have come to appreciate, is like a palimpsest, a manuscript text on top of a text, like dreams to the waking state, where the subtexts are difficult, sometimes impossible, to read, but you sense them. Sometimes you get a glimpse. Freud used the metaphor of a mystic writing pad.

It is like the Greek word for truth, *aletheia,* as interpreted by Heidegger. It is translated as "unconcealedness," nearly unintelligible in English. "Disclosure" or "revelation" do not quite yield the meaning, because what is revealed is still concealed as in an impenetrable mystery, on the order of hide and seek, which is as close to the meaning as I can get. It is a glimpse into the depth of things for which dreams often function as a clue, and this glimpse usually only comes to awareness in retrospect, when you wake up and wonder about it. Did I dream that? Did I see that? What does it mean? This particular subtext is so compelling and amazing I am constrained to tell it, fraught as it is, with potentialities and possibilities we were unable to exploit fully, tap them as we would, if only they had been made clear at the time.

It is my fondest retrospective account, now that I have the luxury of hindsight. Needless to say, I wish I knew then what I know now and had been clear about it from the start. The theme, believe it or not, is the moral equivalent of war.

Chapter Nine

A Moral Equivalent of War

Page Smith had been a student of Eugen Rosenstock-Huessy's at Dartmouth. Nay, more. Page was the recipient of his spirit. He was vouchsafed a spiritual legacy from Eugen that he would ever after marvel at, so that the mere mention of Eugen's name brought tears to his eyes: the tears of spiritual endowment and an appreciation for what was freely given by one of the great teachers of all time. This is difficult to re-count, because it is so rare and so private. I can't do it justice, even though I was initiated into the same spirit and received it in full measure. It is all part of the Chadwick story and the cast of characters involved.

Together, while they were at Dartmouth, Page and Eugen started Camp William James as a leadership training camp for the Civilian Conservation Corps. The year was 1940. It was short lived. The war started and Page was drafted off to the ski corps in the 10th Mountain Division where he became a ma-jor. He was eventually badly wounded, stepping on a mine, in the Italian campaign.

Camp William James was their version of a garden proj-ect on a Vermont farm, within the context of the Civilian Conservation Corps, a successor, of sorts, to the United States School Garden Army during the First World War. I had never heard about it until I found a poster announcing it, showing Uncle Sam as a Pied Piper leading the children off to garden—their hoe, spade, and rake over their shoulders, like soldiers marching off to war. Uncle Sam, but for his goatee, bears a striking resemblance to Chadwick.[1]

Camp William James was named for Harvard's most fa-mous philosopher and psychologist, and was based on one of his talks. James was a visiting professor at Stanford at the time of the 1906 San Francisco earthquake. He witnessed it, and famously said, "Let 'er rip!"[2] He happened to be the one to

Poster for the United States School Garden Army, 1918.

articulate the theme for a century. Voluntary work service on behalf of a passionately held militant cause is the moral equivalent of war, be it land reform, civil rights, community service, or a conservation corps. Draft off the gilded youth and give them a share of the shit work that a segment of society is stuck with for a lifetime; they will become better human beings as a result of the sacrifice. Blow on the spark of civic virtue glowing in the breast of every American and watch the blaze when it ignites. I have seen it for myself.

The Civilian Conservation Corps of FDR was the first national expression of this appeal, even though it was run by the army and included only welfare recipients and delinquents—you had to pass a means test proving that your parents were very poor to get into the corps. If you were found guilty of a crime, the judge would give you the option of going to jail or into the corps.

The theme of voluntary work service was definitely in the air. Rosenstock-Huessy had already tried something like it in Germany in his work with German youth under the banner of voluntary service. Hitler mobilized them as the Hitler Youth.

As a contemporary to William James in Europe, Joseph Popper-Lynkeus sketched out a program in a manner comparable to William James—a German army of youth, an equivalent of soldiers—he called it a *Nahrpflicht,* in contrast to the *Wehrpflicht,* a nourishment army in contrast to the conscription army. They would go to work to establish the foundation for the necessities of life for everyone in the state during peacetime: providing food, clothing, and shelter. He calculated how many recruits it would take and how long. It was a period of self-sacrifice in the interest of a national economy: an economy of gift. His adopted last name (Lynkeus) was the name of the seer/pilot of the Argo, the ship Jason and the Argonauts took in search of the Golden Fleece. He was a visionary after my own heart.[3] It was an odd moniker for a boiler engineer.

The boys and girls at Dartmouth, with the blessings of Mrs. Roosevelt, Dorothy Thompson, and the sons of William James, were going to get middle-class college kids into the corps and imbue it with the spirit of William James and his summons for a century.[4] They were going to actualize the moral equivalent, and they saw the Civilian Conservation Corps as their vehicle. James knew that volunteerism was a key theme in the constitution of the American psyche. He called it civic virtue.

If only I had known this story when I started the garden project. If only over lunch Eugen had said, "Paul, you should talk to Page about Camp William James. He was the first director and I was his mentor. It was our effort to carry through the moral equivalent of war in the service of conservation. You can do it here! You can develop another version of the conservation corps with Alan as the charismatic leader. It is the perfect program for all these hippie students who think they are entering a new age and want to get back to the earth and a renewal of organic nature."

But he didn't. I don't think he liked Alan. Too much theatricality tied to gardening. Too much bombast. Too ill tempered. I don't know. As a matter of shared experience, the theme of the moral equivalent of war and voluntary work service was to come true later, under the most fortuitous circumstances, when the subtext, as a kind of vexing and perplexing spiritual process, surfaced again.

I read William James's essay, "The Moral Equivalent of War." The subject turned out for me to be one of the major themes for the twentieth century. I will always be grateful to Page Smith, who introduced me to it. I went in through the gate of Camp William James. I read the companion essay, "The Energies of Man," where James talks about the remarkable reservoirs of energy released under stressful conditions such as wartime, and of a second, third, and fourth wind phenomenon, like that of a great athlete, allowing one to continue beyond all normal limits of human endurance and ability. He marveled at the reservoirs of untapped energies, and at why only certain conditions allow for or provoke their release. James wanted to tap these reservoirs of energy in the moral equivalent and apply them to peacetime. He knew what Americans were capable of when they are put to the extreme test.

Although it was the Civilian Conservation Corps under Roosevelt that was thought to be the best expression and response to James's call, the moral equivalent was also discovered by Gandhi in his dedication to *Satyagraha* (Truthforce), which he explicitly called the moral equivalent of war, ostensibly with William James in mind. To be grasped by the force of the truth of the moral equivalent of war was Gandhi's message and to be able to resist compliance with evil and accept the penalty for such resistance was the nonviolent part. Accepting the penalty for noncompliance was the militant edge he gave to the theme. It revolutionized India in throwing off the British yoke. Fasting was its most powerful spiritual technique.[5]

Civil disobedience energized Martin Luther King Jr. and the civil rights movement in America. The moral equivalent of war was repatriated from India in one of the most remarkable cross-cultural transmissions of the theme.

I took an interest in the successor to Gandhi—Vinoba Bhave—and the mutation of civil rights to land reform, and the remarkable career Bhave had collecting land given him by wealthy landowners in his land-gift movement, the Bhoodan. We saw something comparable in the move from King to Chávez and the plight of the farm worker in America, as well as the Land Trust and Green Belt land-conservation efforts that developed in many communities beginning in the 1970s. All of this exemplified the land-reform theme.

In the spirit of Gandhi and King and Bhave, the theme of the moral equivalent of war was transmitted to Cesar Chavez and the land reform movement of the migrant worker: from civil rights to land reform.[6] I include Rosenstock-Huessy and Chadwick in the lineage. Eugen for his devotion to the conservation theme as the aim of voluntary work service and for founding Camp William James as a predecessor of the Peace Corps, and Alan for land reform through organic and sustainable farming and gardening, a renewed vision of a land ethic and right livelihood.

John F. Kennedy was grasped by the theme of the moral equivalent when he almost off-handedly proposed a Peace Corps to a group of University of Michigan students during his presidential campaign. They immediately mobilized to ensure its happening. Harris Wofford tells the story in his history of the theme: *Of Kennedys and Kings*. Harris was responsible for taking

REGIONAL LAND
REFORM
CONFERENCE

Look at the world, *rocked by the weight of its over*
hanging dome; *look at* the lands, *the farflung*
seas *and the unfathomable* sky.
See how *the whole creation* rejoices
in the age that is to be.
[Virgil 25b.c.]

Santa Cruz Civic Auditorium June 5-6, 1973
Sponsored by the William James Association.
Printed at the Greenwood Press, S.F.

Broadside for the Land Reform Conference.
The Greenwood Press, 1975.

King to India to meet Gandhi's successors, and he became the close adviser to Kennedy and Sargent Shriver in the formation of the Peace Corps, just as he eventually headed AmeriCorps, the organization of national service developed by Clinton during his presidency. And now President Obama has increased the budget for AmeriCorps and has given it a new life.

I proposed a conference on the theme on the occasion of the one hundredth anniversary of the publication of William James's essay, and we gathered at Dartmouth College in November of 2010 under the auspices of the Rosenstock-Huessy Society. We recounted the origins of Camp William James and the significance of the theme for those who came under Rosenstock-Huessy's inspired leadership. Harris Wofford gave the keynote speech, and participants came from Norway, Holland, and Germany. It expressed my debt to Page Smith. There was even a visit to the very farm where Camp William James was organized.

It was the theme for a century, a century of the most terrible wars ever in the history of the human race. Like the environmental movement, the theme is a ground for hope.

When I was denied tenure and unceremoniously shown the door, Page Smith walked out with me. He said, "Any place that doesn't have room for Paul Lee doesn't have room for me." Even today it has a nice ring to it. Together we went off into the sunset.

I remember vividly the day Page walked into our home, sat down at the kitchen table, and said, "Let's start the William James Association." I said, "Okay. What are we going to do?" He said, "We're going to reestablish the Civilian Conservation Corps." If it had been anyone but Page, I would have blanched, but he was larger than life. He gave me the sense we could do anything we wanted. There was this impression that we had magic wands and could wave them, and whatever we wanted would come to pass. We were free spirits, released from the institutional confines of the university and their "dead works," if I may borrow a term from Rosenstock-Huessy's account of his dropping out of German academic life after World War I, in what he calls an act of *metanoia* (a Greek term for "conversion" or "change of mind," as in the escape from Plato's cave). He went to work in an automobile factory. We were going to start a voluntary service corps.[7]

Eugen Rosenstock-Huessy eventually became a professor of law at the University of Breslau from 1928 to 1930. He organized voluntary work-service camps, which brought workers, farmers, and students together to work on the land. When he applied this experience to his involvement with Camp William James, he became a source of inspiration for all of those involved. Page Smith was elected the first director of the camp and his experience there, before he had to go to war, made up some of the fondest memories of his life. He especially liked singing the camp song; he taught it to me, and we would sing it at the drop of a hat. "We are the boys and girls from William James, we have high and lofty aims...."

We went to Washington, DC, and met with people involved in proposing a national service corps. After all, the Peace Corps had been one of Kennedy's most innovative and spontaneous efforts, following on the wings of Roosevelt's CCC. National service was a natural, but for Republican opposition; because it was regarded as a Democrat cause, we didn't get anywhere. We met with Senators Alan Cranston, Ted Kennedy, and others, to no avail. Washington was a revolving door.

I met Jack Preiss, who came to town because we were beating the drum. He had been in Camp William James with Page and had written an account of it, a wonderful book that captures the whole flavor of the time: the naïve idealism, the willing spirit, the hope for the future, the youthful enthusiasm for the cause, *the unreflective striving for what is noble,* the impressive intellectual standard expressed in the letters exchanged over the project. I met Frank Davidson again, the man who had started the process with his vision of a leadership component for the CCC. When we met on another occasion in Boston, he took me to meet Mrs. Henry Copley Greene, who had supported Camp William James and was a great follower of Rosenstock-Huessy, whom she and her husband provided financial aid over the years. She was very old and bed ridden and about to die, but she was the epitome of the Boston grande dame in the best sense of the figure. I was being ushered into the presence of someone of great culture and charm.

When I was introduced to her as Page Smith's colleague, she said, "Oh how wonderful to have that name come back to me now after all these years!"

Penetrating the corps with college students was Frank Davidson's idea and he was a motivational force in its realization. When Frank first proposed it to Rosenstock-Huessy, Eugen said, "Have you ever worked?" Meaning had he done physical work? As the pampered son of a wealthy New York lawyer, Frank hesitantly said, "No." Eugen responded, "Well, go and work for a year and then come back and talk to me." So he did.

This anecdote doesn't need any embroidery; it is the fullest expression of Rosenstock-Huessy's personality. He cut to the quick and he had a rapier-like stroke to his voice that made the cut count. That Davidson returned after fulfilling the command is the astonishing part. And it was the foundation moment for Camp William James.

Because the Camp was so short lived, with the war interfering, the memory was so intense and so fraught with unrealized promise it seemed that it was meant to rise again at some future point, like our effort in Santa Cruz. In a talk he gave about teaching too early and learning too late, Eugen expressed his lament over the sense of unfulfillment and the problem of timing. After speaking of his experience with the CCC, Eugen ends with these uncanny words:

But let me also hope that some years from now the word spoken out of season tonight may ripen into the maturity of timeliness.[8]

This is exactly the sense I had about the forces he represented and were brought to Santa Cruz, when he taught there, in the company of Page Smith, his devoted student, and took part in the occasion for Chadwick to arrive and accept the challenge.

When we were in Washington, DC, Frank took us to the Cosmos Club. That was fun. We met with Don Eberle, who had devoted his life to the cause of voluntary service; he told us of the dismal prospects for our cause under the current administration. We didn't get anywhere. It didn't seem to matter. We knew we were part of a process that would find its expression sooner or later, so we hoped.

We developed programs in Santa Cruz and were very successful. We started the William James Work Company and found short-term part-time jobs for people. The count went to thirty thousand—not too bad for a community about twice that size. It was the issue of the time for what was called the "undesirable transient element," or UTEs, anticipating our work with the homeless a decade later, when we opened the first public shelter in Santa Cruz, in 1985.

One day, Eloise, Page's wife, said to me, "Paul, you know Baker-roshi and he knows Jerry Brown. Tell Baker to ask the governor to appoint me to the chair of the State Arts Council." I said, "Okay." And it happened. The day Eloise was to be named she was in Brown's office with Page; it was the day Brown gave his State of the State Address. It was a famous one, because it lasted only a few minutes. Brown was in his "less is more" Zen phase, but in that address he took time to call for a California Conservation Corps. Page's mouth dropped. He had a great way of looking astonished. Flummoxed to the max. Page told Brown of our efforts; Brown said, "well, go ahead, organize it." I still remember the excitement and bewilderment in Page's voice when he returned to Santa Cruz and told me what had happened. We had our corps. Our hopes had come to fruition.

We were in business. I saw it as a way of extending the work of Chadwick through the agency of a voluntary corps. We were going to see through the theme of the moral equivalent of war. The corps could become a small army of Chadwick gardeners. There was a great rose garden in Berkeley that the CCC had planted, for example. We could do that. Roses were one of Chadwick's specialties. We would have Chadwick Rose Gardens planted by the California Conservation Corps up and down the state.

We organized a number of encampments to discuss the formation of the corps, one at an old CCC camp in Mendocino. Alan came down from Covelo and spoke, and state representatives in attendance looked stunned at the performance, trying to figure out what they were getting into. Who was this guy in their midst with the Shakespearian manner? We designed the uniform. We had a ball. We organized a subsequent encampment in Covelo. Frank Davidson came out for it. He and Page slept on the lawn out in front of Alan's home.

I sneaked in and slept in Alan's bed, as he was up in the mountains with Freya von Moltke, staying at a wilderness lodge owned by Wilson. After all, Alan had been a guest in my home a number of times. Nevertheless, I felt like Goldilocks.

The next day he sensed someone had used his bed, even though I had a sleeping bag. Besides this, we had cleaned his filthy refrigerator, which probably embarrassed him. And I had found a library book from UCSC, Steiner's *Goethe the Scientist,* which I put in my car to return. It was out on my name. Whatever the cause, Alan had a monstrous fit and walked off, missing a big banquet in Freya's honor. We were all ready to sit down, and when I asked where Alan was I was told he had had a fit over the fridge and had stalked off into the hills where he was not to be found. I thought of his—"I'm all right, Jack"—saying and using it on him. I was pissed off. Even I had my limit. I didn't talk to him for almost a year.

He came down to Santa Cruz and called me up and we made up. He was staying at a motel down on the beach, and we sat and discussed the future of his work. He may have already known he had cancer, but he didn't say a word about it. He was very cryptic, referring to the Round Table of King Arthur and the twelve knights and the Holy Grail and other related symbols. I tried to act like I understood what he was talking about, even though I didn't have a clue. Sensing this, he grew agitated and asked me if I understood. I lied. I said I did. He liked to say, "Agreed?" I nodded again, although I was completely perplexed. About what? He was issuing some kind of charge. I thought whatever transmission was at stake, I already had it. What did he mean by the Round Table? And who were the twelve? I preferred the legend of Robin Hood, having found out we shared the same birthday, September 20. But Alan was trying to convey something to me, something he could only express in mythical symbols. Was I too obtuse to get it? Now I realize how he operated in such cryptic moments of great import. He meant to transmit to me the spiritual substance of his work. Be a member of the Round Table, Paul, you can be a knight of faith, in the message of organic integrity. Carry the banner. Do what you can. There are other knights at the table.

163

One day, a man walked into our office and introduced himself as Boyd Horner, the newly appointed director of the California Conservation Corps. He had driven over from Sacramento. He said he was told of the work we had done to help organize the corps and he wanted to make a courtesy call as his first official act. I asked him what he had done before this. He said he worked for the blind in Washington, DC. I resisted making a smart remark about working with politicians. Something prompted me to ask him what he had done before working with the blind. He said he studied for the Rudolf Steiner priesthood in England.

It is the only time in my life where I raised my arm and looked up my sleeve and wondered if something had crawled out.

Something named Boyd.

I thought it was too good to be true and, of course, it was. I was sent to England, to Emerson College, devoted to Steiner studies, to recruit for the corps. Horner wanted to make it a Steiner Corps, not a Chadwick Corps, although he knew about biodynamics and was all for it. He wanted to put the moonbeam into the governor's office. Or at least add some anthroposophical sparkle. Steiner cuisine; Steiner gymnastics; Steiner eurythmy; Steiner you-name-it. Copper plates in your shoes.

Well, it was a free trip to England.

So I went. Harrison Ford, my brother-in-law, was acting in *Star Wars* in London, some thirty miles from Emerson College. I went in on weekends and hung out and had the time of my life. We discovered single malt scotches: Macallan's 18-year-old. Now he drinks 24-year-old private reserve no one else can get. I put on my tuxedo and danced with Princess Leia and we made the round of pubs. I met Alec Guinness and George Lucas. Somehow *Star Wars* seemed an appropriate accompaniment for a Steiner adventure.

I met a number of wonderful people at Emerson, and, of course, Francis Edmunds was there to welcome me and return the hospitality we had extended to him on his visits to Santa Cruz. I remember going into a local pub in Forest Row, and they all laughed right off, identifying me as a Yank from California. They wanted to know what I was doing there. I told them I was lecturing at Emerson College up the hill.

They instinctively ducked, as if a bat had flown in the window. Did I say Count Dracula?

I gave a lecture at Emerson about the physicalist/vitalist conflict and the historical context for Steiner's work, detailing where Steiner fit in the scheme of things in the move from organic nature to matter. It was the only time an audience sat in stunned silence for an interminable five minutes after I was through. For a moment I thought I had put them to sleep. I had to sit down and wait it out. I impressed myself. I had hit a home run.

But it all came to naught. Horner was replaced and the corps took a more militant turn, first with an ex-Jesuit colleague of Brown's, who was succeeded by a Vietnam casualty famous for drinking a glass of malathion on television when Brown was spraying it against the fruit fly; it provoked a big reaction. Why worry about a little spray? He was an advocate of tough love, emphasis on tough. The Steiner influence was over and so was any chance to insinuate Chadwick gardening into the corps, let alone eurythmy or Botmer gymnastics. So much for the rose gardens. Another force fit; only this one didn't take.

Chadwick at East Harmony,
West Virginia, around 1979.

AND THIS WORLD

'*And this world* you must see and receive,'
    he said: Look! And my eyes sowed the seed
    racing faster than rain even
    over a thousand virgin acres
Sparks taking root in darkness and sudden jets of water
            I was clearing the silence to plant
            seeds of phonemes and golden shoots of oracles
The hoe still in my hand
    I saw the great short-legged plants, turning their faces
    some barking, others sticking out their tongues
        There the asparagus, there the kale
        there the curling parsley
        acanthus and dandelion
        liatris and fennel
Secret syllables through which I strove to utter my identity . . .

ODYSSEUS ELYTIS
from THE AXION ESTI [THE GENESIS]

Seventy-five copies printed at the Greenwood Press in honor of Alan Chadwick and his
Vision of the Garden. The Chadwick Conference, Wheelwright Conference Center, Green
Gulch Farm, Muir Beach, California. 16 February 1980 Trans. (Greek) by Edmund Keeley & George Savidis

Broadside in honor of Alan Chadwick.
The Greenwood Press, 1980.

Chapter Ten

The Death of Chadwick

Alan came down with cancer of the prostate. He went into partial seclusion after leaving Covelo, living in a cottage someone had made available to him. We had tried to develop a project to procure Lemon Soda Springs, an old abandoned spa tucked away up in one corner of Napa Valley, overlooking the valley, a magnificent setting with Wagnerian ruins, where a lemon-flavored spring gushed forth its curative water. Presidents had visited there in its heyday. A fire had destroyed it, but large walls of burned-out buildings remained, as though a setting for an opera. It looked like just the place for Alan to do his most heroic effort. And presumably it was for sale. We had meetings. Nothing came of it.

The next thing I knew, Alan had been invited to New Harmony, West Virginia, in the Shenandoah Valley by a guy named Paul Solomon. (Both names assumed, just to give you an idea of the size of his ego and spiritual pretensions—I mean St. Paul and King Solomon, hence, Paul Solomon.) His real name was William Dove. He had started a New Age community in the tradition of Steiner, thinking he was the successor to Edgar Cayce, a famous clairvoyant, if you can call it a tradition. The Paul Solomon Foundation was a kind of ersatz version of Rudolf Steiner's community at Dornach, as our eponymous hero envisaged it. It was going to become a world center for the revival of human spirituality. So Alan went.

Alan had been identified as the world's greatest living gardener.

E. F. Schumacher had called him that.[1] So Alan was perfectly in tune with the spiritual aspirations of the group. After they heard about him, someone remembered a letter applying for the position. He looked in a drawer. It was from Alan; just the sort of psychic event they lived for. He was given the task of developing an enormous garden project with the followers of Solomon and some of his own apprentices. Tara Singh, an Indian mystic, was also in residence; he looked very good in white silk.

Solomon organized a large conference partially around Chadwick to celebrate the effort in June of 1979. Buckminster Fuller; Sir George Trevelyan, who was a famous anthropop from London; Barbara Marx-Hubbard, that New Age follower of Bucky's; Peter Caddy of Findhorn; Swami Kriyananda; Elizabeth Kubler-Ross; Paolo Soleri; and some others of note. I talked them into inviting me. I wanted to see Alan. I knew he was gravely ill.

Walking across the grounds, I noticed Buckminster Fuller emerging from a portable toilet set up on an open field. With Bucky stepping out, it looked like a space capsule had just landed. He didn't remember me. We had met a few years before at a large cocktail party in his honor in Saratoga, where, along with a hundred other people, I had a chance to shake his hand. Months later, he walked into The Wild Thyme Restaurant in Santa Cruz, which I managed for a while, and said, "Hello, Paul." I thought this was an impossibility. I asked him to speak informally to a small group I had gathered in the restaurant to develop a journal for the bicentennial, and he gave the most engaging and personable account of his trips around the world and the state of things. He walked around the room, affectionately touching everyone, his hand on their shoulders, as he spoke. I thought, "this is one unique guy for whom I had organized the restaurant." He made all the vexing work worthwhile. He said it was one of the most interesting restaurants he knew of, and he sent me a drink recipe to express his appreciation.

When I met Paul Solomon, whose most distinguishing feature was his basketball-sized belly, I asked him how he could be a guru and not be able to tie his shoes. He didn't laugh. I got to give my physicalist/vitalist spiel, and according to my notes, it went over very well. I wore my tuxedo.

My pal Rolf von Eckartsberg drove in for the occasion, and we drove out one morning into the mountains and had breakfast in a cafe where they acted like the South had *won* the Civil War or like the outcome, at least, was still a matter of dispute. I had a shorty beer with my eggs to mitigate the shock of this unexpected insular mentality. A breakfast shorty in the Shenandoah Valley, the locus of my favorite song.

Tara Singh gave a talk based on the saying that no one can serve two masters, which he identified as one genuine and one phony, meaning Alan and Solomon. He was pro-Alan. I sensed a rift.

They told me how sick Alan was, but I was not prepared for what I saw when I walked into his room. The angel of death was hovering over his shoulders. I think he told me he had undergone psychic surgery. I thought, "Oh god, this mystic business has gone too far." I found a young woman in the community who told me what had happened. She had witnessed it. Adepts, spirits, or whatever—"entities"—came in and fiddled with Alan, one after another, and then took their place along the wall. She could see them all and told me what they looked like. I watched her carefully as she described the event, thinking, "what do I know?"

It obviously hadn't helped. He needed intensive care; if not now, soon. I called the Bakers and asked them if they would take him back to Green Gulch and care for him until he died. Alan had an assistant who had devoted herself to him, and she would come along for the day-to-day. They graciously agreed. They had cared for Gregory Bateson until he died, and for others, such as Lama Govinda, who were terminally ill. They were set up to handle it, a kind of Zen hospice for the dying. Alan arrived at Green Gulch sometime around December of 1979.

I thought it was important to organize a farewell, so I did. I asked Jack Stauffacher to print a broadside to commemorate the event, just as he had done when we began the university garden. I thought it would be a good time to announce the organization of the Chadwick Society, the Chadwick Apprentice Guild, and the Chadwick Newsletter, so Alan would know that his legacy would continue. I was willing to initiate the organizing effort and asked Virginia Baker to help.

So on February 16, 1980, we gathered at Green Gulch to say goodbye to Alan. It turned out to be the day of the most violent ocean storm in anyone's memory. Alan played King Lear on the heath, although he was too ill to rage against the dying of the light. He appeared in his powder-blue Goodwill suit and recited his favorite fairy tales, which most of us knew: The Emperor and the Nightingale, and the angelic forces that become the herbs Rosemarinus and Lavendula. It was clear he would not live long. I remember a friend coming up afterward and, to my dismay, whispering in my ear, "What a ham!"

I knew what Alan meant when he recited the Emperor and the Nightingale, a parable about replacing a live bird with a mechanical one. In 1738, Jacques de Vaucanson unveiled his masterpiece before the court of Louis XV. It was a gilded copper duck that ate, drank, quacked, flapped its wings, splashed about, and, most astonishing of all, digested its food and excreted the remains.

Alan probably would have stepped on it.

He gave weekly talks from his bed. I remember seeing the governor of California, Edmund "Jerry" Brown Jr., standing outside Alan's room, hat in hand, waiting to go in. Alice Waters told me that her participation in those talks was to enter a mystery.

Wendy Johnson tells of that time in a beautifully nuanced remembrance:

Every week during the last months of his life, seven or eight of us gathered at his bedside for a garden study class. Alan was mortified to be abed. He had always taught in the sanctuary of the living garden. When we came to his bedside each time, he turned to the wall and began the class in a thin frail voice from under a pile of blankets, but after fifteen minutes or so he slowly turned toward us, awakened by the beauty of Angelica Archangelica or by the creak of a woodland bower heavy with pale yellow tresses of fragrant clematis. "Not even a single moment in the garden is reiterated," he whispered from his sickbed, "not a single moment."[2]

I brought my teacher a spring bouquet of his most treasured anemone flowers not long before his death. These flowers. Known since classic times as "the daughters of the wind" or the biblical "lilies of the field" remained on the bedside-table until long after their midnight-blue pollen had dusted the turned-down white linen borders on Alan's sheets. When I brought him fresh flowers to replace the fallen anemones, Alan raised his bony hand to ward me off, flower-bearing infidel. "Please!" he commanded in a whisper, "Leave me to the daughters of the wind. They are still releasing their secrets."

Then he died. Baker-roshi called. It was Pentecost Sunday, when the Holy Spirit was poured out upon the people. Baker-roshi wanted me to know that it looked like Alan was preparing to die. He said Alan had put a bouquet of flowers next to his bed, had hung up a depiction of the *Pietà* by Raphael, and next to it Shakespeare's fifteenth sonnet, "When I consider everything that grows…" and was just then kneeling in prayer next to the bed. "Wait," Baker-roshi said, and he left the phone. A moment later he returned and said Alan had fallen over and was dead.

I put down the phone and had this extraordinary cataclysmic rush of grief, a kind of paroxysm of nature, a force that took complete control of me like an internal tornado, propelling me out of the house on the run, out the front door and onto the front lawn, where something like an invisible sky hook seemed to come down and yank me up into a huge arc of a somersault and then set me back down on my feet. I ran back into the house and propelled myself, like a flying missile, onto the bed, as the force subsided and the howling stopped. The paroxysm of nature had run its course. Nothing of that force had ever happened to me before, and it hasn't since.

It was then that I remembered the words of Schelling, the German philosopher of nature: "Nature, too, mourns for a lost good."

Baker-roshi left Alan in his bed. It is Buddhist practice to sit with the corpse for three days to bear witness to the departure of the spirit. He had inquired about Alan's Roman Catholic faith and had discussed the proper rites with a priest who had been a friend of Alan's in Covelo. He found out that one reads the Psalms out loud as the very prayers of the departing spirit, so he did that at Alan's bedside. The funeral was arranged, and the invitation was passed around by word of mouth. My wife and I drove up to Green Gulch with our friends Jim and Jeannie Houston.

It was a beautiful service, with hundreds assembled in the Green Gulch *zendo,* a spectacular place, redolent with the hushed silence of meditation. Baker-roshi asked for people to speak. I had such a lump in my throat, I couldn't say a word lest I choke on my voice. Virginia Baker said it for me when she spoke about what Alan had meant to her. On the altar was a large photo of Alan from his theater days in London. When the remarks were over, Baker turned to the photo and gestured upward with his arms, and with a wave of his hands, in a firm and commanding voice, as if to release him, said, "Now, Alan, go to your rest. Go! Go!"

We were all undone as we watched his spirit depart.

The man who had been ordained from on high, for me and all the others he touched, to replant the vital root of existence, in the late stage of the self-destruction of industrial society, was gone.

When I consider every thing that grows
Holds in perfection but a little moment,
That this huge stage presenteth nought but shows
Whereon the stars in secret influence comment;
When I perceive that men as plants increase,
Cheered and check'd even by the self-same sky,
Vaunt in their youthful sap, at height decrease,
And wear their brave state out of memory;
Then the conceit of this inconstant stay
Sets you most rich in youth before my sight,
Where wasteful Time debateth with Decay,
To change your day of youth to sullied night;
    And all in war with Time for love of you,
    As he takes from you, I engraft you new.

Sonnet 15

William Shakespeare

The Greenwood Press, San Francisco, 2002
Set in Galliard types

William Shakespeare, sonnet 15.
The Greenwood Press, 2002.

ALAN CHADWICK
1909-1980

Dylan Thomas wrote to his father: "Do not go gentle into that good night; rage, rage against the dying of the light." Alan Chadwick went gently into that good night at Green Gulch, surrounded by people who loved and cared for him in a beautiful setting where he had created one of his great gardens. The "dying of the light" that Alan raged against was the light of our twentieth-century civilization so heedless of the rich bounty of the earth. More than an inspired horticulturist, Alan was like a furious Old Testament prophet, warning of the wages of our sinful treatment of the land. A visionary, he looked at a barren plot of ground and saw it bloom; the herbaceous border would go just there, opening to an enchanting view of the mountains or the ocean. The herb garden, the garden's soul, would be here, in inviting terraces. The arbor would be over there. And magically, and by incredible labors, they appeared in time, or at least anticipations of them—at Santa Cruz, in Saratoga, at Green Gulch, Covelo, New Market, Virginia, wherever he paused in his flight from the unendurable realities of our technological society, or simply the obtuseness of humankind.

Every garden contained a penance, concretelike hardpan, often the result of ceaseless tractor tracks, which had to be broken up so that the soil could breathe. This nourished that. That looked like a weed but drew necessary nutriments up from the deeper levels of the ground. Something rested in the shade of something else; and it in turn encouraged another flower or vegetable. It was all a marvelously intricate world of interdependent growing things: nature lovingly domesticated.

In an age of "collective leadership," Alan Chadwick was as imperious as a king. In a day of carefully modulated tempers and self-conscious "interpersonal relations," he stormed and raged not just at abstractions like laziness or indifference or inattention but at the poor frail flesh of those who were the destined instruments of his terrible, unflinching will. And then suddenly, being the consummate actor for whom all the world was a stage, he would be as sunny, as playful, as irresistible as the prince of a fairy tale. An exotic past lay dimly behind him—British naval officer, Shakespearean actor, painter of pale watercolors, the remnants of Puddleston china and silver brought out for state occasions, reassuring evidence that he had not, after all, come from outer space as one was sometimes inclined to suspect.

Everything about him was remarkable and distinctive. His physique, his height and angularity, his face, his hair, his walk. Those who fell under his spell had generally to put up with a good deal. That so many were willing to do so is the best possible testimony to the power of what he had to teach, which was inseparable from the way he taught it and the person he was. Mystic, seer, creator, lover of fine wines, coffees, caviar, and champagne, man of prodigious energy and prodigious fury—his life taught us that "nothing great is accomplished without passion." We will find his spirit in the gardens he or his disciples built, exhorting us to do better, to care more, to work harder, to recklessly expend love on an intractable world, to make the world a garden. And we will find his spirit in his vision of gardens never built but only dreamed of.

Page Smith

Verbena communis

Broadside by Jim Robertson, Yolla Bolly Press, Covelo, California, 1980.

Chapter Eleven

California Cuisine and the Homeless Garden Project

On a visit to Green Gulch to see the Bakers, sometime after Alan's death, I met Alice Waters, who had recently started Chez Panisse and was scouting for the best produce for the restaurant. Where else but a Chadwick production garden? The word had gotten around about the quality of the stuff. I knew that she had been party to Alan's deathbed talks, before he died, where some sort of transmission of his vision occurred, and although she could not remember what Alan said, the mystery of his presence, shortly before his death, was evident, powerful and unforgettable.

Alice was cutting a deal to obtain Green Gulch produce for the restaurant and I was glad to witness it and to meet her: she who would become the doyenne of American restaurateurs. We sat in the cozy front room of the Bakers with the great stained-glass windows framing the view out onto the fields, the Scandinavian stove heating up its beautiful blue tile to make the room toasty, the paintings they had collected with an unfailing aesthetic sense, the photographs of their many friends, the Japanese and Zen Buddhist artifacts serenely filling the atmosphere, manifesting a refined sensibility my wife and I had come to love and admire.

I like to credit Alan with having an influence on California cuisine and the movement that Alice initiated and represents. I was sure she would pay homage and credit to Alan for his influence, and I called her to ask her, just to find out. She remembered fondly of the mystical encounters and talks from his deathbed at Green Gulch. Deborah Madison, a graduate of UCSC and a Zen student, took her training at Chez Panisse. She became the original chef at the Greens, the restaurant begun by Zen Center at Fort Mason, supplied by the farm Alan started at Green Gulch. She credits Alan's influence in one of her popular cookbooks. Alan's production techniques and style of horticulture and agriculture perfectly suited a religious community—the Zen Center—in its vitalist roots. Alan's main apprentice at Green Gulch, Wendy Johnson, along with Virginia Baker, were all part of a group that admired Alan and wanted to dedicate themselves to the style of life he espoused. Catherine Sneed should also be mentioned. She started a famous garden project at the San Francisco County Jail on the site of what had been the jail farm. She is much admired for her work and the influence on the prisoners, who learned the Chadwick technique in working the soil. I remembered how dismayed I was to learn that they could not eat any of the food they grew—it could not be brought into the prison kitchen, because all food had to be prepackaged.

Alan was fond of saying, as quoted in an article on the Covelo Garden in the *San Francisco Chronicle*:

There is one rule in the garden that is above all others. You must give to nature more than you take. Obey it, and the earth will provide you in glorious abundance.

Always put back more than you take out was Alan's way of formulating the economy of gift that informed his approach. Be grateful! Give and it will be given unto you: shaken out, pouring out, spilling over, in your lap. And it proved to be true.

In 1985, Page Smith and I realized we had to do something for the homeless of Santa Cruz. The UTEs of the 1970s had turned into the homeless a decade later. In the decade from 1975 to 1985, no one had ever mentioned homelessness. Now it was no longer short-term, part-time jobs for people passing through Santa Cruz—hippie transients—it was the lack of shelter. Forget "affordable." They had nowhere to sleep. Everything in Santa Cruz had become unaffordable to a poor person with little or no means. But it was not just Santa Cruz. It had become a national catastrophe. There was no public shelter facility in Santa Cruz, although there was a soup kitchen run by a self-sacrificing fellow named Peter Carota, whose work inspired us. I asked him to meet with Page and me and talk about opening a shelter for the homeless under the auspices of the William James Association.

After our meeting, Page and I decided to do something. We had to. There was a woman named Jane Imler on a fast to the death lest someone open a shelter for the homeless. So one day we waltzed into the office of the director of Social Services for the county and announced we were going to use the auditorium next to her office for the homeless. It was warm, dry, and empty at night. She squirmed in her seat. To get us off her back, she offered to pay the rent for a space in town as long as it was some miles from her office. So we found the space in an empty family sauna and opened a shelter. The homeless poured in. It turned out to be a season of some of the worst ocean storms ever. We had more homeless than we could accommodate. I appealed to my Lutheran pal, the Rev. Paul Pfotenhauer. He agreed to take in a group, and, starting with his church, we eventually organized about forty churches to take in the overflow. It was called the Interfaith Satellite Shelter Program. Then we had to think of some way of putting the homeless to work. I thought a Homeless Garden Project would be a good enterprise, allowing the homeless to grow their own food. I knew I could call upon resources from the university, and maybe even get some apprentices from the Chadwick Garden to help.

An offer of a thousand or more herb plants from a nursery going out of business prompted me to say yes. I knew if I had the plants I would have to start a garden. We weren't going to stand around and watch them die. So the plants arrived and were, by happenstance, stored in a backyard across the street from the eventual site of the garden; another sign, albeit a minor one.

I thought that was convenient. All we had to do was walk the plants across the street, after Jim Lang, director of Parks and Recreation, offered me the site, adjacent to a community garden site we had started years before under the William James Association. It was city property. I think the project would have made Alan proud of me. It was definitely an expression of an economy of gift. We had no budget, no plan, no feasibility study—we hadn't learned our lesson to temper our freewheeling style—we just started digging beds and all the resources we needed were offered in abundance.

Lynn Basehore Cooper walked up my driveway to my office one day; as I watched out the window, I thought, "Here is the director of our garden project." After she introduced herself and asked me to plant a tree as part of Arbor Day festivities, I told her I would if she would take on a garden project for the homeless. "Okay," she said.

William James comes to mind here.

So far as man stands for anything, and is productive or originative at all, his entire vital function may be said to have to deal with maybes. Not a victory is gained, not a deed of faithfulness or courage is done, except upon a maybe; not a service, not a sally of generosity, not a scientific exploration or experiment or textbook that may not be a mistake. It is only by risking our persons from one hour to another that we live at all. And often enough our faith beforehand in an uncertified result is the only thing that makes the result come true.[1]

Eventually, one of the staff, Jared Lawson, started the first CSA (community supported agriculture) program in the area and that, for me, was the full confirmation of an economy of gift. One hundred families paid some hundreds of dollars for a share in the coming harvest and would go to the garden to pick up a box of assorted greens and vegetables, herbs and fruits every week, for the season. They got more than they paid for—an example of "too much zucchini"—my slogan for an economy of gift. They became passionate advocates of the project, although not enough to deter the city from finally selling the site for development.

Another site was found, and the Homeless Garden continues to develop its program there in the hope of eventually locating at Pogonip, the 614-acre city park directly below the university campus and a stone's throw from the Chadwick Garden.[2]

I helped save the property by organizing the Greenbelt Initiative in 1978, with the hope of making it a major botanic garden in Alan's memory. It would be a culminating link in a chain of gardens, beginning with the world-famous UCSC Arboretum, devoted to subtropical plants; the UCSC Farm and its Agroecology Apprentice Program; and the Chadwick Garden, all within a stone's throw of one another, in a continuous sweep across an elevation that looks out over Monterey Bay, one of the great visual spaces in the world. The Homeless Garden is the only sanctioned project for the development of the Pogonip Park. So far so good.

I went to Lotusland, a famous botanical garden in Santa Barbara developed by a Polish beauty and opera singer, Madame Ganna Walska, on some thirty-seven acres. A psychic accompanied us. She was a friend of the woman who took me into the garden, which was closed to the public at the time. Madam Walska was blind, confined to bed in her remarkable home, surrounded by huge *Euphorias* out of Hieronymus Bosch. The psychic saw an aborigine behind a tree. I couldn't glance fast enough, I guess, because I missed it. I neglected to ask her what she thought about psychic surgery.

She was asked sometime later to access Alan in a trance. Alan appeared. He spoke about his nurse, Acacia, calling her by her real name, Cathleen, which she didn't use, and thanking her for the care she had given him. Then he gave me a message that one day a botanic garden would be developed at Pogonip, or maybe that it was already a botanic garden. *Fait accompli!* He had us standing together observing the vistas and marveling at the sight as we looked out over the city of Santa Cruz and Monterey Bay. All you had to do was realize it or visualize it. I have a transcript of the tape of the séance. I don't know what to make of such things any more than you do.

I kept a horse adjacent to Pogonip and I used to ride there regularly. In the course of my jaunts I discovered what I came to call the Sacred Oak: a great tree in the form of the Crucified. A central branch had been lopped off and formed a semblance of a head with barely perceptible eyes and mouth; the great limbs extending outward from the trunk were like arms. It was Santa Cruz, Holy Cross, in an oak tree. I started having services there every Christmas, Easter, and Thanksgiving. It led to my developing the Greenbelt Initiative and the conservation of the property. Sometimes even I wonder if this is a true story.

I was worried that Pogonip would be developed. It was owned by the Cowell Foundation, and they were mad at the university. I can't remember why. So they were going to put multimillion-dollar homes on one of the great sites in the region. Over my dead body! And my horse's! I asked my friend Sim Van Der Ryn, professor of architecture and design at UC Berkeley, to organize a senior design class around Pogonip to make it a venue for a Chadwick-style botanic garden on a grand scale and whatever else they deemed appropriate for the site. Sim had founded the Farallones Institute, one of the visionary environmental projects in the country, and had hired Michael Stusser to develop the gardens at their rural center. Stusser was a Chadwick apprentice, who had done the film on Alan with the Norman O. Brown soundtrack.

At one point, Sim had invited Paolo Soleri to debate Alan. I was asked to introduce Alan. Alan was in fine form, with his usual awe-inspiring stage presence and stentorian delivery. Soleri showed slides of Arcosanti, his utopian project in Arizona. He sat in the front row and talked over his shoulder to the audience. People kept shouting, "speak up!"

Sim organized his design class around Pogonip. Before the first session, we had lunch at Chez Panisse with the head of the Cowell Foundation, owners of the property. Measure O, which we sponsored, had passed, so we informed him that his development plans had been superseded by our plans to preserve the land and turn it into a garden. He paid for lunch. We were accompanied by Mark Primack, who had done the poster for the Greenbelt Initiative, depicting the Sacred Oak I had found in the middle of Pogonip. We looked up the word Pogonip and it turned out to be an old Shoshone Indian name meaning "white death" referring to the fog that is characteristic of the area. We had taken it to refer to the new meaning that the bourgeois members of the Pogonip Club gave to the word—polo, golf, and nipping. In a superb drawing, Mark rendered the Sacred Oak and a clairvoyée view of the landscape sweeping down to the town, Holy Cross Church, and the Pacific Ocean of Monterey Bay, the very spot Chadwick had indicated in the psychic account I have referred to. Sara Boutelle, the architectural historian and biographer of Julia Morgan, and a friend of mine, also came along.

Sim's class produced a wonderful booklet of designs and did a topographical model of the site. After a long community process of committees and an endless series of meetings, we have what should be the result: the Homeless Garden project is selected as the only sanctioned development for the property. Nevertheless, the obstacles to this ever happening have been enormous, and the project is still in the planning phase many years later.

The story does not end there. Sometimes I wish it had. I still wanted to bring to fulfillment what we had begun. I wanted a corps of Chadwick Gardeners out there building organic gardens to supply families with high-quality food. I tried calling the new directors of the California Conservation Corps in succession. To no avail. I insinuated myself into a CCC annual meeting, where I gave a talk on the moral equivalent of war tradition and named all the players in the history of the theme and their contributions to make it the theme of the century. I had the impression no one understood what I was talking about. They didn't get the linkage. What did William James, whoever he was, and that German with a hyphenated name have to do with whipping ghetto kids into line out on the wilderness trail? There was no interest whatsoever in any intellectual heritage. Try selling that to university students, but not here. It fell on deaf ears. Page came along and we heard Jerry Brown give the main address, in which he acknowledged our work in starting the corps. We stood up to brief applause. That was it. We talked about it on the way home and decided that once you said "Eugen Rosenstock-Huessy" people turned off their hearing aids rather than continue getting more confused.

I kept calling. Somehow I got to the district director and he came for a visit. He turned out to be a really nice guy! Moreover, he liked my idea. He said we could write a grant to AmeriCorps, and he would be the fiscal officer, running the money through the California Conservation Corps. We could get one and a half million dollars from AmeriCorps and we could organize a crew and put organic gardens into local schools. That should have been my first clue. One and a half million dollars? And Chadwick had gone out and bought his own spade! What happened? Had I forgotten everything? Didn't I remember that when we got a government grant to run our William James Work Company practically all the money went to reporting on the money we received, a self-serving loop of wasted energy if I ever saw one.

I remembered one thing. Alan had come down to Westlake

School, my daughter's school just below the campus, and had started a garden there for the schoolchildren. I think it is still there; there was no money involved, least of all for Chadwick's time and services. And when Page and I started the William James Association, we started a community gardens program in the city for seasonal gardeners who could rent a plot on public land. Again, there was no money involved to get it going, but for a small stipend that we paid Rock Pfotenhauer to manage the project.

I had heard about the Martin Luther King Jr. Middle School's organic garden in Berkeley. It was in the Chadwick tradition and had been started by Alice Waters on a challenge from the principal of the school. She had complained how bleak the place looked. She walked by it every day on her way to work. So? Do something![3] The garden she organized turned out to be so fabulous that afterward the state superintendent of schools announced that she had a goal: to put a comparable garden in every school in the state by 2000 (which has long since passed). Good luck! No money and no delivery system. What worked for us does not transfer to a bureaucracy.

A beleaguered bureaucrat from the school nutrition department was put in charge with a part-time assistant. They were clueless. We met at a small conference organized by Sim Van der Ryn. When I told her about my interest in the mandate and my willingness to help on the basis of my experience with the Chadwick Garden, she said the state could not favor organic over synthetic as far as gardens go. I wondered if her father worked for Monsanto. Undeterred, I still thought we had the delivery system. We'd do it in Santa Cruz. With our abundant resources, it would be a demonstration of the delivery system and then take it statewide. It was an easy arithmetical extrapolation. So many schools in Santa Cruz County, so many counties in the state, times what? A million and a half seemed like a good sum to start with.

So we wrote the grant to AmeriCorps and got it. Unfortunately. The AmeriCorps program at the state level was administered by Republicans under a Republican governor. They didn't like the program. It was a Clinton idea,

in line with Kennedy's Peace Corps and Vista, going back
to that supreme Democrat, Roosevelt. They resented being saddled with it and balked at administering it, at least as
far as our proposal was concerned. They didn't like organic
gardening, following the line of the state school nutritionist.
As Republicans, they couldn't favor organic over industrial,
although they were probably pro-industrial. They didn't like
gardening because they smelled another hippie plot. Weren't
there hippies still living in Santa Cruz, only now they were
homeless, under the bridges along the San Lorenzo River?
They didn't think organic gardens in schools fitted their idea
of service. We thought that was pretty retrograde. How could
gardening be construed as community service, they wanted to
know. Will I never be free of obtuse bureaucrats? And then,
when I tried to recruit gardeners from our Homeless Garden
Project as a step up for them in pay and commitment, they
thought I was soliciting under a bridge.

Instead of assisting in the implementation of the program,
they thought up every possible obstacle. We had to deal with
a blonde woman named Circe, who was in charge of the obstacles. I knew right away we were in trouble. Every time I talked
to her, I felt like those swine her namesake had changed men
into in the *Odyssey,* even though, in this feminist day and age,
I thought turning men into swine was redundant. Anyhow,
she was impossible to work with, and I finally walked, after
struggling for a year and a half. So much for gardens in every
school! Most of the local schools said they weren't interested
anyhow—their plate was full—a favorite phrase of educators
when you make any additional demands on their time or their
imagination. And it wasn't full of organic greens, I'll tell you!

Although I'm getting old, I haven't given up. I still think a
statewide movement devoted to school gardens is possible,
although it would probably take a major crisis in the food
supply to promote it. An awareness of the encroachment of
junk foods and junk drinks in the school system has made that
crisis evident. The great example in Berkeley of the Martin
Luther King Jr. Middle School, and whatever additional gardens it inspires, is enough to know that the Chadwick legacy
is alive and well somewhere. I am reminded of this every time

I receive a newsletter from John Jeavons and Ecology Action in Willits in Northern California. John and his devoted group have carried the torch for years throughout the world.[4]

It would have been appropriate to develop profiles of a number of Chadwick apprentices to show how the work has been carried on. There are so many of them. I remember the first apprentices who joined Alan in the garden at the university—John Powell, Michael Stusser, Phil Armour, Michael Zander, Will David, Maureen, Beth, and Jim. It is a very long list, and most of their names are recorded in the list of Chadwick apprentices at the agroecology office at UCSC, a continuation of our effort to start an apprentice guild.

Chapter Twelve

A Biodynamic Garden
on Long Island

Rachel Carson, as everyone knows or ought to know, is credited with starting the environmental movement, practically single-handedly (as Rosa Parks did for the Civil Rights movement), with the publication of *Silent Spring,* which first appeared in the *New Yorker* and then as a best-selling book. Reading a recent biography, late at night, I almost fell out of bed when I read how *Silent Spring* came about and what had inspired her to write it.[1] She was good friends with a gardener, a biodynamic gardener, on Long Island. She was alerted by her friend to an issue having to do with the integrity of her garden—it was being compromised by aerial spraying of DDT, and she wanted it stopped.

The occasion that was the spark for the environmental movement was a biodynamic garden sprayed with DDT. The garden was planted and developed by Marjorie Spock, Dr. Benjamin Spock's sister. You remember him—the famous baby doctor, who advocated permissive child-rearing techniques. Marjorie, it turns out, was a passionate follower of Rudolf Steiner and had gone to Dornach, the Steiner center in Switzerland, to learn about biodynamic gardening in the Steiner tradition. She returned and applied her training to a garden site at her home on Long Island.

Then they started to spray. The local authorities, worried about gypsy moths, had hired aircraft to spray the area, sometimes multiple times a day. Marjorie was furious. Not on her biodynamic garden! She sued; she lost; she appealed; she lost; she appealed again; she lost again. The suit went to the Supreme Court, where she lost for the last time, but guess who followed the course of the suit and did the science on the ill effects of DDT—at every step of the way?

At the outset, Marjorie recruited a witness to the process who happened to be a close friend and who would take a scientific and environmental interest in every step of the campaign, as well as a deep and abiding critical interest in the damage caused by DDT, not only on a biodynamic garden, but on the entire ecosystem—especially bird populations.

You already know the answer. Marjorie called her dear friend Rachel Carson.

Silent Spring was the result.

Chapter Thirteen

Chadwick's Legacy

How does the legacy of Chadwick look from the vantage point of over forty years? Only two of the gardens remain—at UCSC and Green Gulch. Saratoga was given over to development. Covelo was abandoned long ago as a Chadwick Project. However, Steve and Gloria Decatur maintain their Live Power Community Farm as a Chadwick showplace. They have a successful community supported agriculture (CSA) program from March to December. Members in the San Francisco area pay thirty dollars a week for a basket of organic vegetables. East Harmony is long gone. Apprentices from all sites abound and a list of them is maintained and updated by the UCSC agroecology program. They gather for reunions at appropriate times.

There is a Chadwick Archive in Special Collections at UCSC's McHenry Library, which was started with the help of Carol Champion and Margaret Gordon. The Herbst Foundation gave a grant to begin the process of collecting and copying Chadwick tapes, thanks to the beneficent offices of my friend George Malloch, with a matching grant from Alan's great-nephew Richard Senior.

I had boxes and boxes of stuff in my garage and one day asked Chris Jagger, a young friend, to sift through it all and see what he could find with special reference to Chadwick material. He found dozens of letters from Alan and much of the documentary material about the development of the UCSC garden. Even Page Smith's nasty letter about our champagne reception for Alan showed up. We have slides, photos, films, and books, all to be catalogued and placed in the archive. Peter Rigg, Alan's nephew by marriage, sent me the Chadwick family lineage demonstrating the aristocratic line of Alan's ancestors and clearing up the issue of Pudleston and other large family estates. We are searching for other material. Richard Wilson has tapes, and recently Larry Herschman, a student devoted to Alan's legacy, sent me a four-hour video interview with Alan, which is painful to watch only because of his searing intensity. We hope to get whatever is out there for those who want to study the Chadwick contribution. We had great hopes at one point that Bernard Taper's proposed *New Yorker* profile of Alan would put him in the lineage of Rachel Carson's *Silent Spring* and Reich's *The Greening of America*, all *New Yorker* pieces before they became best-selling books. But Taper never finished it. He did supply the reviews of Alan's theater work in London, which are of interest, and they attest to his acting ability. They are in the Chadwick Archive at UCSC.

There is no question that Alan gave us grounds for hope in the midst of a self-destructing industrial society. He satisfied our need for roots—not an inconsiderable contribution. Some have dedicated their lives to the Chadwick lifestyle. Our own Camp Joy, a small farm and garden begun by two of Chadwick's apprentices, is one of the best local examples. It is still going strong after all these years, a small oasis in Felton, some miles up in the woods above Santa Cruz. The Flower Ladies of Santa Cruz have developed a garden of two acres with over a hundred varieties of roses, flowers, and shrubs, which they use to prepare bridal bouquets, corsages, and garlands for weddings and special occasions. They are as wonderful an example of the Chadwick legacy as I could think of. My hunch is that Santa Cruz has the highest concentration of organic farms and gardens in the country. Dennis Tamura, Alan's staunch apprentice in Covelo and longtime member of the Chadwick Garden staff at UCSC, now has Blue Heron Farm, one of the best organic farms in the area. He sells at the local farmers' markets.[1]

Now more than ever the earth hangs in the balance. In the August 20, 2002, issue of the *New York Times,* in a section under the title "Managing Planet Earth. Forget Nature. Even Eden Is Engineered" (a lovely sentiment), two articles express the divide. One is in reference to a Russian—Vladimir Vernadsky—who, it is said, argued that "people were becoming a geological force, shaping the planet's future just as rivers and earthquakes had shaped its past." He argued that "global society, guided by science, would soften the human environmental impact; earth would become a *noosphere,* a planet of the mind." Can you believe it? I never thought my garden in the mind would come out of the mouth of a Russian: "life's domain ruled by reason." To borrow the term *noosphere* from Teilhard de Chardin is untoward, as Teilhard meant something other than instrumental reason, but Marxists have always had a strong utopian element in their thought, as with Ernst Bloch and his principle of hope.

At Harvard, Dr. William Clark is leading international efforts to use scientific technology to save the environment. "Aided by satellites and supercomputers and mobilized by the evident environmental damage of the last century, he thinks humans have a real chance to begin balancing economic development with sustaining earth's ecological webs."

"We've come through a period of finally understanding the nature and magnitude of humanity's transformation of the earth," Dr. Clark said. "Having realized it, can we become clever enough at a big enough scale to be able to maintain the rates of progress? I think we can." One hundred world leaders and thousands of participants were about to meet in Johannesburg at the United Nations' World Summit on Sustainable Development. Clever enough?

In the second article in the *New York Times,* Daniel Botkin, author of *Discordant Harmonies: A New Ecology for the Twenty-first Century,* and President of the Center for the Study of the Environment at UC Santa Barbara, is quoted in reference to the Johannesburg Summit:

The good news is that there is a lot more talk about sustainability than ever. The bad news is about people doing things sustainably: nothing much has improved. People have always been profligate with resources. But the facts are clear. There aren't enough resources to go around for everybody to live at the level we in America live at. My belief is that we will not attain sustainability until we learn to love both nature and people. To love nature, you have to find a way to make a deep connection with it.

That's what Alan showed the way to: a deep connection with nature and the connection was love. I think everyone who was touched by what he transmitted would agree that he showed the way to a deep and loving connection with nature.

On Organic Monday, October 21, 2002, the government instituted "Certified Organic" labels, which has to be some kind of milestone. The Department of Agriculture instituted a new seal labeling food organic, designating produce that has been raised without conventional pesticides or fertilizers, antibiotics or growth hormones.

In an editorial on October 20, 2002, the *New York Times* observed:

Organic farming depends on the concept of the soil as a "living system." In an organic system, which relies on crop rotations, animal manures, green compost, and biological pest control, the soil grows richer and richer, more and more fertile. Organic farmers do not contaminate groundwater, nor do they create toxic runoff. Their soil doesn't blow or wash away. This stands in direct contrast to the rest of American agriculture over the past half-century: a tale of grievous erosion, poisoned wells and rivers, and an agricultural effluent that has created an enormous dead zone in the Gulf of Mexico. Buying certified organic food is a way to support the health of the soil itself.

Nora Pouillon's restaurant, Nora's, the famous organic restaurant in Washington, DC, was the first to be certified as organic. A few years ago she had a fabulous dinner to celebrate the event. Wes Jackson, of the Land Institute in Salina, Kansas, was there as a guest. Festivities are in order when such a gain has been made.

So, in spite of all the signs that look so ominous regarding the future of the earth, we hang on to hope against hope. The signs of the late stage of the self-destruction of industrial society are all around us. We read about them every day. The salvation of nature is no less inscrutable than before, but all the more longed for in the face of the predicament we share. I have just walked out into my garden on a gorgeous day, smelled the Santa Cruz ocean air (always invigorating and vitalizing), and looked at the pears and figs and apples in the late Fall; the Arkansas Black, always the last to ripen, hard as rocks. I can walk up to the Sacred Oak in the middle of Pogonip, as I will at Thanksgiving or Christmas or Easter, and conduct another service, as I have been doing for twenty-five years. It reminds me that, no matter what, creation as creation is good.

Paul Tillich, in his sermon "Man and Earth," reaches his conclusion after a triple reference to quotes:

190

THE PSALMIST

The heavens are telling the glory of God; and the firmament proclaims his handiwork. Day to day pours forth speech, and night to night declares knowledge. There is no speech, nor are there words; their voice is not heard; yet their voice goes out through all the earth, and their words to the end of the world.
—Psalm 19:1–4

THE APOSTLE

For the creation waits with eager longing for the revealing of the sons of god; for the creation was subjected to futility, not of its own will but by the will of him who subjected it in hope; because the creation itself will be set free from its bondage to decay and obtain the glorious liberty of the children of God. We know that the whole creation has been groaning in travail together until now.
—Romans 8:19–22

THE PROPHET

Then I saw a new heaven and a new earth; for the first heaven and the first earth had passed away, and the sea was no more.
—Revelation 21:1

Therefore, commune with nature! Become reconciled with nature after your estrangement from it. Listen to nature in quietness, and you will find its heart. It will sound forth the glory of its divine ground. It will sigh with us in the bondage of tragedy. It will speak of the indestructible hope of salvation!
—*Paul Tillich,* Man and Earth

The last word goes to my revered teacher in church history, at Harvard Divinity School, George Hunston Williams:

   ...we know with St. Paul that the whole creation has been in travail together with us until now. Only amidst the circumambient wilderness of tundra with its musk oxen, of the sea with its whales, the mountain fast-ness with its condor and puma, the jungle with its tiger, the woods with its warblers and crows, the veldt or prairie with its gnu and its bison, can we tend the garden and maintain our hold on life which God created and called good.
(*Wilderness and Paradise,* 136).

Alan Chadwick on *Thymus vulgaris*

When Alan introduced me to the field of medicinal herbs, I already knew he thought herbs were a key ingredient for a sophisticated cuisine. He used them generously in his cooking for meals at the garden, and grew varieties none of us had heard of. In fact, we were almost ignorant of the botanical basis of cuisine and health care in the utilization of herbs. Moreover, practically all of the herbs used for cooking also had medicinal properties. I wish I had known then that I was going to enter the herbal field a few years later with responsibilities for organizing the national industry and that Alan's influence on me would have a logical extension from flower and food production to the botanical basis of health care in the active constituents of medicinal herbs. I would have paid more attention to his knowledge.

Medicinal herbs would provide me with the best-case scenario for the decline and fall of vitalism and the rejection of organic nature in favor of the synthetic productions of the experimental laboratory. The nearly total triumph of synthetic drugs to the near exclusion of medicinal herbs in the pharmaceutical industry in the practice of medicine attests to this state of affairs.

The scientific study of medicinal herbs is a subfield of pharmacology known as pharmacognosy, which has almost disappeared as a subject matter and profession. To take the issue to its furthest extreme, compare homeopathy as strictly vitalist health care and medical practice, using herbs and minerals in inverse doses (below the level of Avogadro's Law regarding the molecular basis for drug dosage), and allopathy or industrial-society medicine dependent on synthetic drugs and extremely high doses as in millions of units of penicillin.

This contrast—practically self-cancelling, so at odds are the two systems—is one of the sharpest examples of the physicalist/vitalist conflict. Homeopathy almost disappeared from the American health scene as a result of the industrialization of medicine and the shift to synthetic prescription drugs. It has enjoyed a very minimal revival due to the herb renaissance and the interest in natural products on the part of the health consumer.

In order to provide a sample of Alan's talks I decided to include his lecture on my favorite herb—thyme, or *Thymus vulgaris.* I have had a strange history with the herb ever since finding out that *thymós* is the Greek word for "courage." I learned about *thymós* from Paul Tillich and his exposition on the word in his book *Courage To Be.* It is a Homeric term, *thymós* widely used in the *Iliad,* best exemplified by Achilles; it means "courage," "vitality," or "spirit (spirited)." Tillich traces the term through the history of Western thought and defines it as

1. the unreflective striving toward what is noble,
2. the bridge between reason and desire,
3. vital self-affirmation (or the courage to be).

It is a rich word and figures prominently in Plato, where it also represents the middle realm, the bridge between reason and desire. It drops out of favor after Descartes and is replaced by the subject/object split. Do me a favor and learn this word.

The thymus gland is just below the chin in the upper chest. The name of the gland and the herb thyme come from the same linguistic source. They both bear out the meaning of *thymós* and the association with courage and vitality. The thymus gland is the master organ of the immune system, and is our defense against illness and disease. The herb is a germicidal disinfectant (it kills germs), besides smelling and tasting good, and it is used extensively in cooking, especially in French cuisine.

I ran a restaurant in Santa Cruz in the early 1970s—The Wild Thyme. We served *ris de veau* or sweetbreads (thymus glands) as the specialty of the house. Page Smith was maître d' and our wives cooked. I went around and spoke to diners about *thymós* and the physicalist/vitalist split. Hey, it was my restaurant!

When I came across Alan's tape (I think it was Craig Siska who sent it to me), I thought Alan must have heard me talk about thyme, he was so well versed in the story of the herb, the one herb I had studied in depth. It is a good example of what Alan knew and imparted with such zeal.

The herb today is *Thymus. Thymus serpyllum* is what you would call the common wild thyme. It is a perennial; it is governed by the sun…. I'll describe the performance of the plant after talking about it…. It is a revivifier of the spirit. The Greek word, *thymós,* which is what the word *thymus* is derived from, refers to the model carriage that welcomes and does not shun crossing the threshold into the invisible world. If you take the plant sage, which gives us the word *sagacity,* here you've got a comprehensive plant related to thymus. They complement each other. Now, sage—sagacity, wisdom—continues with man throughout life into old age. Thymus is the beyond. It always is the uplifting of the world and the light and the heat of the sun. It was always used as incense in Greece and for embalming in Egypt.

It grows as an alpine plant, as a rock plant, and it grows on undulating down, if not exceptionally good drainage, except not like bogland. It's an adorer of the sun, and as you know, is very stalky, with little tiny leaves and little tiny flowers, and has this enormous relationship to the marriage of the sun for warmth and blankets created by that marriage. The fragrance is out of this world, not in it, and its use is serenity. It grows then in alpine areas over rocks, in very shallow soil, in turf amongst other plants, and is perfectly happy, is very low growing. There are several varieties of it, which we will talk a little bit about. But it is a very low-growing plant at all times and likes to grow in and for other plants. It is social. It can't bear to be topped, neither does it appreciate what you call a lot of water. And other than that, it grows anywhere from the African border of the Mediterranean up into Iceland, where it grows extremely well, and into Scandinavia and all of those mountain regions.

The garden variety is *Thymus vulgaris,* and you should put a little note to that, irregular performance, which I'll explain later. Not only does it grow from that region of the southern Mediterranean up, but it also grows extremely well in the Himalayas, anywhere from two thousand up to eight thousand feet, perfectly satisfactory and very happy.

Now the medicinal values are tremendous, as are the culinary. From a medicinal point of view, it is chiefly used from the part of the plant fresh. From the culinary point of view, it has more potency used dried. Here are performances of its virtues, a plant concerned with the world invisible beyond this world, you must realize that you must connect it somewhere with the cypress, the tree connected very much with the beyond world, and that when you do, you'll realize this is used to adorn graves, burials.

Medicinally, it is a strengthener of the lungs. It is excellent as a curer of cough, colds, and bronchials, for cramps and colic, for the digestion generally, particularly in children and rheumatics, against dizziness, against poisoning, and also in particular it is an infallible against nightmares.

The scent of thyme is used in cosmetics and is assigned in that area to nobility and bravery and to dispel fear. The oil of thyme is a hot oil. The whole plant is a heat giver, a heat creator. So the oil of thyme, thymol, is a hot oil and is made only from the leaves, and is a fast cure for toothache and headache. The ointment, which is a balm, is excellent for healing and made from the blossoms only.

In the period when they dealt with the individual and not what you call disease and illness, it was one of the great cures for melancholia.

It is extremely good for nervous people, particularly as an odor, and sheep in particular are improved enormously by feeding upon it. It is one of the supreme herbs used in the preservation of olives and one of its greatest relationships is connected with the bee, which refers us to Mount Hymettus. The whole mountain is covered with thyme. And whenever you have honey made, connected from the nectar of thyme, you have got a honey which is uplifted out of the realm of this world into the invisible, and it therefore does contain spiritual influence. And this connects with the word *love,* for Mount Hymettus was considered the Olympus, with affection, and the thyme growing there connects, of course, with Hymen. Hymen is that creature who brings two people together out of the secret invisible world, when they suddenly see each other and say "Oh!" That is Hymen. And that is connected with Hymettus, of course.

Therefore, the great magic of this particular mountain, covered with this incredible herb that lives literally in the uplift of the invisible world, that when the bees collect that nectar and when people in particular use that honey, you will perceive that they have a secret which you can't talk about. The variations on *serpyllum* and *vulgaris* are numerous, of course. We have lots of little creeping thymes that grow only very, very low, creep over the rocks. *Citriodorus* is the lemon-scented thyme, very, very much appreciated in the kitchen. Those are just some of the variations of the hundreds of varieties of thyme.

Now there's a very interesting matter concerning *serpyllum* that you see, I nominate this, as it's correct to do as a perennial. Anybody who grows thyme and watches it would see that the plant is named annual and perennial. But all of those shoots that we talk about, and you will see this vast difference on the same plant, the medicinal coming from one area and the culinary from the dried. Now you will find on *serpyllum* this extraordinary effect, that all of the growth which is green goes out along the ground and is lateral and stays along the ground, and that is perennial. But all that which comes up from the lateral and goes up toward the stars, vertical, that is annual, and that is the one that blooms. And when it has bloomed, it perishes. And that is the one that you use for the cosmetics, for the flower, but it is very distinct that you have this annual performance and perennial performance on the same plant, and that, therefore, many people think it is an annual plant and can't understand what's happened; only if you perceive what you've got to look for and look out for.

It is enormously disliked by mites. All insects, literally birds, butterflies, bees, have an adoration of this plant and the working of it. It has total effect upon atmosphere where you root it, where you know areas where it grows, the charm of sitting amongst it and the atmosphere it creates.

"... and wear their brave state out of memory."
Shakespeare, sonnet 15.

Alan Chadwick
b. 27 July 1909
d. 25 May 1980

Elizabeth Rarp
b. 11 Jan 1876 at 22 Great James St.,
London
d. 21 Sept 1942 at Canford Magna,
Poole, Dorset

"Harry" Henry Strettell Chadwick
b. 25 Aug 1847 at Parish of
St. James, Kent
d. 26 Feb 1929 at Branksome Park,
Dorset

Charlotte Rarp nee Henry George
Harrison

Elizabeth Pierce
b. 1810-1820
d. 1852

Henry Strettell
Chadwick
b. 1807
d. 29 Mar 1889 at
90 Kensington
Gardens Square,
London

Elizabeth Harrison ??
b. 1780
d. ?

Alice
Arrowsmith

Elias Chadwich
of Swinton Lancs
b. 1775
d. 1825

Unknown   William Harrison
b. 1728
d. ?

Ellen of Swinton
Lancs Strettell
b. 1738
d. 1799

Elias Chadwich
of Wigan
b. 1730
d. 1808

Elizabeth Scott   John Harrison
b. 24 Mar 1693 at
Nostell Priory,
Barrow, Yorkshire
d. 24 Mar 1776

Elias Chadwich
of Winstanley
b. 1700
d. ?

Alan Chadwick genealogy

Notes

Preface

1. E. A. Burtt, *The Metaphysical Foundations of Modern Science,* tells the story in a way that should be carved in stone.

2. Paul Tillich, *The Spiritual Situation in Our Technical Society,* 127.

3. Hans Jonas, *The Imperative of Responsibility,* 10.

4. There is a nice German word for this—*Spurensuche.*

Introduction

1. The definitive interpretation of the painting is given by Erwin Panofsky, *"Et in Arcadia Ego:* On the Conception of Transience in Poussin and Watteau," in a festschrift for Ernst Cassirer: *Philosophy and History*, ed. by Klibansky and Paton. Panofsky defines it best: "the retrospective vision of an unsurpassable happiness, enjoyed in the past, unattainable ever after, yet enduringly alive in the memory" (223). Cf. Adam Nicolson, *Arcadia: The Dream of Perfection in Renaissance England;* Peter Dawkins, *Arcadia, Studies in Ancient Wisdom,* (Francis Bacon Research Trust, 1988); Simon Schama, *Landscape and Memory,* which has a trenchant discussion of the theme. Gervase Jackson-Stopes, *"Arcadia Redesigned,"* chap. 9 in *An English Arcadia 1600–1990.*

2. Goethe, *The Italian Journey.*

3. Löwith, 3-4. My Earth Day talk (2000) encapsulates this line: "Who Killed Cock Robin?" It is available on my website: http://ecotopia.org/who-killed-cock-robin/.

4. Torchiana, *Story of the Mission Santa Cruz,* 349.

5. Cf. Ernst Cassirer, *The Problem of Knowledge.*

6. The raised bed, the double-digging, and scale of Chadwick's gardening style are reminiscent of a grave.

7. Cf. Bruno Snell, "The Discovery of a Spiritual Landscape," in *The Discovery of Mind*.

8. Paul Tillich, *The Meaning of Health*, 16.

9. Tillich, "Man and Earth," in *The Eternal Now*, 55.

10. Ibid., 60.

11. Ibid., 61.

12. Hans Jonas, *The Imperative of Responsibility*, 138.

13. This phrase "but something is missing," comes from Brecht and Weill's *The Rise and Fall of the City Mahagonny,* their operatic tour de force on the late stage of the self-destruction of industrial society. It is uttered as a cry from the depths.

14. E. A. Burtt, *The Metaphysical Foundations of Modern Science*, 90.

15. *The Meaning of Health,* 13.

16. Mircea Eliade, "The Yearning for Paradise in the Ancient Tradition" *Diogenes* 3 (June 1953).

17. Cf. Adelbert Stifter, *Witiko,* a novel about a twelfth-century knight.

Chapter One

1. In a lighthearted moment, or lightheaded, I see myself walking across the campus and suddenly, in an astral hit, I am possessed by the ghost of Rudolf Steiner. He was looking for a likely candidate, a professor of philosophy and religious studies, at a new university in California, where his biodynamics

might take root and develop as a program of organic horticulture and agriculture for the students of the New Age as a major form of spiritual renewal. My knees buckled imperceptibly. Thanks to the hit, the idea of a garden came to mind. We had our walk. Then Chadwick arrived.

2. George Hunston Williams, *Wilderness and Paradise.* I write about coming to Santa Cruz on my website, in "Oceans of Desire," http://ecotopia.org /oceans-of-desire/.

3. One of Page Smith's last books is an indictment of higher education, *Killing the Spirit.*

4. This was the title of a famous book by Simone Weil, *The Need for Roots,* who was an influence on me in her witness to the atrocities of World War II, which, in her despair, drove her to starve to death.

5. I have written a play about this, *A Lullaby for Wittgenstein,* dealing with von Moltke's discussions with Dietrich Bonhoeffer over the assassination of Hitler. Von Moltke was against it; Bonhoeffer was for it. The play was inspired by my friendship with Freya and her *Memoirs of Kreisau.* Helmuth James von Moltke's *Letters to Freya* is one of the great documents of the war, as is the *Letters and Papers from Prison,* by Bonhoeffer.

6. For an interesting account of the role of the muse in history, cf. Etienne Gilson, *The Choir of Muses.*

7. Recently an audiotape surfaced of a talk Alan gave at the "Spirit of Friendship" Conference, at Carmel-in-the-Valley in 1979. He tells a very long fairy tale about a gazelle. After listening to it together, my wife and I were at a loss as to its meaning.

8. The text of "My Georgics" appears in Norman O. Brown, *Apocalypse and/ or Metamorphosis* and also his *Closing Time.*

9. Andrea Wulf has written a charming and informative book, *Founding Gardeners: The Revolutionary Generation, Nature, and the Shaping of the American Nation. (Founding Gardeners* was published in the United Kingdom with a different subtitle, *Founding Gardeners:* How the Revolutionary Generation Created an American Eden.) She features Washington, Jefferson, Adams and Madison. Cf. also Andrea Wulf, *The Brother Gardeners: Botany, Empire, and the Birth of an Obsession,* and Andrea Wulf and Emma Gieben-Gamal, *The Other Eden: Seven Great Gardens and Three Hundred Years of English History.*

10. I am grateful to my friend, the cookbook author and food scholar William Rubel, for these concluding paragraphs on the French intensive method, as well as for his annotated edition of *The French Gardiner,* by Nicolas de Bonnefons, trans. by John Evelyn, commemorating the 350th anniversary of the first edition (1658).

Chapter Two

1. The only comparable figure I know about who initiates his readers into the mysteries of nature is Guy Murchie, whose books, though scholarly, approach Chadwick's sensibility regarding nature, albeit from a scientific point of view.

2. Patricia Unterman, "Savoring Slow Food," *San Francisco Chronicle,* December 31, 2000.

3. As a member of the Slow Food organization, I started a local chapter with Carmen Tedesco, called a Convivio. For information about membership and joining a local chapter, google "Slow Food."

4. Kazuko Masui and Tomoko Yamada, *French Cheeses,* foreword by Joël Robuchon, Eyewitness Handbooks (New York: DK Publishing, 1996).

5. For Brown's meditation on the garden, "My Georgics: A Palinode in Praise of Work," in *Apocalypse and/or Metamorphosis.*

6. John Cage, *A Year from Monday* (Middletown, CT: Wesleyan University Press, 1967).

7. For a pictorial indictment of the industrial form of food production, cf. *Fatal Harvest, The Tragedy of Industrial Agriculture,* ed. by Andrew Kimbrell.

8. Rene Descartes, *Oeuvres,* ed. Charles Adam and Paul Tannery, 314; quoted in Ron Millen, "The Manifestation of Occult Qualities in the Scientific Revolution" in *Religion, Science, and Worldview,* ed. Margaret J. Osler, 198 (Cambridge: Cambridge University Press, 2002). Huxley attributes the elimination of animism to Descartes: "the first person who gave expression to this modern view of physiology, who was bold enough to enunciate the proposition that vital phenomena, like all other phenomena of the physical world, are, in ultimate analysis, resolvable into matter and motion, was Rene Descartes..." John Merz, *A History of European Thought in the Nineteenth Century,* 2:378.

9. Paul Tillich, "Nature and Sacrament," *The Protestant Era*, 100.

10. Ibid., 104.

11. Paul Tillich, "The Freedom of Science," *The Spiritual Situation in Our Technical Society*, 62–63.

12. Cf. Hans Jonas's brilliant discussion of the Physicalist Oath, in "Impotence or Power of Subjectivity, A Reappraisal of the Psychophysical Problem," appendix to chapter 3 (3.5), *The Imperative of Responsibility*, 1981, 205ff. Julian Jaynes in *The Origins of Consciousness* mentions the oath was taken in blood. I have no idea how he knew that.

13. Hans Jonas, *The Imperative of Responsibility*, 205.

14. St. Augustine, *Confessions,* 10.16, R. S. Pine-Coffin translation.

15. Cf. Allen S. Weiss, *Mirrors of Infinity: The French Formal Garden and 17th Century Metaphysics.* And cf. Anna-Teresa Tymieniecka, *Gardens and the Passion for the Infinite*.

16. Pietro Redondi, *Galileo: Heretic,* tells the story of the atomism of Galileo as the threat to a sacramental worldview.

17. Owen Barfield, *History in English Words,* 197. Barfield is one of the foremost scholarly figures in the Steiner tradition. A quote from Merz adds to Barfield's observation, "A popular philosophy founded upon the unknown principle of matter, and the equally unknown and even less clear principle of force, promulgated the notion that science had succeeded in banishing all spiritual entities, and was able to explain everything on purely mechanical principles. Vitalism and animism were at an end; there only remained mechanism and materialism." Merz, 2:399.

18. Cf. Edward Espe Brown, *The Tassajara Bread Book*.

19. Cf. Deborah Madison, *The Greens Cookbook*.

20. Heraclitus is a good reference for a number of points. "The name of the bow (bios) is life (bios), but its work is death" (B48). Heraclitus also acted out the significance of compost when he buried himself in cow dung to demonstrate how consciousness is a product of spontaneous combustion, although the tradition has it that it was to cure dropsy. When I went on a retreat with Alan and my friends the von Eckartsbergs in the Trinity Alps, above Covelo,

and drank of the wilderness waters, I understood what Heraclitus meant when he said you can't step in the same river twice, meaning the vitality of wilderness waters makes them unique at every step Unfortunately, since then, these waters are contaminated and unfit to drink. It was a sight to behold when we all took off our clothes and held them over our heads when we had to ford the Eel River, to get to Richard Wilson's cabin, hoping not to slip and be carried away by the swift current. Alan averted his eyes and acted embarrassed.

21. For the quasi-bodily basis of conceptual terms for consciousness in Homer, cf. Bruno Snell, *The Discovery of Mind*. For a full-blown account of *thymós* in the history of Western thought, cf. Tillich, *The Courage To Be*.

22. Paul Tillich, *The Courage To Be,* 78.

Chapter Three

1. Robert Pogue Harrison, *Forests: The Shadow of Civilization,* 28.

2. Rosenstock-Huessy, "Liturgical Thinking," from *The Rosenstock-Huessy Papers,* vol. 1. Cf. also Robert Pogue Harrison, *Gardens: An Essay on the Human Condition.*

3. Husserl is the absolute master of this discussion. He is the primary critic of physicalism as the crisis of European science. "Galileo, ... a discovering and a concealing genius. He discovers mathematical nature, the methodical idea, he blazes the trail for the infinite number of physical discoveries and discoverers. By contrast to the universal causality of the intuitively given world (as its invariant form), he discovers what has since been called simply the law of causality, the 'a priori form' of the 'true' (idealized and mathematized) world, the 'law of exact lawfulness' according to which every occurrence in 'nature'—idealized nature—must come under exact laws. All this is discovery-concealment, and to the present day we accept it as straightforward truth. In principle nothing is changed by the supposedly philosophically revolutionary critique of the 'classical law of causality' made by recent atomic physics. For in spite of all that is new, what is essential in principle, it seems to me, remains: namely, nature, which is in itself mathematical; it is given in formulae, and it can be interpreted only in terms of the formulae." *The Crisis,* 53. Heidegger continues the discovery/concealment theme in his interpretation of the Greek meaning of truth, *aletheia,* which he translates as "unconcealment." This development of Husserl's critique of Galileo and its meaning for modern science and technology in Heidegger's work on *aletheia* has not been clearly seen. It is important for the epistemological consequences of the Cartesian *cogito* and the mentality of the physicalist scientist. It would have to be shown how mathematics is implicated in this dissimulation. Cf., *The Ethics of Geometry*. The point is that Galileo obscures what he reveals; he is guilty, in this account, of occultation! I have pursued Husserl partly as a result of my association with the chaos mathematician, Ralph Abraham, who motivated me through our interest in John Dee, the Elizabethan magus, who introduced Euclid to British students of mathematics, as well as Abraham's Euclid Project to study the history and philosophy of mathematics in order to understand the "turn" taken by Galileo as the beginning of the defeat of vitalism. In this sense, vitalism is not only the argument in behalf of the integrity of organic nature, it is the defense against the Galilean reduction of nature to mathematical physics. This point is little understood by the critics of vitalism.

4. John Merz gives an overview of the conflict in his *A History of European Thought in the Nineteenth Century,* 4 vols. This is an indispensable source.

5. There is a running debate on the synthesis of urea and the defeat of vitalism in the *Journal of Chemical Education*. McKie's article in this journal made a big splash when he debunks the urea legend as if to remove the embarrassment of a smoking gun in the death of vitalism. I hope to organize *A Urea Reader* at some point and feature those articles.

Chapter Four

1. B. J. T. Dobbs, "Newton's Alchemy and His Theory of Matter,*" Isis* 73 (1982). Hume continues this philosophical reflection on primary and secondary qualities. Cf. F. A. Paneth, "The Epistemological Status of the Chemical Concept of Element," 2 parts, *The British Journal of the Philosophy of Science* 13 (1962).

2. Hans Jonas, *The Phenomenon of Life,* 9–10.

3. E. A. Burtt, *The Metaphysical Foundations of Modern Science,* 90.

4. Armytage is the best reference for this history of European gardens and the relation of botany and the other sciences. Cf. *The Rise of the Technocrat*. He credits John Tradescant with the transformation of the herb to the botanic garden proper, the best known of the Guild of Gardeners, chartered in 1606.

5. John Prest, *The Garden of Eden*. This is one of the best books I have read on the subject, as though written for me. The book you are holding is an attempt to return the favor. Simon Schama sums up the theme: "Some years ago John Prest, in a beautiful and brilliant study, explained that the creators of those gardens were driven by the desire to re-create the botanical totality of Eden. The walled-in paradise had, of course, been the standard form of the monastic garden, where Cistercian monks, for example, were each given their own little allotment of Eden to tend. But the exploration of the New World, with the discovery of a marvelous range of hitherto unknown species, had created a rich new topography of paradise. Eden, it was speculated, not least by Columbus himself, might be in the southern hemisphere. If these wonders of the tropics and the Orient could be shipped home, collected, named, and arranged within the confines of the botanical garden at Padua or Paris or Oxford, an exhaustive, living encyclopedia of creation could be assembled that would again testify to the stupendous ingenuity of the Creator." *Landscape and Memory*, 537.

6. Francis Bacon thought of the botanic garden as a seedbed of science. He lays down the view for the future: "Nature cannot be conquered by obeying her. Accordingly these twin goals, human science and human power, come to an end in action. To be ignorant of causes is to be frustrate in action." Quoted in Armytage, 17.

7. "The Historic Roots of Our Ecologic Crisis," *Science* (1967). It should be obvious that my view is quite contrary, putting the blame at the throne of scientism and the physicalist/reductionist/positivist trend with the focus on matter to the neglect of organic nature except for purposes of exploitation.

8. It is interesting to think that the wilderness theme, prior to the ambiguity of the garden, as cultivated wilderness, the scene of the Fall, is symbolically appropriate to the first creation account, i.e., wilderness equals original creation and the unambiguous affirmation. This distinction pertains to the debate over the role of human beings in the realm of nature and the mistake

made by nature to bring forth humans. Martin Buber opened my eyes to this reading of Genesis in his wonderful essay "Abraham the Seer," *Commentary* (1947). Eric Voegelin discusses it in his magisterial study of the Old Testament, *Israel and Revelation,* and G. H. Williams continues the meditation in his already mentioned *Wilderness and Paradise*. It was the Voegelin account that I referred Williams to when he was working on his book. Cf. also the fine study by Paul Ricoeur: *The Symbolism of Evil*. Ricoeur, more than anyone, has held the line on the unambiguous goodness of the original affirmation. Cf. his discussion of original sin in *Conflicts in Interpretation*. It turns on the misleading term *original.* As Kierkegaard said, sin presupposes itself.

9. John Prest, *The Garden of Eden*, 27.

10. "That the term 'plant' should be used today for a chemical engineering works has a fine historical implication." Armytage, 62. He details the development of chemistry within botanic gardens and mentions H. M. Rouelle, who isolated urea from urine, anticipating Woehler's synthesis.

11. Goethe probably took a hike because the Duke of Weimar piled on responsibilities, as Herder details to Hamann in a letter, "He is ... at present time Working Privy Councillor, President of the Chamber, President of the War College, Superintendent of Construction, including road building, in addition *Directeur des Plaisirs*, Court Poet, arranger of beautiful festivities, court operas, ballets, masked balls and pageants, inscriptions, art works, etc., Director of the Drawing Academy, in which he last winter gave lectures in osteology, himself everywhere the leading actor, dancer, in short the factotum of Weimer..." Quoted by Gordon Craig, "Germany's Greatest," *The New York Review of Books* (April 13, 2000), 54–55.

12. Goethe quoting Schiller. cf. Heisenberg, "Goethe's View of Nature and Science" in *Across the Frontiers*. It is of great importance to notice the holistic thinking of Goethe vs. the technical, mathematical thinking of Newton. Two discrete epistemologies and methodologies are involved, 87.

13. Ernst Cassirer, *The Problem of Knowledge,* 137.

14. The designation of the *Urpflänze* is something of a floater. The Paduan Palm is as good a candidate as any given the symbolism of the palm but it is more of a projection than a correct identification. It is thought that Goethe saw one in the botanic garden in Palermo as he meditated on the *Odyssey.* I have given a talk on this in commemorating the two hundredth anniversary of the *Italian Journey,* and it is included in the festschrift for Frank Barron, *Unusual Fellows,* ed. by Montuori. Jack Stauffacher of the Greenwood Press produced a stunning handset broadside for the occasion of the talk (see p. 15). The talk is available on my website, www.ecotopia.org.

15. For me, the key to Goethe's perception is to be found in Homeric similes. There the cohesion of metaphors, in an interpretive nexus, provides the unifying principle. Henri Bortoft, *The Wholeness of Nature: Goethe's Way toward a Science of Conscious Participation in Nature.* Cf. Paul Tillich, "Participation and Knowledge: Problems of an Ontology of Cognition," *The Spiritual Situation in Our Technical Society*, ed. by J. Mark Thomas. Bruno Snell discusses the role of comparison in Homer in his *Discovery of Mind*. And the best essay on Homeric similes is Kurt Riezler, "Homer's Contribution to the Meaning of Truth," *Philosophy and Phenomenological Research* 3, no. 3 (March 1943): 326ff.

16. Erich Heller, *The Disinherited Mind*.

17. Martin Heidegger, *Kant and the Problem of Metaphysics*. I went into the

herbal industry after my university career went kaput, and I exercised my fascination for the herb thyme, derived from *thymós*. I opened a restaurant in Santa Cruz called The Wild Thyme. I plan to write a cookbook to spoof Heidegger, with the title *Being and Thyme,* with thyme as the vital root Heidegger was looking for, growing right under his nose in the Black Forest.

18. I know that this vital root theme is tied up with the romantic movement and especially its effect in scientific inquiry. There is a straight line from Goethe to Blake on this theme. Cf. Marjorie Hope Nicholson, *Newton Demands the Muse: Newton's Opticks and the Eighteenth Century Poets* and Frederick Burwick, *The Damnation of Newton: Goethe's Color Theory and Romantic Perception.* "As presage of the Romantic denunciation of science, she (Nicholson) cited the poetry of William Blake. His aggressive anti-Newtonianism she finds, among other examples, in his annotation to the Laocoon: 'Art is the Tree of Life. Science is the Tree of Death.' In Nicholson's judgment, 'William Blake presided at the poetic damnation of Sir Isaac Newton.' Blake's opposition to 'Newton's Sleep,' however, cannot be aggrandized into a Romantic rejection of science. Blake, after all, had great company, scientists and poets alike, in the growing anti-Newtonian controversy. For Blake, and for most of the Romantics, the foe was materialism not scientific inquiry.... If there was a poet of the age who 'presided at the poetic damnation of Sir Isaac Newton,' that poet was Goethe." Burwick, *The Damnation of Newton,* 8.

19. I remember reading about Heisenberg and Bohr laughing over the rejection of metaphysics by the squeamish positivists when they accepted meta-logic and meta-linguistics and meta-anything-else.

20. Tillich's essays are collected in *The Spiritual Situation in Our Technical Society*, ed. J. Mark Thomas. Cf. the discussion of "tools" and "things" on 118.

21. Ibid., 82.

22. Voegelin is the sharpest critic of the antispiritualist character of the scientist revolt. It informs all of his authorship. His sharpest attack is his "The Origins of Scientism," *Social Research* 15, 462–94. For a brilliant account of Voegelin's views, cf. Barry Cooper, *Eric Voegelin and the Foundations of Modern Political Science*. For Voegelin's critique of Saint-Simon and Comte, cf. *From Enlightenment to Revolution*.

23. Frederick Hayek, *The Counter-Revolution of Science*.

24. John Weiss, *The Making of Technological Man: The Social Origins of French Engineering Education*.

25. Everett Mendelsohn, *Revolution and Reduction, The Sociology and Methodological Concerns in Nineteenth Century Biology,* 415.

26. Ibid., 135.

27. Armytage, *The Rise of the Technocrat,* 37–38.

28. Hence the classic study by Andrew Dickson White, *A History of the Warfare of Science with Theology*.

29. "Excepting in medicine and at a few military schools, scientific education scarcely existed before the foundation of the École Polytechnique in the last decade of the eighteenth century. The model spread rapidly, however, first to Germany, then to the United States, and finally, more equivocally, to England. With it developed other new institutional forms, especially teaching and research laboratories, like Justus von Liebig's at Giessen or the Royal College of Chemistry in London. These are the developments that first made possible and then supported what had previously scarcely existed, the professional

scientific career. Like a potentially applicable science, they emerged relatively suddenly and quickly. Together with the maturation of the Baconian sciences of the seventeenth century, they are the pivot of a second scientific revolution which centered in the first half of the nineteenth century, a historical episode at least as crucial to an understanding of modern times as its older namesake. It is time it found its way into history books, but it is too much a part of other developments in the nineteenth century to be untangled by historians of science alone." Thomas Kuhn, "History and the History of Science," *The Essential Tension*. For Hayek's splendid account, cf. "The Source of the Scientistic Hubris: L'École Polytechnique," in *The Counter-Revolution of Science*.

30. Hayek, "The Source of the Scientistic Hubris: L'École Polytechnique," in *The Counter-Revolution of Science,* 196, 202–3.

31. Lewis Mumford, "The Organic World Picture," *The Pentagon of Power*, 385.

32. Michael Pollan gives a succinct account of Howard and King in his *Omnivore's Dilemma,* 145–51, as well as the work of Fritz Haber and his work in fixing nitrogen. Cf. Vaclav Smil, *Enriching the Earth: Fritz Haber, Carl Bosch, and the Transformation of World Food Production*. He calls Haber's work (Carl Bosch commercialized it) the most important invention of the twentieth century. In his Global Catastrophes and Trends, Smil writes, "Only 25%–40% of all fertilizer nitrogen applied to crops is taken up by plants; the rest is lost to leaching, erosion, volatilization and denitrification. Because the photosynthesis of many aquatic ecosystems is limited by the availability of nitrogen, an excessive influx of this nutrient (eutrophication) leached from fertilizers promotes abundant growth of algae and phytoplankton. Subsequent decomposition of this phytomass deoxygenates water and reduces or kills aquatic species, particularly bottom dwellers," 202. Pollan puts it in perspective: "When humankind acquired the power to fix nitrogen, the basis of soil fertility shifted from a total reliance on the energy of the sun to a new reliance on fossil fuel," 44.

33. Hans Jonas, *The Phenomenon of Life,* 12.

34. Paul Ricoeur, in his *Freud and Philosophy,* which I had the pleasure to help edit, characterizes the split as that between energetics and hermeneutics, his version of my physicalist/vitalist conflict. For Ricoeur it was a conflict between a play of forces versus a play of meanings in the pursuit of a philosophy of culture. The fate of psychoanalysis and the dispute over its being a science hangs on this split as does the quandary over the meaning of human consciousness.

35. E. R. Curtius, *European Literature and the Latin Middle Ages*, 240.

36. Ibid., 240.

Chapter Five

1. I remember a cocktail party conversation where a chemist told me that as far as chemistry was concerned artificial didn't *really* mean artificial and synthetic didn't *really* mean synthetic. He meant they were technical terms abstracted from their common meaning. I asked him if he wanted another drink. This is reminiscent of another brief encounter that occurred on a boat trip through Hong Kong harbor on the way back from China. I was talking to a remarkably handsome and impressive physicist from Georgia Tech (no rambling wreck he). I asked him about Enrico Fermi's worry over the wayward reaction when he smashed the atom in Chicago and that the world might be destroyed as a result. The physicist said there was no such thing as a wayward

reaction, it was just atoms colliding. Nothing unusual. No need to worry. I thought of Oppenheimer quoting the Bhagavad Gita, after the bomb was exploded: "We have become death. We are the destroyers of worlds."

2. The French critic, Baudrillard, carries on the most extreme and yet instructive discussion of this confusion. Cf. his *Simulacra and Simulations.*

3. Kerner von Merilaum, cited in Merz, 2:376.

4. Cf. *An Awareness of What Is Missing: Faith and Reason in a Post-Secular Age*, Jürgen Habermas, Michael Reder, and Josef Schmidt. Also, Ernst Bloch, *The Utopian Function of Art and Literature, "Something's Missing: A Discussion between Ernst Bloch and Theodor W. Adorno on the Contradictions of Utopian Longing."* Google *Paul Tillich: The Right To Hope.*

5. Bernard Jaffe, *Lives of Great Chemists,* 154–55.

6. Jacques Loeb as quoted in Cassirer, *The Problem of Knowledge,* 207.

7. Paul Tillich, "The World Situation," in *The Spiritual Situation in Our Technical Society,* 6.

8. Ibid., 6.

9. Ibid., 6ff.

10. To date the end of the Protestant era, I refer to the execution of Bonhoeffer, April 9, 1945. His *Letters From Prison* is the epitaph. Tillich's first collection of essays was to be titled "The End of the Protestant Era?" He was talked out of it, but there is an essay with that title in *The Protestant Era.*

11. Hans Jonas, *The Phenomenon of Life,* 36.

12. Countering this trend, Stanford University has added a program in compassion and altruism, partly funded by the Dalai Lama.

13. Cf. Frank Donoghue, *The Last Professors: The Corporate University and the Fate of the Humanities.*

14. Hans Jonas, *The Phenomenon of Life*, 37.

15. Ibid., 37.

16. Ibid., 37–38.

17. Ibid., 38.

18. Paul Tillich, *The Spiritual Situation in Our Technical Society*, 26.

19. Adolf Meyer: see Cassirer, *The Problem of Knowledge*, 208.

20. In technical Kantian terminology this is an antinomy of judgment, as though physicalism and vitalism were the antinomy: mechanism without purpose or purpose without mechanism. It was the conflict of cause and form. As a logician Kant wanted to make the point clear and he accomplished this to the disadvantage of vitalism in his celebrated distinction between regulative and constitutive principles, a distinction in value between two sorts of concepts. Causal concepts are constitutive—they cut the mustard, just as they "count" for knowledge; formal concepts are regulative, merely regulative, inasmuch as purpose or form is only an "idea" or a "heuristic maxim."

21. Mark Walker, *Nazi Science.* Anna Bramwell, *Ecology in the 20th Century* is the place to find out about the Nazi interest in biodynamics largely on the part of Rudolf Hess.

22. Tillich addressed the German nation in over one hundred radio talks during the war unmasking and denouncing the mutilated, self-destroying vitality united with bestiality and absurdity that was Nazism. They are a triumph of spiritual sympathy and solicitude. Paul Tillich, *Against the Third Reich: Paul Tillich's Wartime Radio Broadcasts into Nazi Germany.*

23. Tillich, *The Spiritual Situation in Our Technical Society,* 128.

24. Tillich, "The World Situation," in *The Spiritual Situation in Our Technical Society,* 12.

25. Tillich, "How Has Science in the Last Century Changed Man's View of Himself?" in *The Spiritual Situation in Our Technical Society,* 82.

26. Ibid., 3:18ff.

27. Ibid., 1:19.

28. Ibid., 1:19.

29. Susan Freinkel, *Plastic, A Toxic Love Story*. "Plastics freed us from the confines of the natural world, from the material constraints and limited supplies that had long bounded human activity," 14.

30. Merz, 2:377.

31. Stuart A. Kauffman, *The Origins of Order: Self-Organization and Selection in Evolution*, quoted in Theodore Roszak, "Nature and Nature's God," *Alexandria* 5, 115.

32. Cf. Freud's Project in the letters to Fliess, *The Origins of Psychoanalysis*, ed. Masson. It is reviewed by Karl Pribram and Morton Gill, *Freud's Project Reassessed: Preface to Contemporary Cognitive Theory and Neuropsychology*.

33. Francis Crick, *Astonishing Hypothesis: The Scientific Search for the Soul*.

34. Merz gives a number of examples of chemists eliminating vitalism, as though to line up and then readmitting it after brushing it off and combing its hair. "Virchow, in 'Old and New Vitalism' returns the word after its banishment: 'I see no objection to designating this force…(an impressed derived force in addition to the molecular force)…by the old name of vital force.'" Merz, 2:377.

35. Rudolf Steiner, *The Origins of Natural Science*, 113.

36. Quoted in Jonas, *The Phenomenon of Life*, 203. On LaPlace and the significance of mathematics as the solution for everything: "It seemed time to abandon the familiar conception of a special vital force, and to hand over the physiological problems likewise to the physicist, the chemist, and the microscopist. A crusade was accordingly started in Germany by philosophers, as well as by naturalists and biologists against the vitalists—those who believed in a special principle of life; and an impression was created in the minds of thinking outsiders that a purely mechanical explanation of life and mind was finally decided on, and within possible reach." He cites Lotze. (Merz, 2:400).

The work of Henri Atlan came to my attention just as I was reading the proofs of this book, thanks to my friend Rolf Pixley, and has turned out to be an excellent counterfoil to my point of view. Atlan is a self-avowed physicalistic reductionist, but one who knows what is given up in the rejection of vitalism. I never thought I would encounter the following quote from Albert Szent-Gyorgi, which Atlan features in his book as an epigram: "Life as such does not exist." Atlan comments, "This does not mean our subjective and linguistic experience of life, which is opposed to death, of course, but life as an object of inquiry or as a concept with some explanatory value in modern biology. Even though they are still called the 'life sciences,' these fields of research no longer seek to understand the nature of some entity or essence known as 'life,' but the mechanisms by which certain compound physical bodies assemble themselves, grow, reproduce, and die…. these disciplines could equally be called the 'death sciences'—the study of the death of organized physical objects." *The Sparks of Randomness,* trans. Lenn Schramm, vol. 1, Spermatic Knowledge (Stanford, CA: Stanford University Press, 2011), 92. According to

Atlan, contemporary biology, based on the mechanistic model of physics and chemistry, has vanquished the vitalism that depended on the concept of life.

Chapter Six

1. George Hunston Williams, *The Radical Reformation*.
2. "The End of the Protestant Era," in *The Protestant Era*, 232–33. Tillich experienced this himself in his work with Selfhelp, a nonprofit that helped émigrés from Europe.

Chapter Seven

1. Meyer and Smith, *Paris in a Basket*, foreword by Paul Bocuse. The Raspail Market in the 7th Arrondissement of Paris is devoted to organic produce. Biodynamic produce is a centerpiece under the denomination "Demeter": "Bio-dynamic is an agricultural process that follows the same basic principles as organic production but also uses a stellar calendar indicating the best days for planting and harvesting. Initiated by the German philosopher, Rudolf Steiner, in the 1920s, organic methods of cultivation respect the natural harmony of the land. Bio-dynamic takes these principles a step farther, by using the many forces that exist in the cosmos, beginning with the rotation of the sun and the seasons. For example, the morning, which represents spring, is the best time for sowing the fields and for germination, while the evening, which represents autumn, is the best time for the seedlings to be planted and to take root. The land is also homeopathically treated with minute doses of plant extracts to help it renourish itself and fight against the many pollutants that surround us. This very complex and sophisticated method is closely linked to the constellations of the zodiac and follows the traditional methods of crop rotation, composting, and pollination used in organic farming. Bio-dynamic agricultural practices are internationally recognized" 65. I am grateful to Frank DeWinter for showing me this book.
2. Cf. Frederick Burwick and Paul Douglass, *The Crisis in Modernism: Bergson and the Vitalist Controversy.*
3. Rudolf Steiner, *The Riddles of Philosophy*. For a glance at the literature and the many titles of Steiner's work in print, look him up on www.amazon.com. There are a number of works by Steiner on Goethe as philosopher and scientist. As the cofounder of the John Dee Society with Ralph Abraham, I can't help mentioning John Dee as a precursor to Steiner. Dee, the philosopher to Queen Elizabeth I, is one of the most important neglected figures in the history of Western culture, largely due to his angel conjuring, which buried him, comparable to Steiner's clairvoyance and esotericism, isolating him from mainstream scholarship. Francis Yates is responsible for recovering Dee and Nicholas Clulee's *John Dee's Natural Philosophy,* is the best review of his life and work with a magnificent bibliography.
4. In this morning's paper an article tells the story of a group trying to get federal funding withdrawn from Waldorf Schools because they were started by Steiner who had a weird philosophy and was the founder of a cult.
5. Goethe, *The Metamorphosis of Plants*; Rudolf Steiner, *Nature's Open Secret;* Henri Bortoft, *The Wholeness of Nature;* Ernst Lehrs, *Man or Matter*.
6. For an excellent review of the conflict, cf. Frederick Burwick, *The Damnation of Newton.*
7. Steiner, *The Riddles of Philosophy,* 54.

8. Ibid., 54.

9. For the best overview of existentialism, cf. Paul Tillich, *Theology of Culture*.

10. "The very word 'system' is perhaps symptomatic of our short-sightedness. If the schools are allowed to form a 'system' by themselves as all the rest of our social entities are allowed to do—corporations, professions, unions—we cannot be surprised that they all cease to function as one living universe. Life is no system; it is even less a mere agglomeration of school systems and business systems, all kept apart." Rosenstock-Huessy, "Teaching Too Late, Learning Too Early," in *I Am an Impure Thinker,* 106.

11. For a critical discussion of Kuhn and his relation to logical positivism, cf. Steve Fuller, *Thomas Kuhn: A Philosophical History for Our Times*.

12. Orin Martin, "French Intensive Gardening: A Retrospective," in *News and Notes of the UCSC Farm and Garden* 112 (Winter 2007).

Chapter Eight

1. Maria Rodale, Organic Style (November/December 2002), 16.

2. Wendell Berry, *The Unsettling of America: Culture and Agriculture*.

3. Wendy Johnson, *Gardening at the Dragon's Gate: At Work in the Wild and Cultivated World,* 37–38.

4. John Muir is included in our Ecology Hall of Fame website at http://ecotopia.org/ecology-hall-of-fame/john-muir/.

5. Wendy Johnson, *Gardening at the Dragon's Gate: At Work in the Wild and Cultivated World,* 38.

6. Ted Simon, *The River Stops Here: How One Man's Battle to Save His Valley Changed the Fate of California*.

7. Ibid., 341.

8. Page Smith, *A People's History of the United States*, 8 vols.

9. Cf. Page Smith and Charles Daniel, *The Chicken Book: Being an Inquiry into the Rise and Fall, Use and Abuse, Triumph and Tragedy of Gallus Domesticus*.

Chapter Nine

1. Rose Hayden-Smith, *Soldiers of the Soil: A Historical Review of the United States School Garden Army, 2006*.

2. That's how I first heard it. In his letters, he says he said, "Now, go it!" *Letters of William James,* 1:248.

3. Paul Edwards has written the definitive review of Popper-Lynkeus in the *Encyclopedia of Philosophy*. In 1906 William James was the first to issue the call for a volunteer force in the name of the moral equivalent of war. Popper-Lynkeus did so in 1912, although he wrote about such matters as far back as 1878. I make use of Popper-Lynkeus's formulation of a moral social philosophy and the sanctity of human life in my book on homelessness in Santa Cruz: *The Quality of Mercy*. It is available on my website, http://ecotopia.org/the-quality-of-mercy-homelessness-in-santa-cruz-1985-1992.

4. The story is told by Jack Preiss, *Camp William James* (Norwich, VT: Argo Books, 1978). I remember asking Rosenstock-Huessy about Popper-Lynkeus and whether he knew of his work. He said yes, he knew about him, and that he had himself also assumed the name of the Argo expedition in search of the Golden Fleece, calling his group the Argonauts and Argo the name of his press, a coincidence I still find flabbergasting.

5. H. J. N. Horsburgh, *Non-Violence and Aggression: A Study of Gandhi's Moral*

Equivalent of War. My essay on the subject and my portfolio illustrating the theme are found on my website, www.ecotopia.org.

6. The first project of the William James Association was to organize a Land Reform Conference at the Civic Auditorium in Santa Cruz, which seats almost two thousand people. Only the speakers I invited attended. Fortunately, there were a couple dozen. They listened to one another. I thought Land Reform was the Next Big Thing in the wake of Rees Tijerina and the presidential bid of Fred Harris. I was wrong. It did lead me to setting up the first land trust in the state: The Northern California Land Trust, which helped fund our Greenbelt Initiative for Santa Cruz. Measure O passed in 1979 and preserved hundreds of acres in Open Space. I was right about that.

7. "This dissociation [from a God-forsaken institution], however, is more easily formulated than achieved because no social space or field exists outside the powers that be, and the existing institutions are all there is at the moment of one's metanoia, of one's giving up their dead works.... It takes a lifetime and longer to extricate oneself from the established institutions and to find new ways of establishing some less corrupt forms of expression for the living faith." Eugen Rosenstock-Huessy, "Metanoia: To Think Anew," *I Am an Impure Thinker*, 189.

8. Eugen Rosenstock-Huessy, *I Am an Impure Thinker,* 110.

Chapter Ten

1. E. F. Schumacher was famous for his popular book *Small Is Beautiful*. His word carried considerable weight, as he had been head of the Soil Association of Great Britain.

2. Ibid., 39–40.

Chapter Eleven

1. Quoted on the frontispiece of *Camp William James*, by Jack Preiss.

2. I tell the story of our homeless effort in *The Quality Of Mercy,* available at http://ecotopia.org/the-quality-of-mercy-homelessness-in-santa-cruz-1985-1992.

3. Alice Waters, *Edible Schoolyard: A Universal Idea.*

4. John Jeavons, *How To Grow More Vegetables Than You Ever Thought Possible on Less Land Than You Can Imagine.*

Chapter Twelve

1. Linda Lear, *Rachel Carson*: *Witness for Nature.*

Chapter Thirteen

1. An oral history is available from UCSC, McHenry Library, of Dennis Tamura's relation to Chadwick at UCSC and Covelo. Craig Siska and a number of associates, many of whom are former Chadwick apprentices, are enthusiastically at work gathering every piece of Alan's legacy for the creation of the Chadwick Archive, which will be made available to everyone interested.

Bibliographies are my passion. I would rather read them than the book. Footnotes next. They constitute the scholarly apparatus and give you a sense of the authors' reliance on the sources at their disposal. Not all readers will be interested in this disclosure of sources. But I write, as well, for a scholarly and student audience who might want to pursue any of the lines of thought developed here. It is meant primarily for the student who is intent on reading further, and also to give the evidence for the line of thought to the critical reader. That's one of the great aspects of this theme, the literature is there and to be utilized, documenting the historical process and its meaning. Follow the dots, there is a book at every point, adding that jigsaw piece to the puzzle. It is gratifying when they all fall into place.

What follows is a selection of books that have meant the most to me over the years in my pursuit of what the garden has meant to me and what I have learned from it. It is a bibliography of the garden in the mind.

Altieri, Miguel. *Agroecology: The Science of Sustainable Agriculture.* Boulder, CO: Westview Press, 1995.

Armytage, W. G. H. *The Rise of the Technocrat: A Social History.* London: Routledge and Kegan Paul, 1965.

Barfield, Owen. *History in English Words.* London: Faber and Faber, 1953.

Barrell, John. *The Idea of Landscape and the Sense of Place, 1730–1840: An Approach to the Poetry of John Clare.* Cambridge: Cambridge University Press, 1972.

Belasco, Warren. *Appetite for Change: How the Counterculture Took on the Food Industry, 1966–1988.* New York: Pantheon, 1989.

Bloch, Ernst. *The Utopian Function of Art and Literature: Selected Essays.* Translated by Jack Zipes and Frank Mecklenberg. Cambridge, MA: MIT Press, 1988.

Bonhoeffer, Dietrich. *Letters and Papers from Prison.* Edited by Eberhard Bethge. Translated by Reginald H. Fuller. London: Collins Fontana Books, 1953.

Bortoft, Henri. *The Wholeness of Nature: Goethe's Way toward a Science of Conscious Participation in Nature.* Hudson, NY: Lindisfarne Press, 1996.

Bramwell, Anna. *Ecology in the 20th Century.* New Haven, CT: Yale University Press, 1989.

Brown, Norman O. *Apocalypse and/or Metamorphosis.* Berkeley: University of California Press, 1991.

————. *Closing Time.* New York: Random House, 1973.

Burtt, Edwin Arthur. *The Metaphysical Foundations of Modern Science.* New York: Dover, 2003.

Burwick, Frederick. "The Damnation of Newton: Goethe's Color Theory and Romantic Perception." *German Studies Review* 12, no. 2 (May 1989).

Burwick, Frederick, and Paul Douglass. *The Crisis in Modernism: Bergson and the Vitalist Controversy.* New York: Cambridge University Press, 1992.

Cage, John. *A Year from Monday: New Lectures and Writings.* Middletown, CT: Wesleyan University Press, 1967.

Carson, Rachel. *Silent Spring.* Boston: Houghton Mifflin, 1962; Cambridge, MA: Riverside Press, 1962; London: Hamish Hamilton, 1962; Cutchogue, NY: 1994.

Cassirer, Ernst. *The Problem of Knowledge: Philosophy, Science, and History since Hegel.* New Haven, CT: Yale University Press, 1950 and 1978.

Chadwick, Alan. *Performance in the Garden: A Collection of Talks on Biodynamic French Intensive Horticulture.* Edited by Stephen J. Crimi. With a foreword by John Jeavons. Mars Hill, NC: Logospohia Press, 2007.

Channell, David. *The Vital Machine: A Study of Technology and Organic Life.* New York: Oxford University Press, 1991.

Charlesworth, M., ed. *The English Garden: Literary Sources and Documents.* Mountfield, UK: Helm Publishing, 1993.

Childs, Gilbert. *Rudolf Steiner: His Life and Work.* Edinburgh, Scotland: Floris Books, 1995; Hudson, NY: Anthroposophic Press, 1996.

Crick, Francis. *Astonishing Hypothesis: The Scientific Search for the Soul.* New York: Charles Scribner and Sons, 1994.

Cuthbertson, Tom. *Alan Chadwick's Enchanted Garden.* New York: Dutton, 1978.

Dawkins, Peter. *Arcadia: Studies in Ancient Wisdom.* Northampton, UK: Francis Bacon Research Trust, 1988.

Dézallier d'Argenville, Antoine-Joseph. *The Theory and Practice of Gardening.* Translated by John James. London: Geo. James, 1712.

Dijksterhuis, E. J. *The Mechanization of the World Picture.* New York: Oxford University Press, 1961 and 1969.

Dobbs, Betty Jo Teeter. *The Foundations of Newton's Alchemy; or, "The Hunting of the Green Lyon."* Cambridge: Cambridge University Press, 1975.

Donoghue, Frank. *The Last Professors: The Corporate University and the Fate of the Humanities*. New York: Fordham University Press, 2008.

Elul, Jacques. *The Technological Society.* New York: Vintage Books, 1965.

Fink, Karl J. *Goethe's History of Science.* Cambridge: Cambridge University Press, 1991.

Freinkel, Susan. *Plastic: A Toxic Love Story.* Boston: Houghton Mifflin Harcourt, 2011.

Fukuoka, Masanoubu. *The One-Straw Revolution.* Emmaus, PA: Rodale Press, 1978.

Fuller, Steve. *Thomas Kuhn: A Philosophical History for Our Times.* Chicago: University of Chicago Press, 2000.

Galison, Peter, and David J. Stump, eds. *The Disunity of Science: Boundaries, Contexts, and Power.* Stanford, CA: Stanford University Press, 1996.

Giedion, Siegfried. *Mechanization Takes Command: A Contribution to Anonymous History.* New York: Oxford University Press, 1948; New York: Norton, 1969.

Gilbert, P. M., J. Harrison, C. Heil, and S. Seitzinger. "Escalating Worldwide Use of Urea: A Global Change Contributing to Coastal Eutrophication." *Biogeochemistry* 77, no 3 (2006): 441–63.

Goody, Jack. *The Domestication of the Savage Mind.* Cambridge: Cambridge University Press, 1977.

Graham, Frank, Jr. *Since Silent Spring.* Boston: Houghton Mifflin, 1970.

Habermas, Jürgen, Michael Reder, and Josef Schmidt. *An Awareness of What Is Missing: Faith and Reason in a Post-Secular Age.*

Translated by Ciaran Cronin. Malden, MA: Polity Press, 2010.

Hagege, Maya. *The Early History of UC Santa Cruz's Farm and Garden.* Edited by Randall Jarrell. Santa Cruz: University of California, Santa Cruz, University Library, 2003.

Hallock, Thomas, and Nancy Hoffmann, eds. *William Bartram: The Search for Nature's Design.* Athens: University of Georgia Press, 2010.

Harrison, Robert Pogue. *Forests: The Shadow of Civilization.* Chicago: University of Chicago Press, 1992.

Hayek, Frederick A. *The Counter-Revolution of Science: Studies on the Abuse of Reason.* Indianapolis, IN: Liberty Fund, 1979.

Hein, Hilde. "The Endurance of the Mechanism-Vitalism Controversy." *Journal of the History of Biology* 5, no. 1 (Spring 1972).

Heller, Erich. *The Disinherited Mind.* New York: Farrar, Straus and Cudahy, 1957; New York: Meridian Books, 1959; Cambridge: Bowes and Bowes, 1961.

Horsburgh, H. J. N. *Non-Violence and Aggression: A Study of Gandhi's Moral Equivalent of War.* London: Oxford University Press, 1968.

Hortensis, Furor. *Essays on the History of the English Landscape Garden in Memory of H. Frank Clark.* Edited by Peter Willis. Edinburgh: Elysium Press, 1974.

Howard, Sir Albert. *An Agricultural Testament.* New York: Oxford University Press, 1943.

———. *The Soil and Health.* New York: Schocken, 1972.

Husserl, Edmund. *Phenomenology and the Crisis of Philosophy: Philosophy as Rigorous Science, and Philosophy as the Crisis of European Man.* New York: Harper and Row, 1965.

Jackson-Stops, Gervase. *An English Arcadia, 1600–1900.* London: National Trust, 1992.

Jaffe, Bernard. *Crucibles: The Lives and Achievements of the Great Chemists.* New York: Simon and Schuster; New York: Tudor Publishing, 1930; London: Jarrolds, 1931.

Jeavons, John. *How To Grow More Vegetables.* 7th ed. Berkeley, CA: Ten Speed Press, 2006.

Jonas, Hans. *The Imperative of Responsibility: In Search of an Ethics for the Technological Age.* Chicago: University of Chicago Press, 1984.

———. *Mortality and Morality: A Search for the Good after Auschwitz.* Evanston, IL: Northwestern University Press, 1996.

———. *The Phenomenon of Life: Toward a Philosophical Biology.* New York: Harper and Row, 1966; New York: Dell Publishing Co., 1966; Westport, CT: Greenwood Press, 1979; Chicago: University of Chicago Press, 1982.

———. *Philosophical Essays: From Ancient Creed to Technological Man.* Englewood Cliffs, NJ: Prentice-Hall, 1974.

Kalakowski, Leslie. *The Alienation of Reason: A History of Positivist Thought.* Garden City, NJ: Doubleday, 1968; New York: Anchor Books, 1969.

Kaufmann, Stuart A. *The Origins of Order: Self-Organization and Selection in Evolution.* New York: Oxford University Press, 1993.

Kimbrell, Andrew, ed. *The Fatal Harvest Reader: The Tragedy of Industrial Agriculture.* Sausalito, CA: The Foundation for Deep Ecology in collaboration with Island Press, 2002.

Klibansky, Raymond, and H. J. Paton, eds. *Philosophy and History: Essays Presented to Ernst Cassirer.* Oxford: Clarendon Press, 1936.

Koepf, H., B. Pettersen, and W. Schaumann. *Bio-dynamic Agriculture: An Introduction.* Hudson, NY: Anthroposophic Press, 1996.

Kolakowski, Keszek. *Positivist Philosophy: From Hume to the Vienna Circle.* New York: Penguin, 1972.

Kuhn, Thomas. *The Structure of Scientific Revolutions.* Chicago: Chicago University Press, 1962.

Langley, Batty. *New Principles of Gardening.* London: A. Bettesworth and J. Batley, 1728.

Lear, Linda. *Rachel Carson: Witness for Nature.* New York: Henry Holt, 1997.

Lee, Paul. "Goethe's Italian Journey, On the Occasion of the 200th Anniversary." From *Unusual Associates: A Festschrift for Frank Barron.* Ed. Alfonso Montuori. Cresskill, NJ: Hampton Press, 1996.

———. Introduction to *The Meaning of Health,* by Paul Tillich. Berkeley, CA: North Atlantic Books, 1981.

———. "Thymós as Biopsychological Metaphor: The Vital Root of Consciousness." In *Metaphors of Consciousness,* edited by Ronald S. Valle and Rolf von Eckartsberg. New York: Plenum Press, 1981.

Lehrs, Ernst. *Man or Matter: Introduction to a Spiritual Understanding of Nature on the Basis of Goethe's Method of Training Observation and Thought.* Spring Valley, NY: Anthroposophic Press, 1950.

Love, Glen A., ed. *Ecological Crisis: Readings for Survival.* New York: Harcourt Brace Jovanovich, 1970.

Löwith, Karl. *Nature, History, and Existentialism.* Evanston, IL: Northwestern University Press, 1966.

Maccubbin, Robert P. and Peter Martin. *British and American Gardens.* Charlottesville: University of Virginia Press, 1983.

Magnus, Rudolf. *Goethe as a Scientist.* New York: H. Schumann, 1949; New York: Collier Books, 1961.

Marcuse, Herbert. *One-Dimensional Man: Studies in the Ideology of Advanced Industrial Society.* Boston: Beacon Press, 1964; London: Routledge and Kegan Paul, 1968.

Marx, Leo. *The Machine in the Garden: Technology and the Pastoral Ideal in America.* New York: Oxford University Press, 1964.

Matthaei, Rupprecht, ed. *Goethe's Colour Theory.* Ravensburg, Germany: Van Nostrand Reinhold, 1971.

McDermott, John. "A Special Supplement: Technology: The Opiate of the Intellectuals." Review of Fourth Annual Report, 1967–68, of Harvard's Program on Technology and Society. *New York Review of Books* 13, No. 2, (July 31, 1969).

McKibben, Bill. *The End of Nature.* New York: Random House, 1989.

Mendelsohn, Everett. "Revolution and Reduction: The Sociology of Methodological and Philosophical Concerns in Nineteenth Century Biology." In *The Interaction between Science and Philosophy,* edited by Yehuda Elkana. Atlantic Highlands, NJ: Humanities Press, 1974.

Merchant, Carolyn. *The Death of Nature: Women, Ecology, and the Scientific Revolution.* San Francisco: Harper and Row, 1980.

Merz, John T. *A History of European Thought in the Nineteenth Century.* 4 vols. New York: Dover, 1976.

Meyer, Nicolle Aimee, and Amanda Pilar Smith. *Paris in a Basket.* With a foreword by Paul Bocuse. New York: Konemann, 2000.

Miller, Douglas. "Goethe's Scientific Studies." *Goethe: The Collected Works.* Vol. 12. Edited by Victor Lange, et al. New York: Suhrkamp, 1983-89; Chichester, West Sussex, and Princeton, NJ: Princeton University Press, 1995.

Miller, Philip. *Gardeners Dictionary*. London: 1731, and subsequent editions.

Mlodinow, Leonard. *Euclid's Window: The Story of Geometry From Parallel Lines to Hyperspace.* New York: Free Press, 2001; London: Allen Lane, 2002; New York: Simon and Schuster, 2002.

Moltke, Helmuth James von. *Letters to Freya 1939–1945.* Edited and translated by Beate Ruhm von Oppen. New York: Alfred A. Knopf, 1990.

Mulligan, Jim, and John de Graaf. *Gardensong.* Oley, PA: Bullfrog Films (Box 149, Oley, Pa. 19547). [Video].

Mumford, Lewis. *Technics and Civilization.* New York and London: Harcourt, Brace and Co., 1934; Burlingame, NY: Harcourt, Brace and World, 1965.

Nash, Roderick. *Wilderness and the American Mind.* New Haven, CT: Yale University Press, 1982.

Nicholson, Marjorie Hope. *Newton Demands the Muse: Newton's Opticks and the Eighteenth Century Poets.* Princeton, NJ: Princeton University Press, 1946 and 1996.

Nisbet, Hugh B. *Goethe and the Scientific Tradition.* London: Institute of Germanic Studies, University of London, 1972.

Olson, Richard. *Science Deified and Science Defied: The Historical Significance of Science in Western Culture.* Vol. 2. London: University of California Press, Ltd., 1990.

Otis, Denise. *Grounds for Pleasure: Four Centuries of the American Garden.* New York: Harry N. Abrams, 2002.

Perry, Claire. *Pacific Arcadia: Images of California, 1600–1915.* New York: Oxford University Press, 1999.

Polanyi, Michael. *Personal Knowledge: Towards a Post-Critical Philosophy.* Gifford Lectures, 1951-52. New York: Harper Torchbooks, 1964; London: Routledge and Kegan Paul, 1978 and 2002-4; Chicago: University of Chicago Press, 2000 and 2004 and 2009; London: Taylor and Francis, 1998.

Pollan, Michael. *The Omnivore's Dilemma: A Natural History of Four Meals.* New York: Penguin, 2006.

Preiss, Jack. *Camp William James.* Norwich, VT: Argo Books, 1978.

Prest, John. *The Garden of Eden: The Botanic Garden and the Recreation of Paradise.* New Haven, CT: Yale University Press, 1981.

Redondi, Pietro. *Galileo: Heretic.* Translated by Raymond Rosenthal. Princeton, NJ: Princeton University Press, 1987.

Regis, Pamela. *Describing Early America: Bartram, Jefferson, Crevecoeur, and the Rhetoric of Natural History.* De Kalb: Northern Illinois University Press, 1992.

Ricoeur, Paul. *Conflict of Interpretations: Essays in Hermeneutics.* Evanston, IL: Northwestern University Press, 1974.

———. *Freud and Philosophy: An Essay on Interpretation.* The Terry Lecture Series. New Haven, CT: Yale University Press, 1970.

———. *Symbolism of Evil.* New York: Harper and Row, 1969.

Rosenfield, Leonora Cohen. *From Beast-Machine to Man-Machine: Animal Soul in French Letters from Descartes to La Mettrie.* New York: Oxford University Press, 1941; NY, London: Octagon Press, 1968.

Rosenstock-Huessy, Eugen. "Liturgical Thinking." In *The Rosenstock-Huessy Papers.* Vol. 1. Berg, Germany: Argo Books, 1981.

Røstvig, Maren-Sofie. *The Happy Man: Studies in the Metamorphoses of a Classical Ideal.* Oslo: Oslo University Press, 1954; Oslo: Norwegian Universities Press, 1962; London: Aldus Books, 1974.

Roszak, Theodore. *The Making of a Counter-Culture: Reflections on the Technocratic Society and Its Youthful Opposition.* Garden City, NY: Doubleday, 1969; London, Faber and Faber, 1970.

———. "Nature and Nature's Good" In *Alexandria, 5,* edited by David R. Fideler. Grand Rapids, MI: Phanes Press, 2000.

———. *Where the Wasteland Ends: Politics and Transcendence in Postindustrial Society.* Garden City, NY: Doubleday, 1972; London: Faber and Faber, 1973.

Salm, Peter. *The Poem as Plant: A Biological View of Goethe's Faust.* Cleveland, OH: The Press of Case Western Reserve University, 1971.

Schama, Simon. *Landscape and Memory.* New York: Alfred A. Knopf, 1995.

Schell, Jonathan. *The Fate of the Earth.* New York: Knopf, 1982.

———. *The Fate of the Earth; and, The Abolition.* Stanford: Stanford University Press, 2000.

Schilthuis, Willy. *Biodynamic Agriculture.* Edinburgh, Scotland: Floris Books, 1994.

Schumacher, E. F. *Small Is Beautiful.* New York: Harper and Row, 1973.

Sepper, Dennis L. *Goethe Contra Newton: Polemics and the Project for a New Science of Color.* Cambridge: Cambridge University Press, 1988.

Simon, Ted. *The River Stops Here: How One Man's Battle to Save His Valley Changed the Fate of California.* New York: Random House, 1994.

Smil, Vaclav. *Enriching the Earth: Fritz Haber, Carl Bosch, and the Transformation of World Food Production.* Cambridge, MA: MIT Press, 2000.

———. *Global Catastrophes and Trends: The Next Fifty Years.* Cambridge, MA: MIT Press, 2008.

Smith, Page. *Killing the Spirit: Higher Education in America.* New York: Viking Press, 1990.

Snell, Bruno. *The Discovery of the Mind: The Greek Origins of European Thought.* New York: Dover, 1982.

Sorell, Tom. *Scientism, Philosophy and the Infatuation with Science.* London: Routledge, 1991.

Steiner, Rudolf. "Friedrich Nietzsche, a Fighter against His Time." In *Friedrich Nietzsche, Fighter for Freedom.* Englewood, NJ: Rudolf Steiner, 1960.

———. *Nature's Open Secret: Introductions to Goethe's World Conception.* Great Barrington, MA: Anthroposophic Press, 2000. [1883–1897].

———. *The Riddles of Philosophy.* Spring Valley, NY: Anthroposophic Press, 2000.

———. *The Science of Knowing: Outline of an Epistemology Implicit in the Goethean Worldview.* Translated by William Lindeman. Spring Valley, NY: Mercury Press, 1988. [1886].

Storl, Wolf D. *Culture and Horticulture: A Philosophy of Gardening.* Wyoming, RI: Bio-Dynamic Literature, 1979;

San Francisco: Bio-dynamic Farming and Gardening
Association, 2000.

Stuewer, Roger, ed. "Minnesota Studies in the Philosophy of
Science." *Historical and Philosophical Perspectives of Science*, Vol V.

Tillich, Paul. *The Courage To Be.* New Haven, CT: Yale
University Press, 1952. Special reprint with introduction by
Peter J. Gomes, New Haven, CT: Yale University Press,
2000.

———. *The Meaning Of Health: Essays in Existentialism,
Psychoanalysis, and Religion.* Edited by Perry D. LeFevre.
Chicago, IL: Exploration Press, 1984.

———. *The Meaning of Health: The Relation of Religion and Health.*
Richmond, CA: North Atlantic Books, 1981.

———. *The Spiritual Situation in our Technical Society.* Edited by J.
Mark Thomas. Macon, GA: Mercer University Press, 1988.

———. *Theology of Culture.* New York: Oxford University
Press, 1959.

Tompkins, Peter, and Christopher Bird. *The Secret Life of Plants.*
New York: Harper and Row, 1973.

———. *Secrets of the Soil.* New York: Harper and Row, 1989.

Torchiana, H. A. W. van Coenen. *Story of the Mission Santa
Cruz.* San Francisco: P. Elder, 1933.

Toulmin, Stephen, and June Goodfield. *The Architecture of
Matter.* Chicago: University of Chicago Press, 1962.

Voegelin, Eric. "The Origins of Scientism," *Social Research* 15
(1948): 462–94. [Also in *The Collected Works of Eric Voegelin.*
Baton Rouge: Louisiana State University Press, 2000].

Walker, Mark. *Nazi Science: Myth, Truth, and the German Atomic
Bomb.* New York: Harper Collins, 1995.

Waters, Alice. *Edible Schoolyard: A Universal Idea.* San Francisco:
Chronicle Books, 2008.

Webster, Charles. *The Great Instauration: Science, Medicine and
Reform, 1626–1660.* New York: Holmes and Meier, 1975.

Weil, Simone. *The Need for Roots.* Translated by Arthur Wills,
with a preface by T. S. Eliot. London: Routledge and Kegan
Paul, 1952.

Weiss, John. *The Making of Technological Man: The Social Origins
of French Engineering Education.* Cambridge, MA: MIT Press,
1982.

221

Whatley, Thomas. *Observations on Modern Gardening.* London, 1770.

Williams, George Hunston. *Wilderness and Paradise in Christian Thought: The Biblical Experience of the Desert in the History of Christianity and the Paradise Theme in the Theological Idea of the University.* New York: Harper, 1962.

Wulf Andrea. *The Brother Gardeners: Botany, Empire, and the Birth of an Obsession.* London: William Heinemann, 2009.

———. *Founding Gardeners: The Revolutionary Generation, Nature, and the Shaping of the American Nation.* New York: Alfred A. Knopf, 2011.

Wulf, Andrea, and Emma Gieben-Gamal. *The Other Eden: Seven Great Gardens and Three Hundred Years of English History.* New York: Little, Brown, 2007.

Young, Louise B., ed. *The Mystery of Matter.* New York: Oxford University Press, 1965.

Index

Page numbers in italics indicate photographs.

223

About the Author

Paul Lee was born in La Veta, Colorado, and was educated at St. Olaf College, Luther Theological Seminary, the University of Minnesota, and Harvard, where he received a divinity degree and PhD and was a teaching assistant for Paul Tillich. He served as the Protestant chaplain at Brandeis University and was the founding editor of the *Psychedelic Review.* He has taught at Harvard, Massachusetts Institute of Technology, and the University of California, Santa Cruz. He is the author of the children's book *Florence the Goose* and *The Quality of Mercy,* an account of his work with the homeless in Santa Cruz. He lives in Santa Cruz, California, with his wife, Charlene. Visit his website at www.ecotopia.org.